IN PRAISE OF

GOOD IS THE NEW COOL THE PRINCIPLES OF PURPOSE

"Purpose is the growth story of the 21st Century. For any organization wanting to reap the rewards of this new triple bottom line, this book shows them how."

—Paul Polman, former CEO, Unilever Co-Founder, Chair, IMAGINE

"The Principles of Purpose is a must read for every board member who wants to understand the most disruptive force in business today – and unlock the huge strategic advantage that delivers long-term growth for the companies they advise."

—Rob Perez, Operating Partner, General Atlantic, Founder and Chairman, Life Science Cares

"Aziz and Jones masterfully show that in this new values-driven era we are all creating together, purpose is driving business success even higher."

—Kirk Souder, Co-Founder, Enso Social Impact

As the world rightly moves to stakeholder capitalism, how companies lead, market, and transform their culture will require a reexamining of purpose. Good is The New Cool should be their handbook.

—Eve Rodsky, Author 'FairPlay'

"Not just 'must read' but 'must do' – this book is a Masterclass on how every modern company should operate with purpose."

—Paul Woolmington, CEO, Canvas Worldwide

GOOD IS THE NEW COOL

GOOD IS THE NEW COOL

AFDHEL AZIZ AND BOBBY JONES

THE PRINCIPLES OF PURPOSE

ISBN: 979-8707136269 (paperback)

FOR THE WOMEN IN OUR LIVES WHO INSPIRE US, STARTING WITH OUR WIVES, RUKSHANA AND RENEE

CONTENTS

INTRODUCTION

WHY WE WROTE GOOD IS THE NEW COOL: THE PRINCIPLES OF PURPOSE

Since the 2016 release of our first book, *Good Is the New Cool: Market Like You Give a Damn*, we have witnessed (and contributed to) an incredible and inspiring rise in purpose-led companies that are working to transform our world for the better.

In our first book, we explored the rise of purpose-driven marketing, drawing on our experience building, operating, and advising iconic brands like Ford, Adidas, Moet Hennessy, Nokia, Heineken, and Absolut. We realized that there was a shift happening. Because of the rise of socially conscious customers, brands that had spent decades positioning themselves as "cool" had to start understanding that customers wanted them to be "good" as well (hence the title of the original book).

That book was a call to action for brands to join a purpose revolution, driven by a new generation of conscious customers, culture creators who want to use their influence for good, and a new wave of nonprofits working to solve problems at unprecedented levels. Businesses accepted the call to join the movement and are now emerging as leaders of the next wave of change. But in 2016, we could not have predicted the scale and speed of what would happen next.

We saw Nike break the internet with its campaign backing activist Colin Kaepernick and be rewarded by customers with a 31 percent boost in sales. We saw Patagonia sue the president of the United States in a dispute over federal lands, leading to a massive sales and profitability surge. Tesla became the most valuable car company on the planet and achieved a $700 billion valuation by building a sustainable energy future. And the CEO Roundtable letter delivered a commitment from 181 of the world's top companies to exist for the benefit of all stakeholders—customers, employees, suppliers, and communities, not just shareholders.

We've seen remarkable moments like Microsoft announcing carbon offsets for all its emissions since inception and courageous decisions by Walmart and Dick's Sporting Goods to pull specific guns from their shelves to help save lives from massacres, at a real cost to their profitability. Burger King and the Whopper stood up for LGBTQ rights, and the recent COVID-19 pandemic has made brands an indispensable part of the solution to save lives and jobs. In real time, we are witnessing the dawn of a new age of capitalism, becoming something that could create enduring prosperity for the many, not the few—and help save our planet in the meantime.

In this book, we explore the three tectonic shifts that are driving this next age of purpose—conscious consumers who are becoming more steadfast in their belief that brands need to optimize life on our planet, activist employees who want to do work that is meaningful and purposeful, and impact-driven investors who are earning more money by putting their money where their values are. In the upcoming chapters, we will dive deeper into each of these factors and show why we've never had more opportunities to align our lives and dollars with our beliefs as customers, employees, and investors.

As this movement grows, the data are now irrefutable. Doing good is great for business. On every single measure of success—brand value, equity, revenue, brand loyalty, advocacy, price premium, employee engagement, and impact investment—purpose-driven companies are leading the way.

Yet we know we are at the very beginning of this journey. We heard from many of you—at Fortune 500 companies, small businesses, and entrepreneurial start-ups—who want to build and lead more purposeful companies but don't know how. Our mission with this book is to empower you with the knowledge and tools you need to create a purpose-led organization. This book encapsulates everything we have learned from being on the front lines of this purpose revolution in business, the hard-won lessons and insights pulled together in an easy-to-follow process to discover, design, and deploy purpose. We hope that this will help you embrace purpose for its enormous competitive advantage.

This body of work is written for a C-suite-level perspective on how purpose can manifest itself across every aspect of your business—whether it's supply chain and sustainability, employees and talent, or product innovation and marketing. To you, brave leaders, we propose a paradigm shift in how businesses look at social responsibility. Let's not be satisfied with merely restoring what we have broken; our moon-shot goal should be to make society and our planet healthier than we found it. Let's build it back better.

Over the past four years, *Good Is the New Cool* has served a growing movement of leaders using business and culture to create a better world. We will introduce you to these world changers, providing you with immersive access to their work and lives. You will go from meeting inspiring creators working in social innovation hubs like Silicon Valley to traveling into the heart of Uganda to experience the life-altering impact of building schools in the village of Manya. You will meet the incredible people who activate their companies to help tackle hunger, fight modern-day slavery, and end global homelessness. We will introduce you to the teams that are turning disability into an engine for innovation and using the power of inclusive design to create better living for billions of people.

These women and men come from all walks of life, backgrounds, ethnicities, nationalities, and abilities. What is the one thing they have in common? They inspire us as ordinary citizens doing extraordinary things through their work.

As we write this, we are experiencing the COVID-19 pandemic, which is wreaking havoc on populations and economies worldwide. Nations are experiencing unprecedented levels of unemployment and panic. Yet, when asked, 62 percent of citizens globally said their country would not make it through this crisis without brands playing a critical role in addressing the challenges we face.[1] This stat is in stark contrast to three years before, when customers said they wouldn't care if 77 percent of brands disappeared.[2] Companies are needed now more than ever to help support the well-being of humanity and our planet. We think this is a watershed moment in capitalism's evolution, a necessary upgrade to its operating system, which has created inequality and a world in crisis for too long.

In this book, we shift our gaze from the brand to the corporation, from the chief marketing officer to the chief executive officer as the primary unit of

---

1 Richard Edelman, "Edelman Trust Barometer Special Report on COVID-19 Demonstrates Essential Role of the Private Sector," *Edelman* (Website), Daniel J. Edelman Holdings, Inc., Accessed on January 29, 2021, https://www.edelman.com/research/edelman-trust-covid-19-demonstrates-essential-role-of-private-sector, n.p.

2 "Corporate Governance: Business Roundtable Redefines the Purpose of a Corporation to Promote 'An Economy That Serves All Americans'," *BR Business Roundtable*, August 19, 2019, https://www.businessroundtable.org/business-roundtable-redefines-the-purpose-of-a-corporation-to-promote-an-economy-that-serves-all-americans, n.p.

A great CEO should have

the **brain** of a CFO,
the **heart** of a storyteller,
and the **soul** of an activist.

change. This reflects the Business Roundtable declaration on the Purpose of a Corporation, announcing the shift in focus from solely delivering shareholder value to serving all stakeholders: shareholders, customers, employees, community, and the planet[3] Through our work with our purpose consultancy Conspiracy of Love, a certified B Corp, we've met hundreds of international leaders in the corporate world dedicated to transforming their organizations to deliver growth, helping make the world a better place.

We believe the great CEO's of today should have the brain of a CFO, the heart of a storyteller, and the soul of an activist. That is how they are able to use the power of purpose to fuel both growth and social impact.

We asked ourselves what was missing in this space for all those leaders who inspire us. The answer was the "how": how great companies harness the power of purpose to deliver inspiration that leads to innovation and meaning, which leads to motivation.

We have dived deep into these organizations and interviewed the women (we should point out that the vast majority of our clients at Conspiracy of Love are incredibly dedicated and courageous women leading the charge) and men on the purpose revolution's front lines. We have distilled all of these stories, insights, and case studies into a useful framework. A set of principles whereby leaders can evolve their companies to become purpose driven in an era that demands it, in much the same way the expectations of the last decade required them to meet the digital age's challenges and opportunities.

Our friend Max Lenderman, a guru in the purpose space, once said, "Purpose is the new digital," and we couldn't agree more. The companies that we cover in the book harness the power of purpose, like the first companies to harness the power of digital, By building purpose into functions as diverse as supply chain, marketing, recruiting, and product innovation, they create a competitive edge that will be hard to beat. As a leader, you have a choice: either find ways to embrace it as the competitive edge it is and build purpose capability into your organization or see your competition sail past you because they did.

---

3 "Corporate Governance: Business Roundtable Redefines the Purpose of...", 2019, n.p.

PURPOSE
is the
new
digital.
Max Lenderman

Building on the digital analogy, it is essential to note that if "purpose is the new digital," we are still comparatively in the first days of the internet. Purpose is still scattered, and niche, frequently with no fixed definition that allows for easy interchange; much like the early stages of the World Wide Web were isolated groups of people operating small clusters independently. It was the dawn of HTML, which created a common language among these groups and allowed them to access each other's knowledge.

We believe with purpose as its source code, we can reboot capitalism, creating a newer, upgraded version that is more just, equitable, and sustainable.

To achieve this, we focus on the corporation as the vehicle of change. We look at how different functions within the company are harnessing the power of purpose: for instance, how Patagonia and SAP are developing ethical supply chains, how Microsoft and Mattel are fueling purpose-driven innovation, how IKEA and Adidas are innovating new circular economy models and processes. We should reiterate that none of the companies we profile in the book are perfect, and they all have areas they can improve in. But by diving deep into these companies and focusing on what they are doing right, our goal is to show you seeds of change happening that could ultimately lead to the overhaul of capitalism itself.

It may sound like a naïve pipedream. But it was the very rise of capitalism, with its virtues of self-governance and self-reliance, that moved humanity onward from the depths of feudalism, which five hundred years ago was a system which condemned most of humanity to a life of servitude and subservience to their aristocratic overlords.

It's time to reboot the system again.

The reimagining of business as a force for good has begun. You will see examples in the diverse and fascinating stories of everyday people doing extraordinary things inside corporations of every size: from inspiring start-ups like Now, Chewse, and Promise, to medium-sized companies like TOMS, Patagonia, and Chobani, to multi-billion-dollar behemoths like Procter & Gamble, Unilever, and Tesla. We will connect the dots from these diverse examples and give us all a common language and reference frame to learn from each other.

Now let us be clear: we are painfully aware some may construe all of this as "purpose-washing." It is a term coined to describe how companies distract us from all the negative things they do. We will be the first to acknowledge that there are so many things wrong with capitalism today:

- The callousness of the shareholder-driven model, which separates reward from responsibility.
- CEO compensation at outrageous multiples to their workers, guaranteed to them even when they run their companies into the ground.
- The environmental devastation caused by corporations, from oil spills to chemical runoff, that acidifies oceans and truckloads of plastic that pollute our seas.
- The threat of algorithms and automation to blithely wipe out hundreds of millions of jobs.
- The tax dodges which allow companies to stash money in offshore havens without contributing proportionately to the very economies that produce and nurture them and their talent.
- The shady accounting practices that lead to accounting fraud, all in service of hitting quarterly returns.
- The tens of billions of media dollars wasted on ad fraud or even worse, ad dollars funding hate speech, misinformation and genocide.
- The corrupting influence of unregulated corporate money in politics, which reached a flashpoint following the Capitol Insurrection of 2021, with many companies realizing how their contributions had funded some politicians who had fanned the flames of sedition.

For anyone working in business and social impact, we highly recommend also reading Anand Ghiridardas's fantastic book *Winners Take All* and watching the documentaries *The Corporation* and *The New Corporation*, which intelligently and beautifully dissect all the hypocrisies and misdirections in which corporations indulge. As practitioners in this space, we do our best to hold ourselves accountable and not become unwitting agents that support the status quo.

But one of the most promising truths, and what keeps us motivated, is that corporations are made up of people. People like you and us. And we believe that if enough of us lead these corporations with values and models that balance profitability and prosperity, sustainability and social equity, then we

THE PURPOSE FLYWHEEL EFFECT

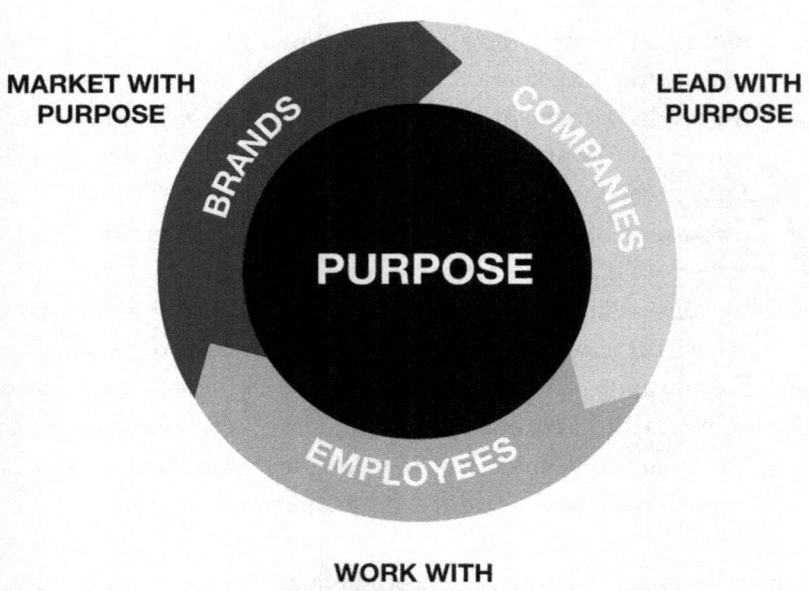

MARKET WITH PURPOSE

LEAD WITH PURPOSE

WORK WITH PURPOSE

BRANDS

COMPANIES

EMPLOYEES

PURPOSE

have a fighting chance of reining in their worst impulses and channeling their enormous power to do good.

This revolution is happening right now in companies. And the secret to unlocking it is what we call The Purpose Flywheel.

The Purpose Flywheel is a phenomenon we have noticed in some of the best examples of purpose-driven companies that we have studied over the past four years: companies like Tesla, Patagonia, Microsoft, and Zappos.

The Flywheel consists of three parts:

Lead with Purpose: It begins with having a clear purpose — an aspirational reason for being that inspires action that benefits shareholders, stakeholders, and local and global societies — which starts at the CEO and leadership level and permeates throughout the organization. This ambition is outlined in a holistic purpose framework: clearly articulating your purpose, vision, mission, values, and positioning.

Work with Purpose: You then invite your employees to contribute their gifts and passions in service to the company›s higher purpose, creating a greater sense of meaning and fulfillment in their work. By creating opportunities for employees to align their passions with the company›s purpose, you can build a corporate culture sought after by top talent in your field.

Market with Purpose: The internal energy that is unlocked when companies and brands make purpose their priority is then outwardly manifested through inspired innovation, authentic storytelling, and impactful marketing that attracts enthusiastic customers, investors, and employees.

Tesla serves as a clear example to bring the Flywheel to life. It set the noble purpose of 'accelerating the planet's transition to sustainable energy' as its overarching goal. It attracts talented people (like designer Sahm Jafari whom we interview in this book's Purpose Must be Profitable to be Sustainable section) who are drawn to this purpose and dedicate their lives to it. These employees produce an incredible flood of purpose-driven innovation (the Tesla Model S,

X, Y and E, the Cybertruck), purchased by millions of purpose-driven customers. This success leads to its shares bought by purpose-driven investors (who made Tesla the most valuable car company on the planet by market capitalization, at 700 billion dollars). In turn, this massive success has triggered every single car company (GM, Toyota, VW, etc.) on the planet to now either have an electric car in their portfolio or announce the move to full electrification. All this gives governments around the world – like the State of California, the world's 10th largest car market– the confidence to announce that they seek a ban on fossil-fuel cars in the next fifteen years, phasing them out by 2035 (and leading to places like the European Union seeking to do the same).

None of this would have been possible without a clear purpose, manifested throughout the company, engaging all of its stakeholders: its employees, its customers, its investors, and society at large. And yes, Tesla has issues just like any other company, ranging from its controversial CEO Elon Musk to allegations around worker safety and quality and reliability issues. All of these need to be addressed as the company grows and matures, and there will inevitably be new ones.

But what it has done to the car category to spark its evolution into one that does not contribute to climate change is truly remarkable.

The number of companies who have achieved this Purpose Flywheel so far is small. But the desire for corporate leaders to become both 'a force for good and a force for growth' is real. And it is gathering momentum, especially in the wake of COVID-19 and the racial justice reckoning that is sweeping America and the world.

In this book, we attempt to show you how to bring that Flywheel to life in your company, using the Principles we have discovered by researching some of the most successful companies on the planet and how they have unlocked and unleashed the power of purpose. We believe in the idea that the secret of change is not in tearing down the old but building the new'. And this book attempts to show you the new model of capitalism being built right now.

While we are skeptics sometimes about what corporations claim to do to make the world a better place, we never descend into cynicism; we have met enough determined people—some of whose stories we share in this book—to see that the movement is real.

You may already be part of this quiet revolution, and we understand your intentions are real, and your convictions are deeply held. We want to equip you with the tools, models, and processes to take control.

Because whether all of you can take control of the companies you are part of will make the difference between whether they continue to maintain a broken status quo or become the instruments of positive change society badly needs right now.

The difference is you. The difference is us.

We hope this book inspires you to take action and start today.

Bobby Jones and Afdhel Aziz

PS: Before we start the next step of our journey together, we thought it would help you to know a bit about us and what has changed in our lives since the last book.

BOBBY'S STORY

"**N**o justice, no peace! No justice, no peace!"

Echoing around the world, those words have been a rallying cry, shouted with passion and pain from people fighting in the face of injustice. I've proclaimed it in chorus many times before in my life, as I marched with others for justice and equality. But on this particular day, it felt different.

Sparked by the outrage of seeing the cold and callous murder of George Floyd at the knee of Minneapolis police officer Derek Michael Chauvin, millions of citizens from the streets of Brooklyn, NY, to almost every continent on the planet were determined to turn this moment of tragedy into a movement for change. As I looked at the people around me, our desperate desire to be seen and heard was palpable. It was in the vigor of our voices, the pulse of our presence, the cadence of our courage.

Marching hand in hand with my nine-year-old son, I thought back to my own experience of being sixteen years old in Washington, DC. Sitting in my parked car, a used Pontiac 6000, with my friend, as two officers pointed their guns at us, ready to shoot because they mistakenly assumed I had stolen my car. I flashbacked to about a year before George Floyd's killing when my young son, tired and hungry, had a meltdown in a gentrifying Brooklyn neighborhood, and someone thought it would be a good idea to call armed police to quiet him down. I remembered as the officer approached us that night, holding my son's trembling hand as I reminded him and myself to stay calm so we could get home safely.

I thought about those who had that same goal but did not have a safe ending: Breonna Taylor, Eric Garner, Michael Brown, Walter Scott, Tamir Rice, Trayvon Martin, Philando Castile, Natasha McKenna, Michelle Cusseaux, and too many others needlessly killed at the hands of police.

As we marched farther, I meditated over all the people who had walked generations before us. I know that we are part of a longer, larger lineage of people who have pushed and pulled us toward a more just and equitable world. As the late great John Lewis would say, the good troublemakers, fighting for all people's liberation and equality. I wanted my son to understand this history and his place in it. I led him through the waves of folks who were moving forward like a current in a sea of change. We reached the sidewalk, and I bent over to look him in the eyes.

I asked him, "Do you know why we are marching?" He said, "I think so." I told him, "I want you to understand what it means to be a citizen, to be part of a community, and a country. To know that your actions affect others, and theirs affect you. I want you to know your life matters, just as much as anyone else's. You have rights. And, with that, you have responsibilities—to be kind, to be fair, and when you see something wrong, to do something about it. I don't want you ever to feel helpless or hopeless. You have the power to change things, and don't be afraid to use your power to do what's right."

We walked home, both processing the world we were in the midst of. The events of 2020 have shaped us in ways it may take a lifetime to understand fully. As I am writing this today, we are on the eve of the US presidential election. The stakes are high. The question millions of Americans and people around the world are anxiously asking is, Who will the president be? But to ask that seems almost beside the point. We must pose a more critical question to ourselves, and that is, Who will we be?

Moving forward, who will we choose to be as individuals, as workers, as communities, as companies? We must not be content or discouraged from the outcome of tomorrow. This opportunity is much bigger. It is the moment to look at our lives and work and decide if this is good enough. And we should not be afraid if the answer is no. If we can envision a healthier planet, a more equitable world where everyone as food to eat, a home to sleep in, safe spaces to learn, and the ability to live a life with dignity, safety, and opportunity, we must do the work to achieve it.

We have to unleash our moral imaginations to see new possibilities for our world and be relentless in our resolve to achieve them. Over the past four years, since the release of our first book, I have seen an incredible display of action from citizens all over the world, doing the work to make this world better. I've seen women worldwide once again lead the way, using their passion and power to drive change in government, commerce, and every other aspect of society.

I'm in awe of the tireless work of Stacey Abrams to protect everyone's right to free and fair elections and Glennon Doyle's work supporting women, families, and children in crisis. Michelle Obama is creating a sense of belonging for women around the world. It is also an honor to share the stories of women business leaders whom I admire in this book.

The power of youth is particularly inspiring at this moment, young people rising, taking action, speaking truth to power, and inviting others to join them. Through my work at Peace First, I have seen young changemakers all over the world. Some are taking matters into their own hands—on massive public stages. Others are creating change through small acts of courage and kindness without recognition or fanfare. For example, Mary-Pat Hector is working to end student hunger on college campuses and has developed youth entrepreneurship programming that has helped hundreds of young people kick-start licensed businesses. Social entrepreneur sixteen-year-old Grace Callwood, a survivor of cancer, founded We Cancerve to bring happiness to homeless, sick, and foster youth. The young entrepreneur Tony Weaver of Weird Enough Productions focuses on combating media misrepresentation through original content production and media literacy education.

I have also seen firsthand how committed employees can reshape companies such as Adidas, Red Bull, Crown Royal, Oreo, and the North Face. We have helped people at Fortune 500 companies like AB Inbev, Diageo, Mondelez, Microsoft, Mars, MillerCoors, and more to unleash the power of purpose in ways that help drive social and environmental impact. And Good Is the New Cool has grown into a global movement of people united by a shared belief in the power of business and culture to become forces for good.

During the COVID-19 pandemic, there have been levels of sacrifice and generosity that have brought tears to my eyes. It turns out there are things more contagious than this virus, such as compassion. Courage also passes from person to person. Love can quickly spread throughout communities and across borders.

On the days I have been down, and there have been many, I think of you all. You keep me going.

I started this journey when I realized my purpose was to feed the good in the world. However, I had no idea how many people around the world would feed the good in me. Every day, you show me how wonderful we can be, the impact we can create, the world we can build. No matter how daunting the problems or depressing the news, I believe in us. I believe in our ability to be and do better—our ability to make business and culture forces for good.

The stakes have never been higher, and the problems we face, like economic disparity, discrimination, and climate change, have never been more significant. Yet, I have no doubt, in this fight, we are all that we need. And as long as you want to create a better world, Good Is the New Cool will connect and serve you. That is our purpose. Now, let's get to work.

AFDHEL'S STORY

After the success of our first book, *Good Is the New Cool: Market Like You Give A Damn*, I was able to find my purpose in being a writer, speaker, and consultant on the topic of purpose. It led to my family making the decision to leave New York for the warmer climate of California, where we settled into life in the peaceful neighborhood of Venice Beach in Los Angeles.

We lived in a beautiful old bungalow on Superba Avenue, one of the prettiest streets in the neighborhood. Our house (literally) had a white picket fence, with bougainvillea and night jasmine blooming in the garden. It's the kind of neighborhood where people stop and chat to each other on the street, genuinely caring for the community. It is the quietest, most charming place I have ever lived in.

One night, my family and I were asleep in the early hours of the morning. Suddenly, we heard a loud *pop pop* and a crash. We woke up. I sat bolt upright and ran into the bedroom of my four-year-old son, who was sleeping across the hall from us, to check if he was OK. He was fast asleep, so I started walking down the stairs, turning the lights on as I went. I saw broken glass on the floor, and I told my wife to call 911, assuming that someone had broken in.

As I got to the living room, I noticed that the ceiling light fixture had exploded, which explained the glass all over the floor. *That's strange*, I remember thinking to myself. *Why would a lamp explode spontaneously?*

That was when I noticed the bullet hole in the front wall of the house.

The bullet had come straight through, and the light fixture was the only thing that had stopped it from following its trajectory—where it would have entered the bedroom my wife and I were sleeping in. Six feet to the left and it would have gone through my son's bedroom.

Within minutes, we had police knocking on our door to check if we were all right. We spent the night dealing with the dozens of police who were sweeping the area, finding bullet fragments all over our house, nestled between the couch cushions. After the police left, my wife and I did what any parents would do—we spent an hour cleaning up the broken glass and vacuuming the house so our son would have no sign of it when he woke up.

I spent months thinking about what this whole episode meant.

I realized that I had always had violence around me in some form or the other. I was born in Sri Lanka, a beautiful island that was plagued with a civil war for thirty years, where I grew up with the constant threat of suicide bombers and terrorism. I moved to London and was there on the July 7 bombings, devastating terrorist attacks that killed so many. I lived in New York City, always with the memory of 9/11 not far away, which had its fair share of terrorist attacks during the time I lived there.

My family and I loved the place we lived in—so peaceful, so quiet, so beautiful. What could go wrong? What happened to us was totally random. We weren't targeted by anyone. So I thought that we were just unlucky: to be in the wrong house at the wrong time.

But on reflection, I realize now that we were lucky—extremely lucky. We were lucky to escape unscathed with our lives. We were lucky to not be among the 38,658 people who die of gun violence every year in the United States, lucky not to turn into yet another tragic statistic. We realized that we had dodged a bullet literally, not metaphorically.

The police never found the person who was responsible, and they could never ascribe a motive. To this day, I don't know what caused that person to randomly fire a gun into our house. Perhaps it was mental illness or drugs or alcohol or perhaps just sheer rage and frustration at the lack of opportunities in his or her life. I will never know.

But what I do know is this: what it triggered in me was an even more burning desire to try to tackle the root causes of why that person committed that random act of violence, to try to engage with the problems of the world. Because if we don't, none of us will be safe. We can't all retreat into gated communities and shut ourselves off from the outside world.

If we want safer streets, safer neighborhoods, and safer cities, we have to become part of the solution. Otherwise, we're just part of the problem.

Today, we live in what seem like turbulent times. We are living in a country that seems more polarized than ever before, with more hatred, distrust, and fear of "the other" than we have ever seen. And that fear paralyzes us. It allows us to disengage from being part of the solution. It allows us to endlessly cycle through the five stages of grief—denial, anger, bargaining, depression, acceptance—without being able to ever get to the sixth stage.

The sixth stage of grief is action. The sixth stage is where we stop anxiously doomscrolling through our social media feeds or being keyboard warriors. The sixth stage is where we realize the awesome power and responsibility we have as leaders and employees of some of the most powerful corporations on the planet and the enormous potential we have to do good from right where we are seated.

We can do better. We must do better. We will do better.

Corporations have more resources than governments. And unlike governments, corporations have no term limits. They have no geographical boundaries. They have legal rights and powers that governments can only dream of. And today people want the corporations in their lives to do good. They want them to have a higher-order purpose than just "maximizing shareholder value." They want to see them actively involved in helping to fix the problems of the world.

Your consumers want it. Your employees want it. Your investors want it.

The key to all unlocking of all of this is purpose: the higher-order reason for a business to exist for more than just making a profit, the North Star that guides everything that the business does and how it can be of service to society and humanity.

So let's start by looking at the three tectonic shifts driving the adoption of purpose today: consumers, employees, and investors.

PART I

WHY WE ARE LIVING IN THE AGE OF PURPOSE: THE THREE TECTONIC SHIFTS DRIVING CHANGE

THE RISE OF THE CONSCIOUS CONSUMER: PEOPLE WANT TO BUY FROM BRANDS THAT GIVE A DAMN

I n our first book, *Good Is the New Cool: Market Like You Give a Damn*, we called for brand marketers to think of people as citizens, not just as consumers. It is clear that people want to be seen as more than just buyers of clothes, cars, and cosmetics; they are members of families, communities, and societies who care about the well-being of people and the planet.

Over the past several years, we have seen an unprecedented increase in civic engagement and activism. Of the top five largest protests in American history, four have taken place since 2017—the two Women's Marches, the March for Our Lives, and the March for Science. However, this groundswell of activism is not limited to the United States. Around the world, we are seeing coordinated mobilizations of global citizens to address our most pressing issues. Examples of this phenomenon include the Youth Climate Strikes, inspired by Swedish climate activist Greta Thunberg (age sixteen at the time), which became the largest mass protest for action on global warming in history, with over 2,500 events in more than 163 countries on all seven continents.

In words and deeds, people are showing they are ready to create a more just and equitable world. As citizens, they are using the vigor of their voices to speak truth to power and their passionate presence to demonstrate their frustration and desire for change. Yet, it is as consumers that their influence is perhaps becoming most evident. The message they are delivering as buyers is loud and clear—brands who want their dollars must align with their values, have a clear purpose, and involve them in social change.

By pretty much every measure of brand health, consumers are more likely to try, stay loyal to, pay more for, and advocate for brands that genuinely do good. When it comes to Gen Z (born 1995–2015), the upcoming wave of consumers entering the market after millennials, the trends are even more impossible to ignore. Gen Z's buying power is expected to exceed $2.5 trillion over the next decade, representing a third of consumers worldwide. According to Fuse Marketing, after learning a brand supports a social cause or is socially responsible, Gen Z consumers are 85 percent more likely to trust a brand, 84 percent more likely to buy their products, and 82 percent more likely to recommend that brand to their friends and family.

Simply put, today's consumers want to buy from brands that share their values and vision for the world.

That is not to say that E. Jerome McCarthy's marketing mix of "the Four Ps"—product, price, place, promotion—are no longer consumer considerations. It is still very important to offer a quality product at a fair price. You need to be available in places—online and retail—that are easy to access and delightful experiences to boot. And your promotion needs to be fresh, relevant, and engaging (lead with the cool). However, when all products are in danger of being commoditized, we believe there is a fifth P—purpose—that may be a business's most valuable differentiator and serve to provide an additional reason for consideration. And on a more fundamental level, without knowing why you exist and how you serve the world, how can you decide what product to make and what price to sell it at?

Let's look at the ways purpose is driving the key metrics for consumer behavior.

TRIAL

The most critical step in initiating a new relationship between your offering and a new customer is trial. This is where your targets get to experience for themselves how awesome your product or service is. But how do you get people to switch from what they already know to give you a chance?

It turns out purpose is a key driver. According to a Cone/Porter Novelli survey, researchers found that 66 percent would switch from a product they typically buy to a new product from a purpose-driven company. This figure goes up to 91 percent when millennials (born 1980–1994) are polled.

Simply having a clear purpose gives people more of a compelling reason to make a change in their purchasing habits.

LOYALTY AND ADVOCACY

Once you have gained customers, the goal is to earn their loyalty. Customer loyalty is the act of choosing one company's offerings consistently over its competitors'. When you are able to achieve loyalty, your customers are not easily swayed by price or availability. They will spend more because they know they will get the same quality service and product they know and love. Loyal customers are the lifeline of businesses and the holy grail of customer relationships.

Patagonia is a brand that has cultivated a loyal community of fans. It is revered by its customers not only for its products but also for its purpose-driven environmental practices. They have built a cult following among conscious buyers for their tireless commitment to "saving our home planet," a phrase that is echoed throughout the walls of their stores.

Their customers' love for the brand is so strong that even when they tell people not to buy their products—as they did in their famous "Don't buy this jacket!" campaign—their customers rush to the store to buy products anyway.

So, how did they amass this level of loyalty? Michael Crooke, former Patagonia CEO, explains, "Customers become advocates of brands because they develop an emotional connection with their core purpose. Brands that elicit advocacy provide a value beyond just product quality and experience. This connection is something that deserves analysis, as it is the foundation of true loyalty."[1]

As Russ Stoddard, founder of Oliver Russell—one of the most progressive purpose consultancies—says, "Today the goal of a purpose-driven company is not to tell a story but to become the story."

Patagonia embodies this idea magnificently.

Purpose communicates your values as a business as much as the value of your product or services. In this new business landscape, what you stand for can deepen or destroy your relationships with your customers. For example, the 2018 Edelman Earned Brand study found that "nearly two-thirds (64 percent) of consumers around the world will buy or boycott a brand solely because of its position on a social or political issue."

We have also found that customers who choose to buy based on your purpose will not only give you their money but will spend their social currency with you as well. The Cone/Porter Novelli survey found that 78 percent of

---

1 John Moore, "The Patagonia Way to Customer Loyalty," *Brandautopsy* (Website), Accessed January 29, 2021, http://brandautopsy.com/2015/09/the-patagonia-way-to-customer-loyalty.html

DON'T TELL THE STORY BE THE STORY

Russ Stoddard

consumers would tell others to buy from a purpose-driven company and that 68 percent are more willing to share content from these companies with their social networks over that of traditional companies.

Perhaps the most telling sign of the extent to which purpose builds loyalty, the same survey revealed that customers are also becoming brands' fiercest defenders in the face of criticism. According to the data, 73 percent of consumers are also willing to stand up for a purpose-driven brand if it is spoken badly of.

Truly purpose-led brands optimize life for their customers and the communities they are part of. Those that deliver on their purpose consistently are rewarded royally. Sustainable Brands and Harris Poll found that "80% of people say they are loyal to businesses that help them achieve the Good Life" (defined by balance and simplicity, meaningful connections, money and status, personal achievement, and making a difference in the lives of others).

Building loyalty should be the goal of every business. Without customers who feel connected to your brand and continue to buy from you, the business won't survive. New customers are more expensive to acquire and don't spend as much money as loyal, repeat customers. Therefore, keeping customers coming back for more is critical to business longevity and prosperity. It is why short-term profit thinking doesn't work in the long run. Loyal customers are just better for business: they help you thrive, and they keep profits high.

For business leaders looking to drive loyalty through purpose, Patagonia's former czar of eCommerce Craig Wilson offers some sage advice. "Share your beliefs. Demonstrate how they integrate into your product, design, and presentation. Communicate what inspires your particular esthetic. Those that believe what you believe will become part of your tribe."

PRICE PREMIUM

In addition to loyalty and advocacy, customers are also willing to pay more for purpose-led brands. In a recent survey, Nielsen found that two in three consumers will pay more for products and services from brands that are committed to making a positive social impact.

As citizens become more aware of the urgent threats to people and our planet, they are showing a willingness to use their buying power to help solve these issues. As an example, a 2018 Pew Research Center survey asked people to evaluate eight potential threats to their nation. Most surveyed countries said global climate change is a major threat to their nation. In fact, it's seen as the top threat in thirteen of twenty-six surveyed countries, more than any other issue the survey asked about.

With this heightened level of awareness of climate change and our environment, it was no surprise that when IBM Research and the National Retail Federation (NRF) polled nearly nineteen thousand consumers (ages eighteen to seventy-three) from twenty-eight countries, they found that "on average, 70 percent of purpose-driven shoppers pay an added premium of 35 percent more per upfront cost for sustainable purchases, such as recycled or eco-friendly goods."[2]

Consumers are becoming much more conscious of the positive difference they can make through their everyday shopping choices. Thus, they are willing to pay a little more to contribute to a greater impact.

GROWTH

The Kantar Purpose 2020 study demonstrates that over a period of twelve years, the brands with high perceived positive impact have a brand value growth of 175 percent, versus 86 percent for medium positive impact and 70 percent for low positive impact.

Perhaps one of the best examples of this is Unilever, in many ways, the gold standard of purpose-led consumer packaged goods (CPG) companies. They have built a remarkable portfolio of Sustainable Living Brands that generate massive growth and social impact. Unilever's Sustainable Living Brands include Dove, which has helped over thirty-five million young people around the world with self-esteem education since 2005; Lifebuoy, which has reached one billion people with its hand-washing campaigns; Vaseline, which has reached three million people living on the front line of poverty and disaster

---

2   Leslie Park, "IBM Study: Purpose and Provenance Drive Bigger Profits for Consumer Goods In 2020," *IBM News Room* (Website), January 10, 2020, https://newsroom.ibm.com/2020-01-10-IBM-Study-Purpose-and-Provenance-Drive-Bigger-Profits-for-Consumer-Goods-In-2020, n.p.

with skin-healing programs; Ben & Jerry's, which campaigns for social justice and climate change; and Rin, whose Career Academy works with women across rural India through mentoring and career fairs.[3]

This success is the realized vision of its former CEO Paul Polman, who committed to making Unilever more sustainable and profitable when he took over the role in 2009. Over that span, as a purpose-led company, Unilever's (UN) stock price has returned 52 percent higher returns compared to the NYSE composite. And that level of performance shows no signs of slowing down.

In January 2020, Unilever announced that its Sustainable Living Brands are growing 69 percent faster than the rest of the business and delivering 75 percent of the company's growth. As a matter of fact, seven of Unilever's top ten brands—Dove, Knorr, Omo/Persil, Rexona/Sure, Lipton, Hellmann's, and Wall's ice cream—are all Sustainable Living Brands.[4]

Unilever describes its Sustainable Living Brands as "those that communicate a strong environmental or social purpose, with products that contribute to achieving the company's ambition of halving its environmental footprint and increasing its positive social impact."[5] While all of Unilever's brands are on a journey toward sustainability, their Sustainable Living Brands are those that are furthest ahead.

This shows the multitude of brands, industries, and categories of brands that can make a meaningful impact, while growing their businesses. Purpose and profit are no longer competing ideals; they are closely connected drivers for growth.

Unilever CEO, Alan Jope, spoke about the relationship between purpose and growth while addressing the Deutsche Bank Global Consumer Conference

3   "Unilever's purpose-led brands outperform," *Unilever* (Website), June 11, 2019, https://www.unilever.com/news/press-releases/2019/unilevers-purpose-led-brands-outperform.html, n.p.

4   Nicola Longfield, "Achieving growth in a sustainable economy," *KPMG* (Website), Accessed January29, 2020, https://home.kpmg/xx/en/home/insights/2020/02/achieving-growth-in-sustainable-economy.html, n.p.

5   "Unilever's purpose-led brands outperform," 2019, n.p.

in Paris. He said, "We believe the evidence is clear and compelling that brands with purpose grow. Purpose creates relevance for a brand; it drives talkability, builds penetration, and reduces price elasticity. In fact, we believe this so strongly that we are prepared to commit that in the future, every Unilever brand will be a brand with purpose."[6]

This level of commitment shows the massive market opportunity to grow your business among conscious consumers. Now, let's look at how employees are contributing to the purpose revolution.

---

6   "Unilever's purpose-led brands outperform," n.p.

THE RISE OF THE ACTIVIST EMPLOYEE: EMPLOYEES WANT MEANING AND PURPOSE IN THEIR WORK

One of the most fascinating trends we've seen is the rise of the activist employee: on an unprecedented level, we are seeing employees stand up to their leadership and challenge them on issues where they feel like their actions are not in line with their values. Tens of thousands of Google employees walked out on one day to protest their company paying millions of dollars in exit packages to male executives accused of sexual harassment.[7]

Amazon workers have gone on strike on "Prime Day" to protest against unfair working conditions. Facebook employees have publicly spoken out against Mark Zuckerberg's policy on allowing hate speech to thrive on the platform. In another example, the news that Wayfair had been profiting off of selling beds to the detention centers along the southern US border was immediately met with disgust and protest by people both in and outside of the company.

Employees today are empowered to speak up and be the conscience of their organization, even at the risk of losing their jobs. Why is this happening right now? We believe the groundwork has long been laid for a simmering sense of dissatisfaction over the treatment of employees, which is now boiling over in this new age of dissent.

Gallup's *State of the Global Workplace* report summarizes a wealth of data to assess how well employers and countries worldwide are using human capital in their workforces.

Well, according to its most recent survey results, employers are doing a dreadful job.

Worldwide, 85 percent of employees are not engaged (meaning they are emotionally invested and focused on creating value for their organizations every day) or are actively disengaged in their job. The vast majority of employed people across 142 countries are "not engaged" or "actively disengaged" at work, meaning they are emotionally disconnected from their workplaces and less

---

7 Neeti Ubadhye, "Google Employees Stage Worldwide Walkout," *The New York Times*, November 1, 2018, Video, 01:08, https://www.nytimes.com/video/technology/100000006192998/google-walkout-sexual-harassment.html

likely to be productive. In fact, actively disengaged workers worldwide continue to outnumber engaged workers at a rate of nearly 2–1.[8]

Considering that employees are not only the biggest investment of most businesses but also their most valuable resource to drive growth, innovation, and impact, 85 percent of global employees being disengaged is an opportunity cost at an unaffordable scale.

Although the engagement numbers in the United States are higher than average, they are far from impressive. Only 31 percent of employees reported feeling highly involved and enthusiastic about their work and workplace. In our work with companies, we see evidence of this often. Smart, talented employees with ideas and abilities are underutilized because they don't feel a deep attachment to any higher purpose of their work and company. Thus, they are putting time—but not energy or passion—into their work.

With such overwhelming levels of employee disconnection and dissatisfaction, this begs the following questions: what are employees looking for, and how can employers better provide it?

EMPLOYEES' NEW HIERARCHY OF NEEDS

Beyond titles, wages, and perks, increasingly, employees seek fulfillment in their jobs through a sense of deep meaning and connection to the work they do. If we look at jobs through the lens of Maslow's hierarchy of needs (one of the world's most accepted frameworks for ranking the different human needs in life), jobs, at their most essential function, provide us with the means to fulfill our basic needs of safety, food, and shelter. Jobs also give us the ability to gain a sense of belonging to our work communities, building friendships and extended families. Through work, we develop a sense of worth and esteem by achieving accomplishments that make us admirable in the eyes of others. That enables us to get to what was thought to be the highest level of human existence and aspiration, which Maslow called "self-actualization"—the point

---

8 "Gallup Releases New Insights on the State of the Global Workplace," *Gallup* (Blog), October 8, 2013, https://news.gallup.com/opinion/gallup/171632/gallup-releases-new-insights-state-global-workplace.aspx

MASLOW'S HIERARCHY OF NEEDS

OLD

Self-actualization

Esteem

Love/Belonging

Safety

Psychlogical

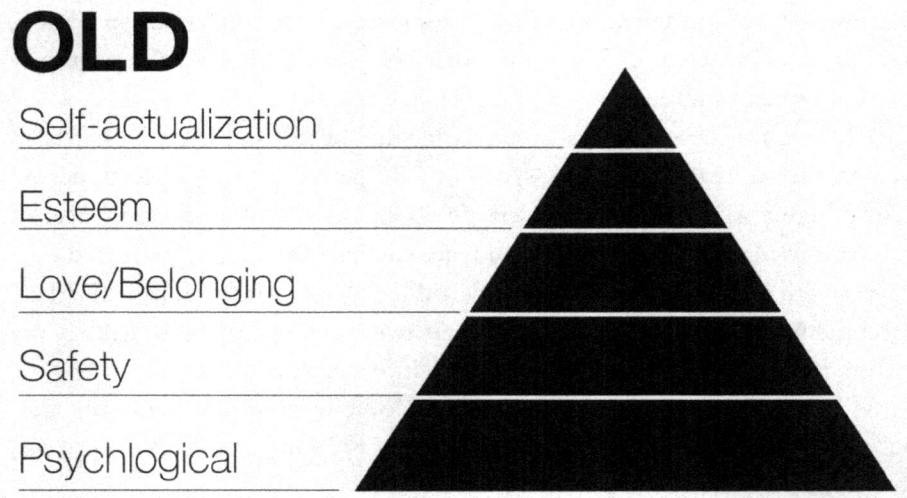

NEW

Self-transcendence

Self-actualization

Esteem

Love/Belonging

Safety

Psychlogical

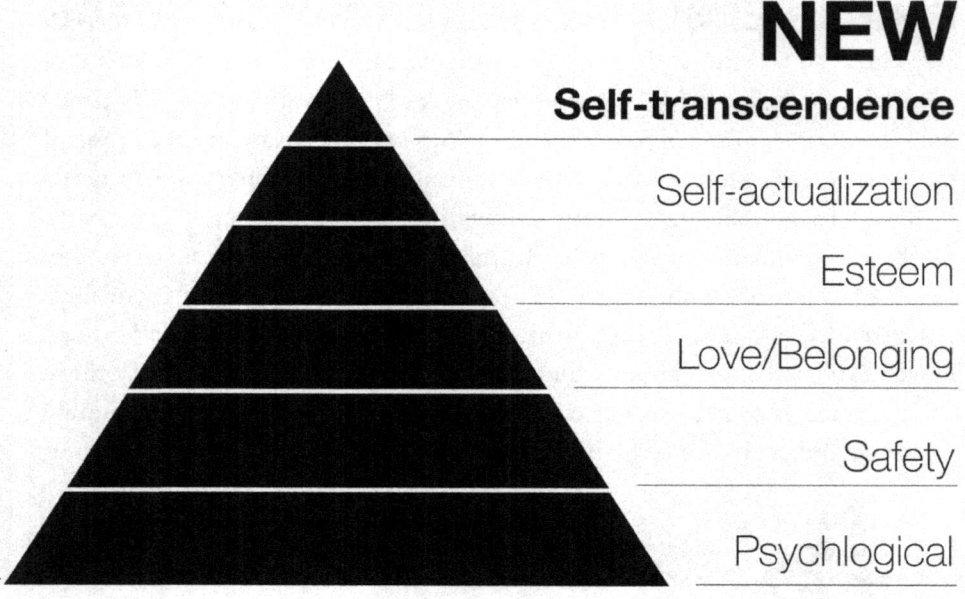

at which we recognize our fullest potential as human beings, the fullest expression of who we are. Throughout history, the goal of life and work has been to get to this level.

However, what we found fascinating in our research was that Maslow amended his model later in his life, and so the widely used illustration of his hierarchy is incomplete. In *Psychology*'s summary of Maslow's self-transcendence, they write, "In his later thinking, he (Maslow) argued that there is a higher level of development, what he called self-transcendence. We achieve this level by focusing on things beyond the self like altruism, spiritual awakening, liberation from egocentricity, and the unity of being. Transcendence refers to the very highest and most inclusive or holistic levels of human consciousness, behaving and relating, as ends rather than means, to oneself, to significant others, to human beings in general, to other species, to nature, and to the cosmos."[9]

Essentially, Maslow realized that our highest level of need is to realize our greatest gifts and apply them in service to others. This paradigm shift is what many employees are experiencing, especially after achieving the other levels of so-called success or seeing others reach those heights only to remain unhappy and unfulfilled. This results in a hunger for more than just making money. People want to make a difference in the lives of others, which is the foundation of purpose.

Employees and job seekers today are looking for career paths in which they are given the chance to give back. The Cone Communications Millennial Employee Study says millennials—who will make up 75 percent of the workforce by 2025—want to see how organizations are committed to solving problems and making a difference, proving that they have a purpose beyond making a profit.

To take that expectation further, the Cone study found that 64 percent of millennials won't even take a job if their employer doesn't have a strong corporate social responsibility (CSR) policy, and 83 percent would be more loyal to a

---

9 John Messerly, "Summary of Maslow on Self-Transcendence," *Reason and Meaning: Philosophical Reflections on life, death, and the meaning of life*, January 18, 2017, https://reasonandmeaning.com/2017/01/18/summary-of-maslow-on-self-transcendence/, n.p.

company that helps them contribute to social and environmental issues—versus 70 percent US average.[10]

The fascinating thing is that these desires to help the world actually go beyond just Millennials. IBM's Institute for Business Value released a report titled *Myth, Exaggerations and Uncomfortable Truths: The Real Story Behind Millennials in the Workplace.* Based on a multigenerational study of 1,784 employees from companies across twelve countries and six industries, it found that about the same percentage of millennials (22 percent) want to "help solve social and/or environmental challenges" as their second most important career goal (after "making a positive impact on my organization") as Gen Xers (20 percent) and baby boomers (24 percent).[11]

Millennials and Older Workers Have Many of the Same Career Goals

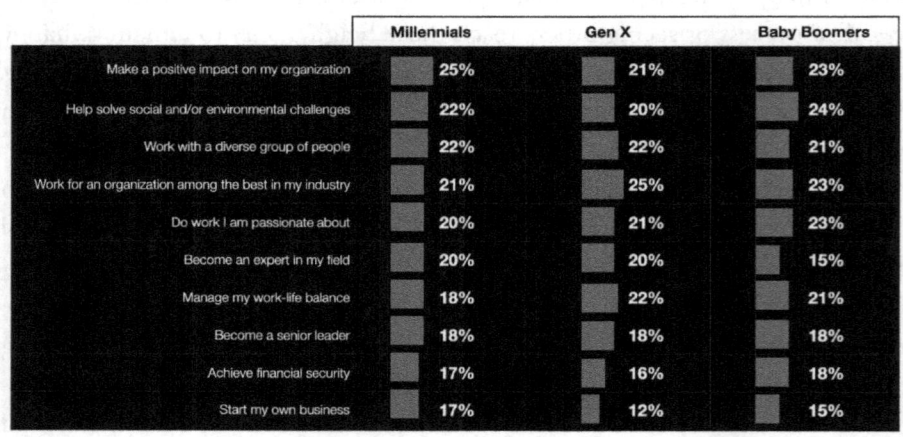

	Millennials	Gen X	Baby Boomers
Make a positive impact on my organization	25%	21%	23%
Help solve social and/or environmental challenges	22%	20%	24%
Work with a diverse group of people	22%	22%	21%
Work for an organization among the best in my industry	21%	25%	23%
Do work I am passionate about	20%	21%	23%
Become an expert in my field	20%	20%	15%
Manage my work-life balance	18%	22%	21%
Become a senior leader	18%	18%	18%
Achieve financial security	17%	16%	18%
Start my own business	17%	12%	15%

10 "Organizational Change:3/4 of Millennials Would Take a Pay Cut to Work for a Socially Responsible Com*pany,*" *Sustainable Brands* (Website), November 2, 2016, https://sustainablebrands.com/read/organizational-change/3-4-of-millennials-would-take-a-pay-cut-to-work-for-a-socially-responsible-company, n.p.

11 Bruce N. Pfau, "Generational Issues: What Do Millennials Really Want at Work? The Same Things the Rest of Us Do," *Harvard Business Review,* April 7, 2016, https://hbr.org/2016/04/what-do-millennials-really-want-at-work

In team-driven organizations, we all have the desire to be part of something bigger than ourselves. Purpose-driven companies show us how we can do so in ways that align with our passions and make the most of our abilities and limited time on this earth.

HOW EMPLOYERS CAN MEET THESE NEEDS

As B Corps wisely stated, "A business can only be a strong force for good with the support and work of committed, purpose-driven employees, and this can only be achieved by building a strong values-based culture."[12]

Jason Mayden, CEO of Super Heroic—an amazing company that was created to empower every kid to unleash his or her inner superhero through play—says, "The first product you create is your culture, and the first consumer is your employee base."

In our experience in working with and researching brands, we believe there are three keys to building strong, purpose-led cultures that make employees feel empowered and engaged:

1. Clearly define and live your purpose

Your organization's purpose is the most important thing to know and stay true to. You should treat it as your North Star, your signal that cuts through the noise. Every employee needs to embody your company's purpose, and it starts with clearly understanding it. It should not just live in annual reports or in PowerPoint presentations; it should be visible throughout the halls of your organization and in your daily communications as a promise to workers and the world for why you show up each day. Your purpose should be the first filter for what to do, or not do. It should create a consistent level of accountability for everyone who works in the organization.

---

12 "New Assessment Helps Employers Find Job Seekers Who Want to Be a Force For Good: Introducing the First Purpose Assessment for Recruitment," *B The Change* (Website), January 16, 2020, https://bthechange.com/new-assessment-helps-employers-find-job-seekers-who-want-to-be-a-force-for-good-f9228f6adc8c

2. Make it personal

Beyond identifying a shared brand purpose, ask people to discuss what gives them personal meaning at work. In our consultancy work, we love doing this exercise with the brands' employees. The variety of responses leads to inspiring insights that make it easier for managers to connect with people in ways that really resonate. Along the way, you are bound to learn something new about your colleagues and possibly about yourself. It also enables compassion and understanding for the whole person and everything he or she shows up with each day, creating a culture with safety that promotes both personal and professional development.

3. Unleash the culture builders

Every organization has a pool of change agents, a network of positive energizers who are open and willing to take initiative and help the common cause. They are a purpose-led organization's secret weapon. These are the hand raisers, evangelists, and action takers who, if property engaged, can assist with every step of cultural change at all levels of the organization.

Companies that embody these qualities have employees who trust and enjoy the people they work with and have pride in the work they do.

THE REWARDS FOR MEETING THESE NEEDS ARE MASSIVE

Research has shown that employees who feel like their work creates a positive impact are more likely to be drawn to your company in the first place, to feel fulfilled and inspired to be innovative, to promote and defend their company publicly, and to stay on the job longer, reducing turnover at great financial upside.

Recruitment

Purpose-led brands attract purpose-led employees. For an example of this, let's look at B Work, who is a leading expert in connecting purpose-driven job seekers with positions at social enterprises who are using business as a force for good. On the B Work job site, purpose-driven employers post jobs, and candidates can search for meaningful work among the thousands of jobs available.

According to their report, B Work data shows that Certified B Corporations—businesses that meet the highest standards of verified social and environmental performance, public transparency, and legal accountability to balance profit and purpose—on average attract more than two times as many candidates as noncertified corporations.[13]

To add even more muscle to their matchmaking abilities, B Work has pioneered a way for companies to identify potential employees who are more inclined to thrive in a purpose-led environment.

This has the ability to be a transformative tool for brands that want to recruit and retain conscious employees to work for them. Not only can you find great talent, but you may be able to do so at more affordable salaries. For instance, a survey by Swytch—a blockchain-based clean energy platform—found that most millennials would take a pay cut to work at an environmentally responsible company. In that study, almost 50 percent of all respondents and 75 percent of millennial workers said they would make that trade-off. As a matter of fact, 10+ percent would take a cut in pay between $5,000–$10,000, and slightly more than 3 percent said they'd be willing to go even further and take a pay cut of over $10,000 a year if they believed the employer had a green frame of mind.

And when it comes to Gen Z, again, the data is even more compelling. The newest entrant to the workforce, Gen Z is expected to make up 30 percent of the US workforce in just four years. For a deeper look, a study by WeSpire found that Gen Z is "the first generation to prioritize purpose over salary. They read Mission Statements and Values documents to select where they work and want their employer's values to match their values."[14] They expect consistency and authenticity and will call you out, often publicly, if they don't see it. They will leave companies they believe are hiding or putting too much spin on bad

13 Certified B Corporation (website), Accessed January 30, 2020, https://bcorporation.net

14 "15 Critical Insights into Gen Z, Purpose and the Future of Work," *WeSpire* (Website), Accessed January 30, 2020, http://www.wespire.com/wp-content/uploads/2018/07/WeSpire_GenZ-2.pdf, p.2.

news or ignoring their negative environmental or social impacts or that have toxic workplace cultures.

A study by Peakon reviewing employee comments also found that Generation Z is "the only generation to reference social concerns within employee comments. Raised in a time when the effects of climate change are making weekly headlines, it shows that they care deeply about the world around them."

So if you want to future-proof your talent for the next two generations and attract the best and the brightest, it is crucial that you show them how their work ladders up to something more than just a quarterly profit goal. That is why to be a place that candidates want to work, companies need to be successful in promoting their purpose through showcasing their culture, values, and impact during the recruitment process.

Satisfaction and Engagement

When an employee is aligned with the company's purpose and is inspired toward doing purposeful work, sentiments and performance improve. As statistics show, employees who derive meaning and significance from their work were more than three times as likely to stay with their organizations. They also report "1.7 times higher job satisfaction"[15] and "1.4 times more engagement" at work. To further the case, LinkedIn's *Purpose at Work Global Report* study revealed 73 percent of professionals who identify as purpose-driven are satisfied with their jobs.

This satisfaction and engagement set the groundwork for forward-thinking to make a positive change in the communities your company aims to impact.

Innovation

Meaningful work is a strong motivator for your employees to tackle problems and challenges with passion and purpose. Deloitte Insights *2020 Global Marketing Trends* report found that purpose-driven companies report 30 percent higher levels of innovation. This illustrates that companies who concentrate

---

15 Schwartz, Tony, and Christine Porath. "Why You Hate Work." *The New York Times*, The New York Times, 30 May 2014, www.nytimes.com/2014/06/01/opinion/sunday/why-you-hate-work.html.

their efforts on providing purpose-driven work experiences to their employees, they will, in turn, be inspired and empowered to contribute to the organization's bigger vision.

This is giving rise to the *social intrapreneur*—a new breed of employee who creates innovative ideas inside businesses that have a social or environmental impact. An example of this we are going to share in this book is Microsoft's Saqib Shaikh (whom we interview in the section entitled, Purpose is about Picking Your Shields – And Sword) who, in his twenties, and inspired by Microsoft's purpose *to empower every person and every organization on the planet to achieve more*, began to look at his loss of sight as an opportunity. He asked, "What if the world thought of disability as an engine for innovation rather than a disadvantage?" With that mindset, Saqib has led internal initiatives breaking new ground through innovations like the Seeing AI app, which is helping solve problems for the millions of people around the world with low or no vision.

The Harvard EY Beacon Institute survey found that half (53 percent) of executives at companies with a strong sense of purpose said their organization is successful with innovation and transformation efforts, while less than one-fifth (19 percent) report success at companies that have not thought about purpose.

At a time when the customers are asking brands to solve problems in their lives more than ever, those that inspire employees to unleash their moral imaginations to solve the biggest problems people are facing will have a big and long-standing advantage over brands that don't.

Retention

Benevity is the global leader in corporate social responsibility and employee engagement software, including online giving, matching, volunteering, community investment, and purpose-driven actions. Their engagement study, which examined the activity of more than two million users on the Benevity platform, found that turnover dropped by an average of 57 percent in the employee group most deeply connected to their companies' giving and volunteering efforts.[16]

---

16 "Benevity Study Links Employee Centric Corporate Goodness Programs to Big Gains in

Given the significant cost of employee turnover, retaining good employees is critical for financial stability and culture building. Studies show that the total cost of losing an employee can range from tens of thousands of dollars to 1.5 to 2 times an employee's annual salary, which for US companies totals more than $160 billion a year. This shows that giving employees a sense of meaning in their work has tangible and hugely impactful benefits.[17]

The good news is creating purpose-oriented workplaces will increase retention. Research by Tony Schwartz and Christine Porath of the Energy Project showed employees who gain a sense of meaning from their work experience are much (three times) more likely to stay with their organization.[18] They can acquire this meaning through their everyday work as well as through opportunities for community service.

CUSTOMERS ARE WATCHING

The world is facing an unprecedented crisis that is already leading to catastrophic consequences for businesses, causing massive layoffs around the world. As of today, the jobless claims in the United States is at forty million.[19]

Customers are paying attention to the ways companies are treating their employees, using their actions as a signifier for how trustworthy and support worthy companies are. According to a research report by Edelman, 90 percent of people say brands must do everything they can to protect the well-being

Retention," *Benevity* (Website), May 31, 2018, https://www.benevity.com/media/media-releases/benevity-study-links-employee-centric-corporate-goodness-programs-big-gains

17 "Retention: A Strategic Challenge," Alex Charles: Search Partners, Accessed January 30, 2020, https://alexcharles.co/retention-strategies/

18 Tony Schwartz and Christine Porath, "Opinion: Why You Hate Work," *The New York Times*, May 30, 2014, https://www.nytimes.com/2014/06/01/opinion/sunday/why-you-hate-work.html

19 "U.S. Jobless Claims Pass 40 Million: Live Business Updates," *The New York Times*, Contributed by Ben Casselman, Patricia Cohen, Kate Conger, Maggie Haberman, Niraj Chokshi, Ben Dooley, Sapna Maheshwari, Geneva Abdul, Mohammed Hadi, Emily Flitter, Jim Tankersley, David Gelles, David Yaffe-Bellany, Tiffany Hsu, Carlos Tejada, Katie Robertson and Gregory Schmidt, January 20, 2021, https://www.nytimes.com/2020/05/28/business/unemployment-stock-market-coronavirus.html

Half the world
has a poverty
of means

**the other has
a poverty of
meaning.**

Justin Dillon

and financial security of their employees and their suppliers, even if it means suffering big financial losses until the pandemic ends.[20]

Not supporting employees right now will have long-term costs for businesses. Seventy-one percent of customers say, "Brands and companies that I see placing their profits before people during this crisis will lose my trust forever."[21] This is the time for businesses to show up for their employees in the ways their employees need them to.

As our friend Justin Dillon (author of the fantastic book 'A Selfish Plan to Change the World') once said 'Half the world has a poverty of means. The other has a poverty of meaning'. Corporations are one of the few things on the planet that can solve both: by giving their employees meaning, they can help provide means for the most underserved on the planet.

20 Edelman, 2021, n.p.

21 "Special Report: Brand Trust and the Coronavirus Pandemic: Edelman Trust Barometer 2020," Accessed January 30, 2021, https://www.edelman.com/sites/g/files/aatuss191/files/2020-03/2020%20Edelman%20Trust%20Barometer%20Brands%20and%20the%20Coronavirus.pdf, p.27.

THE RISE OF THE IMPACT INVESTOR: INVESTORS WANT TO MAKE MONEY WHILE POSITIVELY IMPACTING PEOPLE AND THE PLANET

Finally, let's look at investors and the exponential increase in "impact investing"—investing in ways that generate social impact alongside financial returns.

For those not familiar with this term, it is sometimes also called "ESG investing": "E" is for "environment" and includes issues such as climate change policies, carbon footprint, and use of renewable energies. "S" is for "social" and includes workers' rights and protections. "G" is for "governance" and includes executive compensation, diversity of the board, and corporate transparency.

ESG investing is growing rapidly in the investment community, propelled by three key enablers for growth: an increasing number of citizens who want to become more conscious investors, more resources and support available to help them do so wisely, and the above-average returns purpose-led companies deliver.

MORE PEOPLE (AND INSTITUTIONS) WANT TO BE CONSCIOUS INVESTORS

Beyond making money, people and institutions are thinking more holistically about the legacy they want to build. Morgan Simon, an impact investing expert, observes, "No one wants to tell their grandchildren they built wealth for their family by locking up someone else's in private prisons, or destroyed the environment so thoroughly that there's no world left to enjoy. People are thinking more about a holistic return definition that is not just about making 8% vs 7%, but about societal impact."[22]

Young investors in particular seem to be driven by the idea of contributing to positive impact. According to deVere Group, a survey of millennial investors around the world found that some 77 percent of them say that environmental, social, and governance concerns are their top priority when considering

---

22 Barney Cotton, "What Is Impact Investing and Why Is It on the Rise?" *Business Leader* (Website), August 27, 2019, https://www.businessleader.co.uk/what-is-impact-investing-and-why-is-it-on-the-rise/72276/

investment opportunities, above anticipated returns (cited by 10 percent of those polled).

These values seem to be even stronger among the newest generation of workers. Swell Investing's Money Meets Morals survey found that 84 percent of Gen Z investors are either already invested in socially responsible or impact investments or plan to invest this way in the future. Nearly one in three Gen Z investors (31 percent) said they would be willing to allocate 50 percent or more of their investment portfolio to socially responsible or impact investments. One in four millennial investors would do the same.

However, this trend is not just happening on an individual level. Among institutional investors, we are seeing significant shifts of mindsets that are moving massive amounts of capital toward purpose driven companies.

Perhaps the most powerful institutional investor in this new world of conscious capitalism is Laurence D. Fink, the founder and chief executive of BlackRock, the world's largest asset manager with nearly $7 trillion in investments. Each year, CEOs receive a letter from Fink, which in many ways sets the course for how capital will be allocated for the year. In 2018, Fink's letter informed business leaders that their companies need to do more than make profits—they need to contribute to society as well if they want to receive the support of BlackRock. He noted, "Society is demanding that companies, both public and private, serve a social purpose. To prosper over time, every company must not only deliver financial performance, but also show how it makes a positive contribution to society."[23]

This announcement sent shock waves throughout the business world, but it was this next statement that has served as the ultimate validator of purpose as a driver of performance: "Profits are in no way inconsistent with purpose. In fact, profits and purpose are inextricably linked."

This call to action by Fink coupled with brands embracing the challenge and delivering strong results has catalyzed an incredible increase in impact investing. A Bank of America (BofA) Merrill Lynch report predicted a "tsunami"

---

23 Laurance D. Fink, "BlackRock: Focus on Society and Profits," *The New York Times*, January 16, 2018, https://www.nytimes.com/interactive/2018/01/16/business/dealbook/document-BlackRock-s-Laurence-Fink-Urges-C-E-O-s-to-Focus.html?dlbk, p.1.

of capital flowing to ESG stocks, fueled by high levels of interest among women, millennials, and wealthy individuals. BofA Merrill Lynch predicts that over the next two decades, $20 trillion in assets will flow into sustainable funds and strategies, nearly equaling the market value of the S&P 500 today (some $24.7 trillion).

Furthermore, according to Morningstar, "Net flows into sustainable funds this year are on track to triple their 2018 total, driven by ESG (environmental, social and governance) factors as well as the desire to make a social impact."

As impact investing becomes more widely adopted, with younger workers tying their fortunes to the betterment of the world, we will see even more examples of conversions to more enlightened investment.

CONSCIOUS INVESTORS NOW HAVE MORE RESOURCES AND SUPPORT

As the Good Trade noted, "Where we invest financially is one of the most direct and simple ways we can contribute to values-based positive change in the world."[24] Along with this surge in impact investing are more products, resources, and support available for those who want to invest more ethically. Martine Costello of Impactivate noted, "A January 2018 report by Morningstar found that more funds than ever incorporate ESG or sustainability goals across fifty-six equity and bond categories, with positive short- and long-term performance. Assets under management and net flows have reached all-time highs, and investment choices include both active and passive strategies."[25]

For further evidence of this growth, Global Impact Investing Network (GIIN) estimated that more than half of active impact investing organizations made their first transactions in the last ten years. They estimate that there are

---

24 "5 Socially Responsible Investment Platforms That Help You Invest in Both Purpose & Profit," *The Good Trade* (Website), Accessed January 30, 2021, https://www.thegoodtrade. com/features/socially-responsible-investing-platforms, n.p.

25 Martine Costello, "The Rise of Individual Impact Investors," *Impactivate* (Website), July 26, 2018, https://www.theimpactivate.com/the-rise-of-individual-impact-investors/, n.p.

now more than 1,340 organizations managing $502 billion (£402 billion) in impact investments globally.

This increase of experts in the field has helped solve two of the biggest barriers in getting more people to reallocate their investments into companies that are socially responsible. The first is, according to Teresa Orsolini, formerly of Swell investing, many people don't know where their money is currently going: "It's kind of a 'set it and forget it' mentality and that's becoming an acceptable phrase in America. Do you know the top three holdings in your 401(k)? Most people don't. And so we are challenging people to read the label of their investments. We think that investing should be personal: it doesn't mean you spend hours a day on it, but it means that you know where your money is going and it aligns with your values."[26]

Companies are now helping individuals better understand their current portfolio and identity holdings that may not align with their values. This new generation of socially responsible investment platforms is easy, automated, transparent, and customizable so people can invest their money in green tech, renewable energy, clean water, fossil-fuel-free funds, and more.

THE MARKET IS REWARDING CONSCIOUS INVESTORS

The Business Roundtable "Statement on the Purpose of a Corporation" created shock waves when it announced that 181 of America's leading CEOs had signed a letter signaling a shift away from the era of shareholder primacy (as most famously propagated by Milton Friedman) toward "stakeholder capitalism," focused on creating long-term value, better serving all stakeholders—investors, employees, communities, suppliers, and customers. But the data back up why this move is essential for the long-term success of publicly held companies.

A twenty-year study by the Torrey Project explodes the myth that an ethical, stakeholder-driven approach to business cannot lead to shareholder returns

---

26 Afdhel Aziz, "How Swell Is Riding the Wave of Impact Investing," *Forbes* (Website), August 29, 2018, https://www.forbes.com/sites/afdhelaziz/2018/08/29/how-swell-is-riding-the-wave-of-impact-investing/?sh=73ca97dad470, n.p.

by examining the long-term historical performance of different sets of companies, including the S&P 500, Jim Collins's "Good to Great" companies, Raj Sisodia's stakeholder-focused "Firms of Endearment," and Ethisphere's 2019 "Most Ethical Companies."

After comparing these four sets of companies' financial performance on the NASDAQ and NYSE over the past twenty years, they found that while ethical companies do enjoy a higher level of stock price growth (50 percent higher than that of the S&P 500 over the same period), stakeholder-focused companies (Sisodia's Firms of Endearment) had the highest growth of all in stock price (100 percent higher than that of the S&P 500 over the same period).

These data have two clear conclusions: (1) Ethical business behavior correlates with high financial returns. (2) Companies that take things one step further and adopt a stakeholder-focused model (that explicitly serves employees, customers, suppliers, business partners, investors, local communities, the environment, and society) have historically shown even higher returns than standard ethical companies.

Looking at performance through more of a global lens shows how widespread this is. In a survey of 1,500 global C-suite executives, DDI—a global leadership consulting firm—found that those companies that both define and act with a sense of purpose outperformed the financial markets by a whopping 42 percent.

We are seeing this consistently in an overwhelming majority of purpose-led companies. The global customer-centricity study Insights 2020, led by research firm Kantar Millward Brown, found that when companies or brands are linked to a purpose, 80 percent of them outperformed the market. In comparison, only 32 percent of brands that are not purpose led managed to perform better than the market.

What is most remarkable is how ESG companies are performing even in the midst of the COVID-19 crisis. HSBC analyzed 613 shares of global public companies valued at over $500 million (US) where climate solutions generate at least 10 percent of revenues. In addition, they looked at 140 stocks with the highest ESG scores and values above the global average from December 10, 2019 (the crisis's start), until March 23, 2020, and from February 24, when high volatility began. The climate-focused stocks outperformed others by 7.6

percent from December and by 3 percent since February. The ESG shares beat others by about 7 percent for both periods. Companies that are built to solve problems in the world display above-average levels of resilience in their performance.[27]

A WARNING

Enlightened capitalism is not a new concept, and unfortunately there have been promising moments of businesses placing purpose above profit only to revert back to short-term thinking. The short termism of quarterly reporting means publicly held companies are too focused on hitting a number for their shareholders, which prevents long-term clarity of purpose. Another factor is that the average tenure of a CEO is now five years, meaning that there is no bandwidth to think about the long-term vision.

This is the time for businesses to stay true to their values and purpose. It is also the time for shareholders to give companies the time they need to focus on what matters most: long-term thinking and wealth creation.

Let's begin with exploring how brands can discover their purpose in the world.

---

27 James Murray, "HSBC: Companies focused on climate change 'outperformed' as virus spread," *GreenBiz* (Website), April 6, 2020, https://www.greenbiz.com/article/hsbc-companies-focused-climate-change-outperformed-virus-spread

PART II

DISCOVERING PURPOSE

We enjoy visiting the corporate offices of the people we work with throughout the world. Each office has its own vibe, with a different take on space, design, and culture. Our hosts take great pride in showing off where they work, and they particularly enjoy introducing us to their coworkers, the people who make the company so special. Typically, these informal office tours consist of two phases.

During the first leg of the tour, we meet employees who are working in functions such as marketing, sales, manufacturing, technology, finance, and design. These are the people who wake up each day to drive revenue, or as some would say, "keep the lights on." They are normally frantically talking or typing or on their way to one of the many prebooked conference rooms to come up with the next great idea. After a round of friendly hellos closes, we meet another group of workers. This group is typically clustered in a smaller section of the floor and usually works in functions such as CSR, sustainability, diversity and inclusion, and community relations. They see their jobs as using the resources of the company to keep their workers engaged and doing some good in the world. In most instances, we have found that these groups rarely intersect, coming together occasionally to converse but rarely ever to collaborate.

People often ask how CSR, sustainability, cause marketing, and diversity and inclusion all fit with the idea of purpose. Here's the simplest way we at Conspiracy of Love, our purpose consultancy, can describe it—all of these powerful movements are "strands" that are weaving together into the "rope" of purpose that is much stronger when they are integrated. They are all necessary conditions for purpose—how a business can be a force for good—to flourish.

Today's purpose-led companies understand how to build this "rope of purpose." They have learned that when the "doing good" and "making money" functions of the company intertwine because of a unifying purpose, the business becomes so much stronger. A rope of purpose weaves organizational teams together to encourage the integration of perspectives and exchanges of knowledge. In turn, it inspires more collaboration and decreases divisions and silos, giving everyone a greater sense of contribution to both the company's income and its impact in the world.

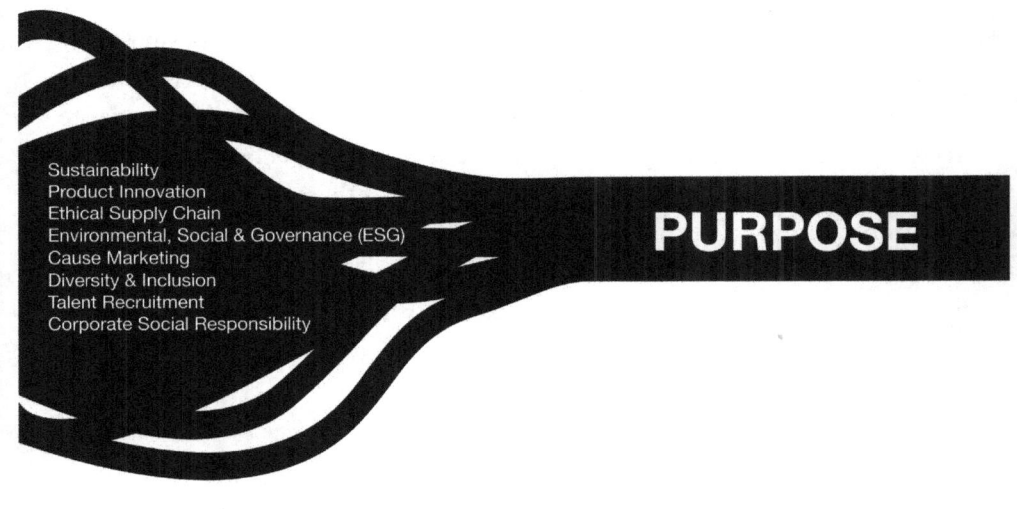

Sustainability
Product Innovation
Ethical Supply Chain
Environmental, Social & Governance (ESG)
Cause Marketing
Diversity & Inclusion
Talent Recruitment
Corporate Social Responsibility

PURPOSE

In addition to these elements, true purpose involves going beyond—into the realm of innovating products and services that create positive social and environmental impact—and embedding that intention into the heart of your business model so that whether a company does well financially or not, the commitment to doing good stays the same.

Each strand is equally important and made stronger by the others. If one strand becomes frayed, then the integrity of the rope is at risk.

Thus, it is not surprising that the results of a ten-year study of 50,000 brands found that the fifty highest-performing businesses are the ones driven by "brand ideals" (another term for purpose), and these fifty businesses grew three times faster than their competitors.[28]

Getting to this stage of purpose-driven performance as a business is a journey that starts with discovering your purpose, which we will discuss in the next section. However, before we begin the next step, we feel it's essential to make sure you understand the language we will use in this book. One of the biggest challenges when discussing this topic is that there does not seem to be a commonly accepted set of terms to define "purpose" and how a company then translates that purpose into action. For the goal of this book, we will share the framework we use in our consulting work with brands.

---

28 "Why Purpose," *Jim Stengel Company* (Website), Accessed January 30, 2021, https://www. jimstengel.com/purpose/

DEFINITIONS

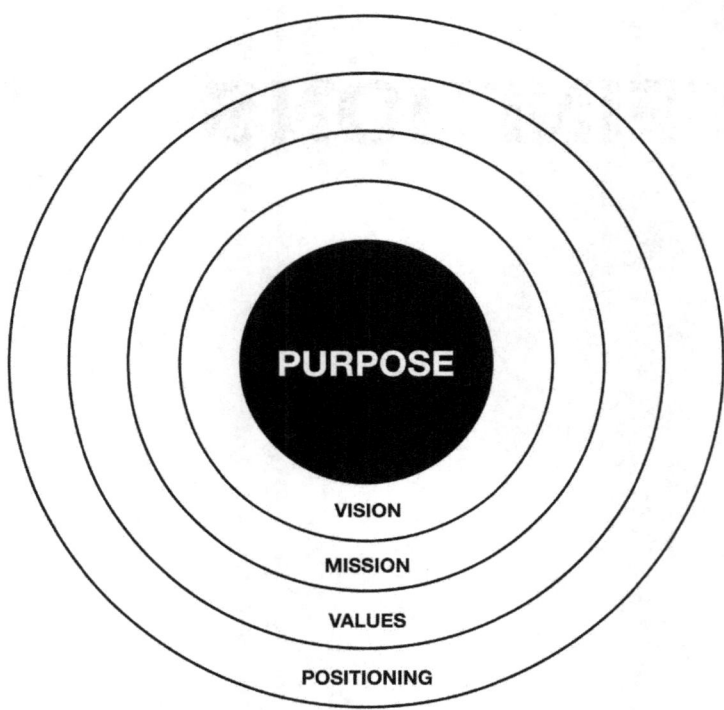

DEFINITIONS

Purpose: Why your company or brand exists

Vision: Where you want to get to by a specific point in time in line with the Purpose

Missions: What bold moves do you need to take to achieve the vision

Values: How you behave as a brand, what behaviors and attitudes you display

Positioning: How all of the above is encapsulated to occupy a distinct place in people's minds

Purpose is why the company or brand exists, the higher-order reason for your company, how it helps serve society.

The best definition of purpose is 'an aspirational reason for being that inspires action that benefits shareholders and stakeholders as well as local and global societies.' Let's look at the three parts of this sentence:

An aspirational reason for being means a company should exist to accomplish an ambitious goal or achievement. It should give people a moon shot goal to strive for every day.

Next, *inspires action*—once you have set the ambition, your purpose should compel people to do something to help achieve it.

And *that benefits shareholders and stakeholders, as well as local and global societies*—instead of creating a false choice between whether a company should serve shareholders, stakeholders, or society, we believe business should reward all three (ideally in equal measure). Organizations should always strive for a win-win-win.

A succinct, well-articulated brand purpose that everyone in the company knows and believes in is crucial to driving differentiation, relevance, and growth. Our favorite story to illustrate the power of purpose to inspire organizations is that of US president John F. Kennedy. He was walking around NASA in 1962 and saw a janitor carrying a broom. When he asked the man what he did, the janitor responded, "Well, Mr. President, I'm helping put a man on the moon." It showed how the purpose of NASA had powerfully spread to every single person within the organization.

Vision is *where* the company wants to go—the destination where you want the brand or business to be in the future. The vision informs the kind of company that you need to create to achieve the purpose. A vision can be more granular and defined by category and time: for instance, a financial services company can set itself the vision of being "Canada's best community bank by 2030." It clearly lays out the geographical territory, a business category, and a timeline to get there. It's what the company must achieve, in a measurable way, in order to fulfil its purpose.

Missions answers the question, *What* initiatives does the company need to enact to achieve the vision? These could be specific initiatives or tactics centered around product development, operational excellence, go-to-market strategies, or brand communications. For instance, in the chapter about Tanyaradzwa Sahanga from Adidas, we explore one particular mission—an initiative to create the world's first truly circular sneaker.

The phrase "one purpose many missions" is helpful in thinking of the relationship between the multiple activities of a company and its higher-order reason for being.

Values refer to *how* the organization/brand needs to behave—privately and publicly—to achieve the missions. It's the attitudes and deeply cherished beliefs that are at the core of everyone who works there. It's how they behave when no one is looking. Choose your values very carefully because they are the biggest drivers of your organizational culture, the foundation for everything else. We believe *your values drive your value* (both in business and in your career).

Positioning is *who* you are in the eyes of the marketplace. At this point, you can tie all of the preceding (which the outside world never sees) together to create the story of who you are and why you exist. Nike's purpose is "to bring inspiration and innovation to every athlete* in the world." However, the outside world only sees "Nike. Just Do It." But in those four simple words is imbued the noble purpose of the company, made powerful by its consistent and deeply authentic focus over time.

YOUR VALUES
DRIVE YOUR
VALUE

SEVEN QUALITIES OF A GREAT PURPOSE STATEMENT

Now that we have defined the components of a brand or corporate purpose architecture and showed how they all fit together, you can see how vital a purpose statement is. It sets the course for the company's vision, mission, values, position, and, ultimately, behavior.

But what are the elements of a great brand or company purpose statement? Crafting one is as much a creative act as a strategic act. We are geeks about purpose statements and collect them like other people collect stamps. Over the past four years, we have looked at purpose statements from hundreds of brands, as well as worked with Fortune 500 brands to help craft theirs. All of this has given us a wealth of insights into how great companies articulate their purpose.

Here are seven qualities we have identified. It is important to note that these are not a checklist—meaning a purpose statement does not need to have all of these qualities, but it should have some combination of these elements. We will also share where we think some purpose statements miss the mark.

1. It is inspiring

A great brand purpose statement should send a shiver down your spine when you hear it. It should be memorable, aspirational, inspirational, and even poetic to be the spark at the heart of your company that keeps the engine running. Remember, the statement's primary goal is to clarify and inspire action.

Our all-time favorite statement is from the Steve Jobs–era Apple. Are you ready? "To make a contribution to the world by making tools for the mind that advance humankind."

Wow. That one sentence is packed with such ambition, such scale, such determination. (It even rhymes!) It communicates both an inspiring goal and how it will achieve it.

Unfortunately, you won't find that purpose statement on the Apple website anymore. What you will find is this: "To empower creative exploration and self-expression."

This statement is OK. But you could apply that same purpose statement to Adobe or other enablers of creative expression. It doesn't have the majesty of the original, which befits a company the size and importance of Apple. That may explain why while the company has dominated the creative tools space, it has lost that sense of world-changing ambition that it once had.

Another great example is Adidas: "Through sport, we have the power to change lives."

Although some may see sports as mere entertainment, Adidas recognizes and embraces the higher power of sports in our world. As Nelson Mandela famously said, "Sport has the power to change the world. It has the power to inspire. It has the power to unite people in a way that little else does. Sport can create hope where once there was only despair."[29]

It is through this lens that Adidas looks at its role in the world, and this purpose inspires not just its employees but also its community of customers. One of Adidas's recent success stories has been its partnership with Parley, whose mission is to end the destruction of our oceans. Adidas recognized that saving the oceans is one of the most important ways to change lives for the better. The company teamed with Parley to create sneakers made out of ocean plastic and activated their running community to wear the shoes and help raise awareness and money for the cause. Adidas donated money to Save the Oceans for every kilometer run by their community. To date, Adidas has sold over eleven million pairs of Parley shoes, generating $2 billion in sales, showing a great purpose statement can inspire innovation, design, retail, and customer action.

Now after looking at Adidas's purpose, let's contrast this with Lyft's (a company we love, by the way): "Improve people's lives with the world's best transportation."

Hmm. Very practical but a bit flat, right?

2. It should be brief
A good purpose statement should be as short and sweet as possible to aid memorability. You should be able to stop any employee in the corridors and ask him or her, and he or she should be able to recite it from memory.

---

29 Nelson Mandela, "Sport has the power to change the world," *Laureus World Sports Inaugural Awards*, February 9, 2000, Monaco, Youtube Video, 04:35, https://www.youtube.com/watch?v=y1-7w-bJCtY

For instance, here's Red Bull's: "To give wings to people and ideas."

The "people" part is self-explanatory: the snowboarders, the skateboarders, the extreme sports enthusiasts who are its core base. But the "ideas" part is also very clever. In essence, it allows them to move into territories like music (with the phenomenal Red Bull Music Academy), as well as social entrepreneurship (the little-known social impact vertical Red Bull Amaphiko, which has now been spun off into a stand-alone entity).

Red Bull Amaphiko (pronounced "amapico," which is the Zulu word for *wings*) originated with the Red Bull South Africa team, who developed the platform to help South African entrepreneurs. The program was so successful that Red Bull has now expanded it into multiple markets, like Brazil and the United States. So far, 110 social entrepreneurs have been through the Red Bull Amaphiko Academy programs in these countries, with over 70 percent running and growing their businesses with sustainable revenue streams and robust social impact.

Now, that's giving wings to people and ideas.

Here's Zappos's: "We deliver wow."

It covers this insanely customer-centric company's zealousness in making sure that the experience of shopping with Zappos is elevated from a purely functional one to a joyous, delightful one. Every word matters in a purpose statement. *Wow* is such a great word. It conveys so much in three letters.

Let's look at Google's: "To organize the world's information."

We admit, at first look, it sounds pretty scientific and dry, but when you consider the size of the task versus the brevity of the intention, it packs a lot into that phrase.

Netflix is another excellent example. Its purpose is "to entertain the world."

It's simple but awesomely ambitious in its scope. The whole world! It also doesn't tell us "how" it's going to entertain the world, leaving the company open to exploring channels beyond streaming. Netflix VR headsets someday?

Contrast this to Disney's, which we would give a B-: "To entertain, inform, and inspire people around the globe through the power of unparalleled storytelling."

Disney is a large company and does many things. So, we get it. This statement covers everything from entertainment (Marvel, Disney, Pixar, Lucasfilm) to information (ESPN, Vice), and there is no doubt that the company's super-power is "unparalleled storytelling." But it sounds like a committee wrote it.

What is our all-time worst in terms of brevity? See if you can guess which company's this is: "To be Earth's most customer-centric company, to build a place where people can come to find and discover anything they might want to buy online."

Any guesses? Yes, it's Amazon. We would craft something more about their relentless ability to get the things you desire into your hands in an almost magical way. How about "We exist to empower anyone to buy anything, anywhere, anytime."

3. It should have a role and an outcome

Our good friend and frequent collaborator Ben Cleaver (who runs the terrific agency BigSmall in the UK) contributed this one to our list. Many good purpose statements have a role for the brand—and an outcome they wish to see in the world. For instance, here is outdoor retailer REI's purpose statement: "To awaken a life-long love of the outdoors."

This statement is beautiful. REI's role is to "awaken"—to spark, to inspire—with the outcome being a passion for the natural world. And what do people with a passion for the natural world need? Camping and outdoor equipment.

However, REI's purpose goes beyond the pragmatic. For example, REI's "Opt Outside" campaign challenges people to forego Black Friday (the most significant retail day in the United States) and instead go out and enjoy nature. This initiative connects with the brand's desire to get customers to find ways to help combat the climate crisis. A good purpose statement can resonate on multiple levels: commercial, emotional, social, in some cases, even political.

Another favorite of ours is Barbie's. This was Barbie's original purpose statement dating back to 1959: "To inspire the limitless potential in every girl."

This statement was crafted by her creator, Ruth Handler (whose daughter's name was…you guessed it, Barbie). Somewhere along the way though, the brand lost its focus on the "every" part, with many girls feeling unrepresented in the thin, white, and blond models. This loss of concentration led to Barbie losing its cultural cachet and being condemned by feminists as being dangerous.

But that very focus on "every" is what led to the brand's reinvention as the most diverse and inclusive doll on the planet now (with Barbies in every shape, size, and color) as we unpack in the chapter with Kim Culmone from Mattel. Today, Barbie's role as inspiration is coupled with a desire to create positive role models for every girl on the planet, regardless of what she looks like or what possibility she can imagine.

Another example is Walmart's, which is simple and powerful: "To help people save money so they can live better."

There is a humble but noble aspiration that is baked into this statement. And when you multiply this by the 140 million customers who visit a Walmart every week, you can see the enormous impact that this has on people's quality of life and the American economy in general.

4. It may have a tension that is unresolvable

Sometimes a great purpose statement may be wrestling with two conflicting intentions that create a space for continuous innovation and growth. The following are some examples of great purpose statements that fall into this category:

Chobani's purpose is "to make better food for more people."

We love this statement. There are two conflicting intentions baked into this statement. To make "better" food (food that is higher quality, has better ingredients, and is organically and ethically made) but for the most people (democratizing access so that that good food doesn't have to come at too high a premium). Resolving that tension can create real energy and innovation at the heart of the brand.

There is a similar tension in IKEA's purpose statement (which also has delightful Swedish overtones): "To create a better everyday life for the many people."

This tension imbues IKEA's mission to make durable, sustainably made furniture and homewares—but at the lowest possible cost. Again, this forces innovation, leading to IKEA's fantastic work toward becoming a circular economy company fit for the twenty-first century. Lena Pripp-Kovac, who is head of sustainability at IKEA, is the person responsible for transformation happening. She states, "A circular business is one that eliminates waste and pollution while restoring natural systems. If the entire global economy could become circular, then human society could thrive without depleting the earth of its resources or destroying ecosystems."

She describes how their purpose inspires their design. "It is turning from the linear to the circular, of course, but the major purpose is to have a completely new take on providing more for more people, but with fewer resources."[30] Beautiful.

5. It strikes a balance between aspiration and precision

A good purpose statement needs to be aspirational but not vague. It needs to be precise but not limiting, allowing room for a company to grow. For example, an unclear purpose statement is "to help make the world better." It is lofty but meaningless, a platitude that serves no one.

We love LEGO, and the company's purpose statement is an excellent example of how to strike the right balance: "To inspire and develop the builders of tomorrow."

It grounds the brand in always seeking to help children experience the transformative power of play. The verb *build* beautifully evokes the core product, the brick that is at the heart of the brand. This purpose is manifested effortlessly in all of its work, ranging from partnering with Sesame Street to help Syrian refugee kids to their ridiculously successful movies, which have grossed more than a billion dollars worldwide, leading to a 25 percent increase in sales (which you can read about in the chapter with Loren Shuster, Lego's Chief People Officer).

Similarly, SAP is also another company we admire. Their purpose is expressed as "Help the world run better and improve people's lives."

The underlying core product truth—the technology platforms that SAP creates are the foundation upon which a trillion dollars' worth of global business runs—is self-evident in this statement. It's great to see this company using its scale in the supply chain world to help tackle problems like modern-day slavery and human trafficking.

---

30 Augusta Pownall, ""We're looking at a change of our total business" says IKEA sustainability chief Lena Pripp-Kovac," *DeZeen* (Website), September 4, 2019, https://www.dezeen.com/2019/09/04/lena-pripp-kovac-ikea-circular-interview/, n.p.

In 2018, SAP proudly announced, "SAP Ariba has a partnership with Made in a Free World, a San Francisco-based company with an application called FRDM (read 'Freedom') that makes it easier for companies to identify forced-labor problems in their supply chain. Through this partnership, SAP is helping its clients identify places where child and forced labor may exist in their supply chain."[31] The tremendous capabilities of SAP allow them to solve this problem on a scale that very few in the world can.

It also answers the question "Can a B2B company have a purpose?" Yes, absolutely, it should. It just needs to consider not only the end user or consumer but also its more immediate customers as part of that ecosystem of stakeholders. As we cover in the Purpose Doesn't Have to Be Political chapter with SAP CMO Alicia Tilman, SAP found a problem their stakeholders wanted to put an end to, and in FRDM, they found a partner they could help to solve it. As Justin Dillion, CEO of Made in a Free World, said, "Our mission is simply to help companies buy better and build a marketplace network that we can be proud of. Partners like SAP help us achieve this mission."[32]

6. It can either be a "general purpose" or a "social purpose" statement

A question we often get from companies that are looking to articulate their purpose is "Does our purpose have to focus on social impact?" The answer is no; there are many types of purpose-led companies.

Some companies are "general purpose" brands, meaning that their core purpose statement does not have to manifest itself as having a social or environmental impact. This does not mean they can't still tackle social problems as part of a broader portfolio of initiatives (missions). It just means that for general-purpose companies, it's not their core reason for being.

Some companies are "social purpose" companies, which means at their inception or their core, they exist to solve a social or environmental issue.

Let's take a look at a couple of examples of each.

---

31 Scott Campbell and Ashley Tully, "Eliminating Forced Labor Around the World, Starting with the Supply Chain," *SAP* (Website), March 5, 2018, https://news.sap.com/2018/03/eliminating-forced-labor-around-the-world-starting-with-the-supply-chain/, n.p.

32 Campbell and Tully, 2018, n.p.

A great example of a "general purpose" company is Microsoft, a company that we are massive fans of. Their purpose after the arrival of CEO Satya Nadella was defined as follows: "To empower every person and organization on this planet to achieve more."

It's a great example of a company that has authentically and successfully redefined its purpose for a new era. When Bill Gates founded Microsoft, their mission was "A computer on every desk, and in every home." Hardly inspiring on a societal level, but it helped drive sales and incredible financial success. Microsoft's new articulation shows that even when you don't start with a purpose at your inception, it is possible to find one that works if it is done thoughtfully and inclusively.

Microsoft's new purpose can manifest itself both in general (its cloud computing business, for instance) and in socially impactful ways. An example is its work to create Xbox adaptive controllers for kids with disabilities. Another is its relentless drive to make Microsoft Office accessible for everyone, such as through its groundbreaking Seeing AI applications, which help the visually disabled use their phones to see.

Another great general purpose statement we love is from Airbnb: "We help people to belong anywhere."

It is simple, clear, and concise. It reflects the brand's belief that you should travel like a local, not as a tourist, and experience a sense of community that a conventional hotel experience does not give you. A purpose is a promise. When Airbnb saw that some members' behavior was preventing other members from getting fair access to rentals, they acted. They ensured all of their users signed a nondiscrimination clause that prohibits anyone being denied based on their race, religion, color, or creed. (We cover this more in our interview with former Airbnb CMO Jonathan Mildenhall in the Purpose Is about Being the Helper, Not the Hero section.)

This policy led to a terrific example of a social purpose manifestation, Airbnb Open Homes, a program that provides free shelter to refugees and victims of natural disasters, with plans for one hundred thousand zero-dollar listings available for nonprofits to use. This initiative also provided free housing to first responders in the COVID-19 pandemic.

Now consider a brand with a "social purpose" built into its core: Tesla.

This is Tesla's original purpose statement: "We exist to accelerate the planet's transition to sustainable transport."

First of all, we love the use of the word "accelerate"—a subtle nod to Tesla's role as a car manufacturer. Using language that is native to the category you are in (or better yet, reflects some core product truth) is a great way to make an intuitive connection between a product truth and a higher-order goal.

But then look at the audacious outcome it seeks to create: to end the era of fossil-fuel transport on this planet. This substantial environmental ambition inspires employees and imbues their work with deep meaning. Similarly, it draws the customers who buy Tesla to the deeper "good" of driving super-cool electric vehicles that combat climate change and are on the cutting edge of a clean energy revolution. As a result, in 2020, Tesla achieved a market capitalization in excess of $700 billion, becoming the most valuable global automaker ever.

Similarly, one of the companies we admire the most, Patagonia, has for decades had a clear focus on the planet: "Build the best product, cause no unnecessary harm, use business to inspire and implement solutions to the environmental crisis."

These are social purpose statements that befit companies that have that as their core reason for being. Whatever the financial outlook of the company, that is its central goal, not an ancillary one.

7. It can evolve with the times

Finally, a great purpose statement does not have to be static. It can evolve as the company grows, or the context around it changes, leading to a need to reframe what it stands for. Let's look at two.

Remember Tesla's original statement?

"We exist to accelerate the planet's transition to sustainable transport."

Here's how Tesla's purpose statement reads now: "We exist to accelerate the planet's transition to sustainable energy."

Did you notice which word changed? "Transport" changed to "energy." With that one word change in their purpose, Tesla announced that they were no longer just a car company: they want to be the "Apple of clean energy" and own the interconnected ecosystem in your life, from solar roofs to Powerwall batteries to the car in your garage. Their competitive context shifted to include not just other automotive manufacturers but also all power utilities. That's the power of a finely crafted purpose statement to signal intent and clarity.

Let's look at Patagonia's original statement again: "Build the best product, cause no unnecessary harm, use business to inspire and implement solutions to the environmental crisis."

This statement has now changed to the much more urgent and provocative "Patagonia is in business to save our home planet."

It reflects this incredible company's determination to raise its game even further to meet the crisis we are all facing, which threatens to make humanity extinct.

We will end by saying that a great purpose statement is meaningless if solid, measurable commitments do not back it. Words without action don't mean anything, and consumers are increasingly demanding that companies "show us the receipts"—the proof behind their promises.

DISCOVERING PURPOSE

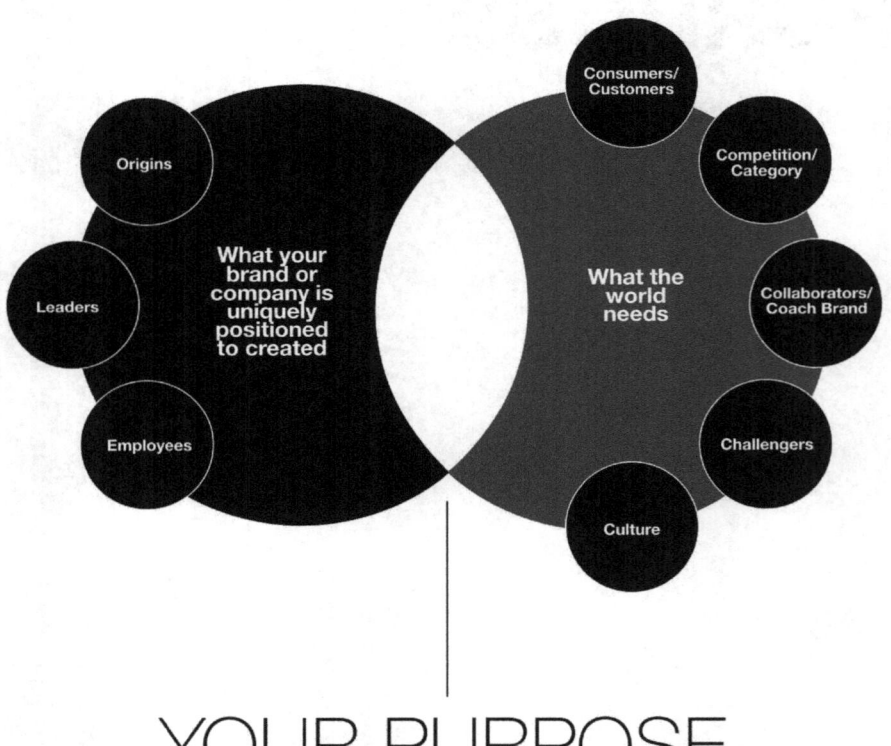

YOUR PURPOSE

One of our most rewarding experiences is seeing people go through the journey of discovering a higher purpose for their business or brand. It is wonderful to see business leaders reimagine the role their company can have in the world, opening their eyes to new possibilities for their work as well as their lives.

The process for discovering purpose essentially boils down to two big questions: What does the world need? What do you do best?

The magic is in finding that intersection—the place where your superpowers as an organization can fill a need that benefits shareholders and stakeholders, as well as local and global societies.

While most of the businesses covered in this book have achieved some level of scale, it's important to note that even if you are a small company, there are many ways your business model can make a meaningful impact in your local community. One great example of the power of purpose in small businesses that we love is the Habana brand, which includes multiple restaurant locations and the nonprofit organization Habana Works. Its founder, Sean Meenan, launched Habana with the purpose of using business as a medium to foster community. Sean recognized that healthy communities need spaces to come together to eat good food and to learn, play, and connect with each other. Communities also need art, music, and businesses that take good care of neighbors and the environment.

Twenty years ago, Meenan launched the first Café Habana in a landmark diner in New York City's Nolita neighborhood, which remains an institution and one of our favorite restaurants in the city. Habana's purpose has inspired it to build businesses that support environmentalism, as well as empower neighbors and residents through free, hands-on environmental education programs. The business has grown to include restaurants in Brooklyn, Malibu, and Dubai.[33] Sean showed love for one Brooklyn community by transforming a building across from his Fort Greene–located Habana Outpost into the

---

33 "About Habana," *Cafe Habana* (Website), Accessed January 30, 2021, https://www.cafehabana.com/story/

Brooklyn Love Building. What is really cool is that Meenan designed a large mural on the facade of the building to honor the one and only Notorious B.I.G. with a transcription of his famous lyric "Spread love; it's the Brooklyn way"—a proud message of local love and community pride and a mantra by which Sean and the whole Habana family tries to live. Baby, baby!

Whether you are a small-business owner or the CEO of a Fortune 500 company, identifying the sweet spot between your offering and what the world (or community) needs is the critical first step. In the following section, we will help you start your journey to discovering purpose by looking internally to understand your superpowers as an organization.

Let's look at what the journey will consist of.

Engage inside

As Socrates said, "Know thyself." Before we can get to where you fit in the world, it's important that you understand what you care about and what you have to offer. Together, we will go through the steps of understanding your "why."

Know your origins

We are often asked, How do you discover the purpose of a company that has been around for decades? We always suggest going back to the founder's story. Many companies have interesting stories of entrepreneurs who created the business to solve an important need. Brand teams are usually surprised to see how clear the founding values are. Over the years, businesses often lose their way. Founders, focused on survival or growth, lose sight of why they started the company. Also, as leadership changes over time, companies lose continuity. Sometimes going back to the beginning is the best way to start the journey forward.

Engage your C-suite

Engage your leadership team and find out what matters to them. What do they wish they had more time to care about? What work do they wish they could do?

Executives often want to move beyond the day-to-day pressure of the job, and many are at stages of their career where they want to leave a legacy of impact. If given the space to talk candidly, this group often reveals itself to be the hungriest for deeper meaning.

Engage your employees

Your employees are the front line of your purpose. Often, they have ideas of how the company can do more, and engaging them unearths great ideas for impact. A question as simple as "Tell us about a day you felt proud to work at this organization" can unleash huge insight.

Next, we will journey with you through the external process of exploring the five Cs that every purpose-led brand needs to consider when discovering its purpose.

Explore Outside

Customers

It's critical that you know your buyers. What do they look for in products and services? What issues and causes are your customers most passionate about as citizens? Purpose-led brands understand the value of their offerings to their customers, but more important, they understand the values that they and their customers have in common. When you and your customers share a common vision for the world, they are not just buying from you; they are buying into you.

Competitors/category

Understand the imperatives of your category and what your competitors are focused on. What are the trends in your industry? What are the contributions—positive and negative—that your category is currently making to society? Fair or unfair, brands in a category often get grouped together. For example, when there was outrage at the effect of fast fashion on the environment, everyone in the category felt the wrath. It's important to look at what issues the category can help address before moving on to individual crusades.

Challengers

Identify the groups that are the most critical of your practices; they may be your best thought partners in solving the problems you want to solve. Sometimes our critics are right, and seeing things through their eyes may help us see more clearly.

Collaborators

Identify those you can create partnerships of common purpose – for instance, with non-profits, culture creators, or even other brands in or out of your category.

Culture

Look at the wider cultural context of where your company operates. As culture changes, so do customer expectations. Movements like #MeToo have caught many companies flat-footed, leaving them looking woefully out of touch.

Now, let's get started on this journey to discover your company's purpose. Are you ready?

ENGAGE INSIDE

Know Your Origins

For any of you who are fans of PBS, you may know the show *Finding Your Roots*, hosted and written by Harvard professor Henry Louis Gates. The show uses traditional genealogical research and genetics to research the family history of famous Americans, helping them discover the surprising stories buried within their past. During the show, celebrities are presented with a "book of life" that allows them to view their ancestral histories, learn about family connections, and discover secrets about their lineage.

It is always amazing to see how people react to their family's history. Guests experience feelings of pride and awe when they learn of a heroic tale of a great-grandparent. Others experience a sense of guilt and shame to know their ancestors were slave owners or committed horrific crimes. There is something both uncomfortable and necessary about discovering the truth of who we are and where we come from. It helps us to understand ourselves in ways we can't just by merely looking at the experiences in our own short lives. Understanding our history helps us to answer two of our most existential questions: Where did I come from, and why am I here?

The question of "why" in business is what purpose seeks to answer. It explains the reason we exist as a business and thus what we are supposed to do with our talent and resources. However, to discover your "why" as a brand, it's essential first to answer the question "How did this all begin?"

For people who are working for founder-run businesses, that answer is clear. Some of the most successful companies today benefited greatly from being led by the creators of the business. To Apple employees, Steve Jobs was a god. Friends we have at Nike speak about the time they randomly bumped into Phil Knight on campus and had the opportunity to hear one of his great stories in a hallway. Founders like Oprah Winfrey and Sara Blakely of Spanx are heroes to their teams, modeling how to build empires on values of service and excellence. Start-up and small-business founders attract employees because of their vision and passion.

Whether you work for a company with a founder you see every day or a business so vast that few can vaguely recall its history, every brand starts with a story. And understanding that story is the first step in discovering the magic that will guide where you can go next.

One of the best examples of the importance of knowing your roots comes from Paul Polman. Paul is the former CEO of Unilever and has been one of the best examples of purpose-driven leadership for over the past decade (he is one of our heroes).

Paul realized early in his life that business should be a force for good. And if it was to do so at Unilever, it had to start at the top with the CEO. However, he also understood he could not do it alone. He needed the C-suite leaders of the company to buy into a higher purpose for the business than earnings. Paul tells a beautiful story of how he used a trip with his team to start a new journey for the company.

It was at the height of the financial crisis [2009]. At Unilever, we unfortunately had had ten years of decline. The company had gone from $55 billion to $38 billion in turnover. It had become a little bit too short-term focused. But we had good brands, good people. Coming in from the outside wasn't easy. Some people said, "Why is that needed?"

I thought if we want to change the company, we would need to do something that Jim Collins talks about in his book *From Good to Great*, which is nurturing the core before you stimulate progress. I had to find that core, so for one of the first meetings with my management team, I brought them to the British village of Port Sunlight, to the former home of Lord Lever, who founded the company.

He built Port Sunlight before the factories were fully running to provide houses for his employees. He had the highest number of volunteers in World War I because he guaranteed the wages and the jobs, and he helped the wives when the men were gone. No smoking and no drinking in Port Sunlight made the life expectancy better. He fought for six-day work weeks. He introduced pensions in the UK. He brought these values to the company, and he believed in shared prosperity.

Going back to our roots gave me the permission to drive change. People would say, "Yeah, he's bringing back values that were at the roots of the success of this company." We were there and saying we needed to have a more responsible business model. We came up with a very bold objective to decouple our growth from our environmental impact.[34]

Discovering the roots for your business, just as in life, can be uncomfortable. Your company's "book of life" may have chapters employees are not proud of. But it will give you a deeper understanding of the problems your business was created to solve, and that can inspire what you seek to improve in the future.

34 David Gelles, "He Ran an Empire of Soap and Mayonnaise. Now He Wants to Reinvent Capitalism," *The New York Times*, August 29, 2019, https://www.nytimes.com/2019/08/29/business/paul-polman-unilever-corner-office.html, n.p.

Today, Paul is the founder of IMAGINE, which creates coalitions of CEOs to drive change across sectors of business, which is at the Jedi level of purpose building. You can read more about his current mission in the Purpose Should Be an Open-Source Pursuit section. His story illustrates two lessons. The first is that by knowing your company's roots, you can better understand the values that are at the heart of your brand's DNA, which show you what you can most authentically stand for. The second is the importance of engaging your leaders early in the discovering purpose process. Now, let's go deeper into this latter point.

Engage Your C-Suite

The process of understanding your origin story can give you a great perspective and appreciation for the voyage of where you have been to where you are today. Now, as a leader, it is your turn to write the next chapter of your company. The first step in reimagining the purpose-led future of your business is bringing together its leaders to help chart the course.

Executive teams play two critical roles in an organization. The first is obvious: they are hired and measured by their ability to provide strategic and operational leadership to the company. They set goals, develop strategies, and ensure they are executed effectively. Since they are the people most responsible for the performance of the business, they understand better than anyone that purpose must help the organization achieve its business goals for it to be sustainable.

Many leaders we talk to speak openly about the pressures of the constant pursuit of the business goals and their desire to move beyond the gravity of growth to find greater meaning and purpose in their work. They are living embodiments of those who have reached the highest level of success, achievement, and recognition—the self-actualization level of Maslow's hierarchy of needs. They have reaped the benefits of long hours and sacrifice only to be left with a feeling of unfulfillment, a deeper desire to do more in the world through their work.

When we spoke with Procter & Gamble Global CMO Marc Pritchard about his journey to purpose and realizing the enormous potential of business to do good, he shared this story.

> Just recently I've been more vocal about it, and I think largely because being in a position of senior leadership and being willing to express points of view or tell personal stories about myself helps create some emotional safety for others to be able to speak up. I have told this story before. About twenty years ago, I was on a spiritual retreat with my family—my wife, Betsy, and our three young daughters, who are all under the age of ten. And at the end of it, the guy who led it said, "I hope you know the good you can do because you're in business—and business will someday be the greatest force for good in the future. It won't be the powers that be today; it'll be business." And he said, "If you choose to do so, you can do a lot of good." And that was kind of the first blinding moment of clarity for me.

Increasingly, executives like Marc are recognizing that they can do good right where they are, and that realization gives them a renewed sense of excitement and drive. By engaging your leaders in an exploration of brand purpose, you can tap into this desire and create the space for leaders to reimagine their work with endless possibilities to connect their expertise in delivering business impact with the opportunity to create social impact. In this case, Marc's epiphany helped him to lead Procter & Gamble to become "a force for good and a force for growth" that serves five billion customers around the world.

The second role executives play is less obvious but just as important. As the Center for Creative Leadership states, "The executive team provides the organizational and cultural DNA for the company. How well the executive team functions as a collective leadership body and how its members interact serve as the model that teams throughout the organization will follow. Anyone who has ever had the displeasure of working for a dysfunctional leadership team knows the ripple effect it has on the performance and morale of the rest of the company."[35]

However, when the leaders come together to create a common vision to build a business that has a more meaningful role in the world, the effects can be profound.

One of the most remarkable examples of a company completely transforming itself around a higher purpose is the story of Microsoft (which recently passed the trillion-dollar valuation mark, joining Apple and Google in that storied club). Ever since CEO Satya Nadella took the reins, the company has been reinvigorated with a new sense of drive and passion. The starting point? A five-month journey that Nadella and the executive team took to reframe the company's purpose into thirteen succinct words: "To empower every person and every organization on the planet to achieve more." We spoke to Microsoft Chief Marketing Officer Chris Capossela about their leadership team's journey to purpose and how it has revitalized the company and its employees, leading to a wave of purpose-driven innovation and growth. He said,

Satya spent the better part of the first five months with his direct reports to ask some pretty fundamental questions about what the

---

35 "Increase the Effectiveness of Your Executive Team," *Center for Creative Leadership* (Website), Accessed January 30, 2021, https://www.ccl.org/articles/leading-effectively-articles/increase-executive-team-effectiveness/, n.p.

mission of the company should be. We landed on those words that most Microsoft employees could give you correctly. I think that was the starting gun for a lot of change at the company. Over the past five years, we haven't changed the words. All we've done is to try to dig deeper into an understanding of what the words mean and how to bring it to life for our employees and for our customers.

Part of the success of the process was the sense of ownership that the leadership team brought to it, ensuring that it was vetted and tested with the rest of the company so that it felt authentic.

We did a listening tour inside Microsoft, pulling in everyone from new employees, young kids right out of college, to corporate vice presidents, and talking to them in small groups to really understand what words resonated with them and what words didn't. It wasn't just something that the marketing team did off to the side and then just lived off some slides that were posted on a poster somewhere.

The next phase involved embedding it into the culture through consistent communication, reflecting the time it takes to become a living, breathing part of the organization. Chris added "We've repeated it at every speech Satya has given; you hear people talk about it all the time in the halls. I don't think that gets done in a week. I think it takes a long time to really own every word, and I'm glad we took the time to make that."

Microsoft is a great example of a company engaging its leaders to empower employees with a clear purpose, vision, and goals and then trusting them to run with it. Capossela agrees.

Satya has this beautiful way of saying, "Hey, you work for Microsoft, but you should make Microsoft work for you." In other words, use Microsoft as a platform for you to pursue the things that give you meaning in your life. If you have a real passion for accessibility, then great. Use the fact that you're a developer at Microsoft to work on accessibility in your product, or in any of our technology. A little push has certainly gone a long, long way. Maybe from the outside, it looks like it was all beautifully orchestrated. In fact, it's been far more organic to be perfectly honest.

That's what leadership should be.

As you look to convene your leadership team to discover your purpose, here are three questions that every leadership team should ask itself:

- What type of world do we want to help create?
  Envision the world you want to live in. Think of the state of humanity and the health of the planet. List the problems that will no longer exist. Imagine the role your company plays in creating this world. This will help you become clear on the change you want to see that you are best equipped to help achieve.

- Do we have the culture we need?
  This question will require deep soul searching but it's critical to be honest about the answer. No purpose can thrive if you do not have the culture to support it. If you have a high-performing culture where people trust its leadership and feel valued, cared for, and passionate about doing good in the world, you have a solid foundation. If you do not, get to work building it.

- Do we have the courage we need?
  Purpose requires risk and vulnerability. You must be willing to make tough decisions, to take chances and make mistakes. You must be brave.

Engage Your Employees

We believe that the real magic in an organization occurs when employees recognize how their gifts and passions can be of service to the purpose of the company. However, this can only happen if employees are engaged in the purpose-creation process. There is a famous mantra in business, often attributed to the author and businessman Stephen Covey, that simply says, "No involvement, no commitment." CEOs and their executive teams can have the best-laid-out plans for building a purpose-led company, but without involving their employees in the process, be assured there will be no commitment to living that purpose each day.

When employees are engaged as active participants and brought along in the journey, they become the most valuable stakeholders in the future of the company. They, too, will begin to imagine the possibilities for their work and the impact it can make in the world.

When Microsoft employees connected their passion for accessibility, specifically addressing the issue of disability, to the purpose of the company, it unlocked groundbreaking innovation. We asked Capossela where this focus was born.

It really came from a combination of the mission, as the North Star for the company, and how our employees interpreted that mission and started doing things in different ways. There wasn't a single day where the senior leadership team said, "We now shall care a lot about accessibility and all product teams need to figure out what that means." Frankly, it came much more bottom-up inside the company.

This purpose has now manifested itself in a wide range of ways, from Microsoft now ensuring all company events, however large or small, feature live transcription on-screen to revolutionary ideas like the Xbox adaptive controller, which allowed kids with disabilities to play games with equal ease.

Chris's story shows that when employees are engaged, they feel a deeper connection to the company and begin to see it as a place where they can bring their passions and creativity to their work in more meaningful ways. This work is the key to truly unlocking the power of purpose in an organization. It has led to Microsoft jumping thirteen places to number 21 in Glassdoor's annual "best places to work" ranking, a fact that no doubt has helped spur its joining Apple and Facebook in the hallowed trillion dollar valuation club (beating Google to the punch).

When we work with brands to help them engage their employees in the purpose journey, we host what we call GPS workshops. GPS is a model pioneered by our good friend and purpose mentor, Tru Pettigrew. Like a GPS in your car, the model he designed guides people on a journey to a more purposeful destination in life. The "G" stands for your *gifts*, your talents, the abilities people see as your superpowers. The "P" stands for your passions, the issues and

GPS

What are your **GIFTS**, Your **PASSIONS**, How can you be of **SERVICE?**

Tru Pettigrew

causes that you care about as a citizen – the things that make you made, the things that break your heart. Lastly, the "S" asks the question "How can you use your gifts and passions to be of service to your company's purpose?"

The GPS experience is transformative for employees and their coworkers. The process asks employees to tell each other what they believe their gifts are. We often find people amazed that others see them as courageous or funny or creative. There is something very moving about having the people you see every day tell you how much value you add to their lives. The workshop also requires vulnerability. People share the causes they are most passionate about, many of which are rooted in very personal experiences, such as bullying or loss. Employees listen to each other's stories and develop a deeper understanding and connection. When people feel seen, heard, connected, and engaged in their jobs, work becomes something more than a means for survival and safety. Work becomes a place to experience love, belonging, and fulfillment. And at that point, the ability to be of service to something greater becomes much more accessible and desirable.

The idea of work being a place to experience love and vulnerability may sound like a hippie concept. But it's a critical part of building a culture grounded in selflessness and trust, which are the bedrock of a purposeful work environment.

"Being part of Unilever Honduras showed me that sense of purpose, a brand with purpose, people with purpose. We are not only a working force, or working capital. We are individuals with family, dreams to be fulfilled, purposes we want to carry on. Making a company become more than a company but a place where you can match your purpose with the company's values it's to where every business must have to move."
—Andres Martinez Landaverde, Quote from LinkedIn

Purpose begins with the understanding that we are all just human beings, harboring a strong desire to be seen, loved, and appreciated. As you do the work to involve your employees in the discovery of purpose, find ways to engage them with love. Create an environment where they can give the best of themselves to each other and the world, and you'll have a workforce that can deliver the level of excellent performance that purpose demands.

EXPLORE OUTSIDE: UNDERSTAND YOUR CUSTOMERS AND CONSUMERS

Consumers

When writing our first book, *Good Is the New Cool: Market Like You Give a Damn*, we challenged brands to think of people as citizens, not just consumers. This notion has never been more important for brands to embrace than now. Customers are making decisions based on attributes beyond product selection or price (although those attributes are still critical). They're now assessing what a brand says it stands for—and what it does.

When customers are buying products, they want to feel like they are contributing to creating the world they want to live in. Accenture's most recent global survey of nearly thirty thousand consumers found that 62 percent want companies to take a stand on current and broadly relevant issues like sustainability, transparency, or fair employment practices.

Customers carry a significant level of power on the success of your business beyond sales. As Accenture noted in their global study, "They aren't just buyers anymore. They've got the power to demand experiences on their terms. They readily influence others to buy (or not buy). They codevelop products or services, invest in brands they believe in, or even act as sales channel partners. Through their words and actions, they provide insights that can enable companies to hone their competitive agility."[36]

One of the ways customers are asserting their power on brands is by demanding that companies participate in social, cultural, or even political dialogues. They believe their actions—from posting comments on social media to participating in boycotts—can influence a brand's reaction to an event or its stance on an issue of public concern.

When a company's purpose aligns with its customers' beliefs, it creates an excellent opportunity to form more authentic and profitable relationships with customers. The customers believe they are part of a deeper connection to the brand based on a shared outlook of the world. The goal of a purpose-led company should be to build long-lasting relationships grounded in a common purpose and built around a shared sense of brand belonging. People want to be connected to brands that do more for the world than just make money.

And they want to feel actively engaged in the efforts for good. Thus, perhaps the most important thing to ask customers—particularly young people—is, How can we best involve you? According to DoSomething.org's study on dollars and change, nearly half of Gen Z says that it is important for a company or brand to have a social change initiative that consumers can be an active partner with them on.

---

36 "To Affinity and Beyond: From Me to We, The Rise of the Purpose-Led Brand," *Accenture Strategy* (Website), Accessed January 30, 2021, https://www.accenture.com/_acnmedia/thought-leadership-assets/pdf/accenture-competitiveagility-gcpr-pov.pdf, p.4.

Understanding how to involve your customers as active stakeholders creates an exciting way to build new relationships with them. An example of this is the wonderful Australian consumer goods company Thankyou.

Thankyou's goal is to help end extreme poverty by 2030, and their purpose statement reflects that ambitious goal. "Our purpose is 'empowering humanity to choose a world without poverty.' I think we've taken a long time to develop it," said cofounder Daniel Flynn. Taking this purpose as a guiding principle, Flynn and his cofounders—his then girlfriend (now wife), Justine Flynn, and his best mate, Jarryd Burns—launched in Australia with a unique approach to getting their brand in stores: leveraging the power of their fans and social media to get major retailers like Coles and Woolworths to stock their products. Their fanbase embraced the challenge to such an extent that a couple of helicopter pilots took it upon themselves to fly banners over the head offices of these retailers, leading them to be successfully stocked there.

But in addition to enthusiastic fans, another considerable part of Thankyou's success has been their attention to creating a great product and a great brand, with beautiful, minimal aesthetics. "It comes from a great book, *Do Purpose*, which says, 'Rule number one, make a great product. Rule Number two, never break rule one.' There's a little asterisk above rule one, and the fine print says, 'Never use a good cause to sell an average product.' And that is the mantra at Thankyou," said Flynn. Their thoughtfulness extends to innovations like a unique tracker ID on each Thankyou product to see the exact details of the project your product is assigned to fund.

Another fantastic idea from this amazingly innovative brand was the launch of their first book, *Chapter One*, with a unique "Pay what you want" model and all proceeds going into funding the next stage of the company's growth.

Flynn said,

The book has worked beyond expectation. Part of it was we wanted to get our story in as many people's hands, but we also wanted to raise money. We do have our own self-inflicted problem of raising funds; because we don't have any shareholders, we don't have any investors. We're not changing our 100 percent model. It's awesome. But it does create this funding gap, and that idea was, well Thankyou has been built by people the whole way along, and people have solved our greatest problems like getting stocked in the supermarkets. And so we thought, what if "we, the people," could help solve that issue of funding?

The book blew past the initial goal of selling 80,000 copies, going on to sell 124,000 copies to date and raising over $2.5 million that went toward the launch of their Thankyou Baby line and their subsequent expansion into New Zealand.

Flynn believes that this is because the brand created a space for their fans to be participants in their journey. "I think people innately love story, but we also love being part of the story and feel like we're contributing our little piece to a bigger story. I think what *Chapter One* does is that it's an invitation to all of us to go, what part can I play?" Flynn reflects on whether the more significant impact of Thankyou may be the inspiration it has been for others to find their purpose. "Part of me wonders whether our biggest impact will be measurable, whether it will be the effect of other people in organizations seeing some of what we've done and then likely doing it better themselves and beyond."

Flynn has parting words of advice for anyone seeking to create their own social enterprise. "Don't fall into the illusion that the 'enterprise' part will be easy because of the social impact. In fact, the social element can create complexity that the average enterprise may not have had. But it is rewarding; it is satisfying. It is not easy, but it's essential. So if that's your dream and vision, chase it, go hard."

As you are writing the next chapter of your journey to becoming a purpose-led brand, make your customers part of the story. Listen to their ideas, desires, and vision for the world, and build a business together that will achieve it.

Engage Your Challengers

Every company has its critics. These could be nonprofits criticizing your supply chain, government watchdogs enforcing environmental legislation, or even unions made up of your employees. We believe challengers play an essential role in helping your company realize its full potential as a force for good. They often see the part you play in society's problems, and your power to help solve them, long before you do. They help shine a light on your blind spots and hold you accountable for your behavior. Challengers push you to be and do better.

For this reason, it's important not to confuse challengers with haters. Haters ultimately are rooting for your demise, and regardless of what you do, you cannot win them over. Haters are fueled by dislike. Challengers are sparked by disappointment. Challengers call brands out because they have expectations that companies should behave ethically and responsibly and want to compel businesses to act more consciously. In a choice between the motivational tools of sticks (punishments) and carrots (rewards), challengers use the sticks of protests, boycotts, and criticism to help drive you to greater action. In many cases, these tactics have caused companies to implement ethical changes in their business with much greater urgency than they would have otherwise.

Challengers will push all businesses, and brands with social impact purposes that are not insulated from their criticism. As a matter of fact, those brands often face greater scrutiny because the expectations are higher. A good example of this is TOMS.

TOMS, which started over thirteen years ago, has been one of the trailblazers in the business-for-good space. They pioneered the "one for one" model of giving, which has proved so successful that the company has now donated ninety-three million pairs of shoes since inception. Moreover, they have given millions of dollars to causes as well (the company donates between 40 and 50 percent of net profits, the highest percentage of any US company). But in recent years, TOMS has come under fire for various perceived problems with its model of giving. We spoke to our friend Amy Smith, chief giving officer at TOMS (whom we interview in the Purpose is About Putting Your Money Where Your Mission Is section of the book about their new work around gun safety), to understand how they responded to a wave of backlash and used the feedback to evolve their giving model.

Along the way, TOMS started to hear criticisms from the very people who were once their most stalwart supporters. Many of the objections came about because of general skepticism about the company's intentions (especially after Bain Capital's 50 percent investment stake in the company) and also some specific misunderstandings of how the company operates its shoe-giving programs.

What TOMS did next provides five lessons that any brand can apply to their business when dealing with challengers.

1. Listen to your critics

It is always essential to understand how society sees your brand. It's easy to focus on the good, but you also need to hear where you may be doing more unintentional harm than good. TOMS used the criticism from their customers to rethink their model. This led to a moment of internal self-reflection. "We got to this point of, hold on: maybe having a new give and a new product every year, it might not make sense for us. And so we've since then been taking a pause to say, Are we having as much impact as we possibly can have with this level of giving?"

By reflecting on the criticism, they were able to explore new pathways to create the level of impact they and their challengers want to see in the world.

2. Get the data

Brands must understand the impact of their business on the planet and the communities they serve. This knowledge helps to create an accurate measure of return on investment (ROI) as well as to dispel myths and misperceptions. One of the biggest myths TOMS faced was that their business model was hurting local economies by destroying existing shoe businesses that could not compete against free shoes.

To address this concern, TOMS carried out extensive academic research to investigate this pernicious myth. The researchers found no proof of the negative impact in the markets where they give. Amy shares, "We commissioned a study to test this. Is this actually true? Are we having a negative impact? Because that's the last thing we want to do. After many months of studies (I have a twenty-seven-page report), the conclusion was that there was no significant set of data that said we were having a negative impact in these communities—because we weren't giving at a significant enough level."

3. Share the facts

Unfortunately, we live in an age where misinformation can travel so fast and far that brands can't stop it. Although some of the questions and critiques directed at TOMS were valid, others, like the negative impact on communities, were not. Since that fact is central to the trust that customers buy into, it was essential to correct. TOMS decided to take a proactive approach in telling its story and correcting inaccuracies point by point. Brands must make a proactive effort to share the facts of their business, values, and impact, especially to the people who trust them most.

For TOMS, the data show the level of impact they have made in their mission to use business to improve lives. To date, they have given away ninety-five million shoes, helped restore sight to 780,000 people, given 722,000 weeks of safe water to others, and donated millions of dollars. When criticism comes, they can always point to this proof of who they are and the value they bring to the world.

We asked Amy to reflect on the journey so far and share any parting wisdom.

I think the most important thing to know is that we're a learning organization. We've not figured it all out. We're committed to progress, not perfection. And I think any of us who are focused on perfection are going to miss the opportunity to have a positive impact. And so we've embraced that. That also means if you choose that model, you have to listen to your critics. You have to embrace what they're trying to tell you and test it out and make sure what they're saying is accurate, and then to make the necessary changes you need to make to constantly be improving.

BE
COMMITTED TO
PROGRESS
NOT
PERFECTION

Amy Smith

Competitors and Category

To develop a social purpose strategy, leaders should begin by identifying a set of social or environmental needs to which the brand can
make a meaningful contribution in a unique and distinctive way. An
excellent place to start is within your category—the competitive set
of companies in the same industry that you are part of. By zigging
where others zag when it comes to purpose and impact, you can
find new ways to differentiate yourself—as the examples of Delta and
Everlane, which we are going to share with you, illustrate.

By looking at the problems your industry is contributing to, you can identify the places where you are the most likely to make a measurable impact in ways that are relevant to your brand. For example, for years, the airline industry has been a rising contributor to air pollution. According to the *New York Times*, greenhouse gas emissions from commercial air travel are growing at a faster clip than predicted in previous, already dire, projections, according to new research. The United Nations (UN) aviation body forecasted that airplane emissions of carbon dioxide, a significant greenhouse gas, would reach just over nine hundred million metric tons in 2018 and then triple by 2050. But the new research, from the International Council on Clean Transportation, found that emissions from global air travel may be increasing more than 1.5 times as fast as the UN estimate. The researchers analyzed nearly forty million flights around the world last year.[37]

According to Business Insider, "With concerns for the environment growing, airlines have been among the most attacked for the part they play in global climate change. They're easy targets for environmentalists; after all, their aircraft consistently leave reminders of their environmental impact whenever they fly overhead." For companies in this sector looking to become more purpose driven, they would serve the world best by starting with reducing the negative impact of their product on the planet. And, increasingly, that is precisely where air transportation companies are starting.

Delta Air Lines and JetBlue Airways in the United States have both announced measures to drastically cut their emissions, with the former pledging $1 billion to do so.[38] To take steps further toward reducing its footprint, Delta Air Lines announced that it aims to be carbon neutral in the next ten years, with a $1 billion investment in reducing and offsetting emissions.[39] These steps are consistent with Delta's mission to "form a force for positive local and global change, dedicated to bettering standards of living

---

37 Hiroko Tabuchi, "'Worse Than Anyone Expected': Air Travel Emissions Vastly Outpace Predictions," *The New York Times*, September 19, 2019, https://www.nytimes.com/2019/09/19/climate/air-travel-emissions.html, n.p.

38 Tabuchi, 2019, n.p.

39 "Bezos And Blackrock Are Pouring Billions into This $30.7 Trillion Trend," *Yahoo Finance*

and the environment where our customers and we live and work"[40], which makes it credible. And it is aligned with its business model, which makes it sustainable.

By committing to move beyond emission cutting to becoming ultimately carbon neutral, Delta has raised the stakes for the entrepreneurial category. The reduction is no longer satisfactory; airlines now have to be replenishing. Paying attention to the ways your industry is addressing its issues can give you a starting point and a bar to meet.

Looking within the category can also create opportunities not only to address an industry issue but to do it so well that it becomes a competitive advantage. Exhibit A is Everlane and how it led transparency in pricing in the fashion industry.

The world of fashion has also come under considerable scrutiny for its environmental impact, labor practices, and material sourcing. Brands, recognizing that the rising tide of criticism will threaten the entire industry if not addressed, have begun to band together to create overdue change. In Europe, under the guidance of French president Emmanuel Macron at the recent G7 summit in Biarritz, thirty-two fashion companies signed a "fashion pact" to emphasize sustainability in the industry.[41] They included some of the largest luxury brands in the market—Chanel, Ralph Lauren, and Prada—as well as "fast fashion" producers, including H&M Group and Zara.

As more consumers looked to buy brands that follow ethical practices and with sustainable materials made for long-term wear, there was a real need for disruption. Everlane founder Michael Preysman saw this opportunity and seized it with a vision that would change the game (and hopefully the world).

(Website), August 18, 2020, https://finance.yahoo.com/news/bezos-blackrock-pouring-billions-30-230100473.html, n.p.

40 "Delta Airlines Mission and Vision Statements Analysis," *Delta Airlines* (Website), Accessed January 30, 2021, https://mission-statement.com/delta-airlines/, n.p,

41 Edward Helmore, "Fashion industry changes might help save the planet," *Taipei Times* (Website), September 7, 2019, http://www.taipeitimes.com/News/editorials/archives/2019/09/07/2003721848, n.p.

Everlane's vision is "Exceptional quality. Ethical factories. Radical transparency." They build this into everything they do.

It is the core of their mission, and they use it as a rallying cry for their customers and stakeholders. As "The 10 Marketing Secrets to Everlane's Success" noted, "They packaged it up for their customers to hear, easily remember, and share."[42]

Everlane believes we can all make a difference, and they want making the right choice to be as easy as putting on a great T-shirt. That's why they work with ethical factories around the world, source only the finest materials, and share each story with their audience. They include stories about finding the factories right down to the real cost of every product they make. Prominent advocates of "radical transparency," Everlane believes that their customers have the right to know how much their clothes cost to build from materials to labor to transport. "Know your factories. Know your costs. Always ask why" is a constant refrain from the brand, with the underlying message: blindly trust no one, including us.

Preysman shared in an interview with *Vogue* where the idea of "radical transparency" came from: "The idea of 'radical transparency' came in when Preysman considered how to convince consumers that his $16 T-shirt was of the same quality as the $60 one. He decided to tell them everything: how much the crewneck cost to make (eight dollars), where it was made (Mola Inc. in Los Angeles), and how much the markup was (100 percent)."

Since launching in 2011 with just two styles of cotton T-shirts, Everlane has grown exponentially. They have doubled sales annually for the past four years, their product line has expanded to everything from outerwear and underwear to stylish sneakers and ReNew backpacks, and they will reach two million customers in 2019. By committing to transparency, they have made a bold decision to back up the promise with the proof.

The company is continually seeking to improve its offerings and reduce its footprint in increasingly ambitious ways. After almost three years of research

---

42 Mark Spera, "The 10 Marketing Secrets to Everlane's Success," *Growth Marketing Pro (GMP)* (Website, February 2, 2019, https://www.growthmarketingpro.com/ecommerce-marketing-manual-10-secrets-everlanes-success/, n.p.

and testing, Everlane has created an entire line of outerwear produced from recycled plastic water bottles, called ReNew, and has vowed to eliminate all use of virgin plastic by 2021. They expect to recycle one hundred million water bottles in the next five years. While many companies have offered one-off products featuring recycled plastic, Everlane aims to be able to tell customers, "You don't have an alternative," says Preysman. By default, all their products will incorporate this urgent environmentalism. He said, "I don't know of any single company that has done that in this short order."[43]

We should note that despite its progressiveness in materials and pricing, Everlane has come under criticism by its employees for issues ranging from union-busting to alleged racism and toxic work culture. Again, our view is that no company is perfect, just like no human being is perfect. We commend the employees of Everlane for standing up for themselves.

By focusing on your category, you can see the most ownable lanes for your purpose. Start there.

---

43 Chloe Malle, "Has Everlane Ushered in a Brave New World of Retail?" *Vogue* (Website), February 21, 2019, https://www.vogue.com/article/everlane-new-world-of-retail, n.p.

Collaborators

Once you have engaged your employees and leaders in identifying a social issue that feels true to your brand and taps into their passions, the next step is determining how you can make the most significant impact – by partnering with other allies to create a coalition for good.

The biggest mistake we see brands make at this point is that they attempt to jump into a cause with the mindset of singlehandedly saving the world. This mindset leads to campaigns such as the oft-maligned Kendall Jenner Pepsi ad that featured Pepsi as the cure for racism and police brutality. Although that campaign has become the poster child for self-aggrandizing approaches to social impact, Pepsi is far from alone in making that mistake. Unfortunately for them, they were the highest profile.

The best way to avoid that mistake is to work collaboratively with the people, communities, and organizations that are also dedicated to these issues to create an impact that is much greater than anything your brand could have done alone. There are three types of collaborators that brands should consider; each of them brings a unique set of superpowers.

The first are nonprofits. They live and breathe their causes. They know the issue inside and out and have deep experience helping to solve the problem. They also bring a great deal of credibility to the table as well as boundless passion. Nonprofits may have been some of your most vocal critics, challenging you to change your products or practices to help solve an issue. Nonprofits need your resources, infrastructure, and ability to scale. When brands and nonprofits collaborate in the right way, they can help to impact society meaningfully. An example of this is the collaboration between Starbucks, Food Donation Connection, and Feeding America.

In 2017, Starbucks announced it would donate all of its unsold food to America's needy as part of its plan to minimize food waste at its US locations. They asked the questions "Where could this food do the most good?" and "How do we do this at the scale of the business?" To develop the solution, it teamed up with the leading nonprofits in the space—Food Donation Connection and Feeding America—in a program known as FoodShare. This collaboration allowed the company to donate all of its leftover prepared meals to food banks, with FDC and Feeding America picking up food at 7,600 Starbucks-operated US locations to redistribute it to the families that need it.

For brands, nonprofits like Feeding America are becoming valuable collaborators. Catherine Davis, chief marketing and communications officer for Feeding America (and one of our favorite clients at Conspiracy of Love), is one of the chief architects in creating win-wins with brands. Before joining

Feeding America, Catherine oversaw the US McDonald's and Esurance businesses at Leo Burnett and was SVP marketing services at Diageo, thus giving her experience on both the for-profit and nonprofit sides. She is responsible for identifying innovative ways to engage the public in Feeding America's mission, as well as enhancing the organization's reputation as one of the most-admired nonprofit brands in the country.

Catherine speaks about the scale of the hunger problem.

About 40 million people face hunger—and Feeding America believes that's 40 million too many. It is hard to reconcile that there are kids in our country who go to bed hungry, while at the same time, good food gets thrown away. Feeding America's purpose is "to alleviate hunger today and end hunger tomorrow." To do this, we rescue good food that is going to waste—like fresh produce—and work with our nationwide network of food banks to provide meals to the people who need them. Working with partners, we also work to identify the best methods for helping families overcome hunger and get back on their feet.

As companies become increasingly purpose-driven, we're working closely with them to help them achieve their objectives as we fulfill our mission. For example, our partnership with Starbucks enables the company's employees to play a key role in carrying out Starbucks's commitment to ending hunger. Starbucks employees help ensure that 100 percent of the food available to donate from Starbucks stores reaches people facing hunger through the Starbucks FoodShare program.

The COVID-19 pandemic has exacerbated the problem, leading to one of the highest levels of food insecurity the United States has seen since its 2008 financial collapse. This epidemic has created an even greater need for brand partnerships to help fill a $1.5 billion gap in necessary resources. Companies across the board have stepped up in unprecedented ways, helping to raise hundreds of millions of dollars. When brands partner with nonprofits to align their superpowers, it can save lives.

The second type of collaboration is with culture creators. These are the creators, artists, designers, and storytellers who reshape the way we see the world.

They can harness their influence and celebrity to draw critical attention to an issue. A young lady who exemplifies this power is Yara Shahidi. Anointed the "Face and Brain of Young Hollywood" by the *Hollywood Reporter*, Yara is best known as the breakout of ABC's hit *Black-ish* and star of its spinoff, *Grown-ish*. She is a fierce advocate for racial and gender equity, youth political engagement, and ensuring the marginalized have equal access to opportunity.

So when Bombas, which has successfully built a one-to-one give model that donates millions of items of essential and comfortable clothing to homeless shelters, decided to expand its impact to vulnerable communities beyond the homeless, Yara was an ideal partner. Together, they created the UNITE collection: limited edition socks, designed to celebrate people who believe in the uniting power of bettering communities around us. For every pair of Bombas x Yara Shahidi socks purchased, they will donate funds to organizations that are working toward equity in education and providing support for underprivileged communities. Shahidi's collaboration with Bombas helps the brand to expand into new territory credibly. Equally important, it celebrates her dedication to educating young people and highlights the idea that change is a powerful force that unites us.

The third type of collaboration that we are excited to see is more brands collaborating with other brands. As the size and scale of problems such as the climate crisis, our dying oceans, and economic inequality threaten the well-being of all of humanity, it's time for brands to become less competitive and more collaborative.

We are seeing the ways brands can come together, facing a common crisis in the COVID-19 pandemic, which is threatening physical and economic health around the world.

Anna Vogt, chief strategy officer, TBWA\London, chronicled examples of how brands throughout Europe were working together in unprecedented ways.[44]

For example, when McDonald's had to shut down all of its restaurants, its German staff were encouraged to work at Aldi to help the supermarket cope

44 Anna Vogt, "All hail the recent rise of frenemies," *Campaign* (Website), April 14, 2020, https://www.campaignlive.co.uk/article/hail-recent-rise-frenemies/1679919, n.p.

with the surge in demand and serve the public. In another example, Virgin Atlantic and easyJet contacted about four thousand of their CPR-trained staff, grounded during this pandemic, and encouraged them to volunteer at the NHS Nightingale hospital.

But perhaps most impressive is Project Pitstop—a collaboration between University College London, Mercedes Formula One (F1), and their respective technology arms, coordinating a response to the UK government's call for assistance with the manufacture of medical devices. Pooling the resources and capabilities of their member teams, they doubled down on the core skills of the F1 industry: rapid design, prototype manufacture, test, and skilled assembly.

Anna observed, "Considering how closely guarded the technology and engineering around F1 teams is, and the competitive advantages they present, it's no small feat to put that to one side for a moment and work as one team. It took a mere 100 hours from first being briefed to producing the first device, which is now NHS-approved."

Purpose is powerful. It can transform our ability to harness the power of business for good. But purpose without collaboration misses the point. There are things more significant than ourselves to be of service to. We need all hands on deck, working together, to save the world.

PART III

THE NINE PRINCIPLES OF PURPOSE

COMPANIES MUST GO FROM CHARITY TO SOLIDARITY

As we emerge from the aftermath of COVID-19, we have a golden opportunity to reboot capitalism, and we believe purpose is the source code that we need to start with. Our aim should not merely be to restore what's been lost but also to build society and the planet back better than ever. To do this, we need to do more than restore the status quo—which created a situation of extreme inequality and the climate crisis, both evidence of the systemic failure of capitalism.

Our situation requires us to repair and restore, resulting in a net positive contribution to the planet and humanity. We have massive damage to undo if we are to survive and thrive. Businesses will need to rebuild, for a new reality and purpose is the fundamental and foundational starting point for all companies to reimagine their role and potential.

There has never been a more opportune time to make this shift. Companies must advance a mindset of giving more than taking, choosing for the future over the present, of public good over self-preservation. Brands must move from seeing customers as passive audiences of ads to seeing them as active participants in change. We must promote listening, learning, compassion, and involvement as the new pillars for innovation and growth.

Companies must step up, not step back, if we are to have a chance at fair and enduring prosperity for all. They must move from charity to solidarity, standing beside the people and organizations seeking to build a better world.

With the political world in tumult, unemployment at record levels, and the fragmentation of the international world order that has been the bedrock of progress since World War II, people expect businesses to fill voids that governments and nonprofits can't address alone. We need today's companies to show the will and wherewithal to lead the way in addressing urgent social and environmental issues.

Like companies that embraced digital first, organizations that adopt purpose before others can have a huge competitive advantage, especially around three key stakeholders: consumers, employees, and investors.

Companies that take the time to deeply understand their DNA and relationship with society and build purpose-led strategies into their operations are much more likely to win over consumers. These consumers will pay attention to the nuances of how a company operates and will share that information with their networks once delighted.

Beyond integrity in products and processes, consumers today want brands to take a stand on issues that matter and to invite them to be part of the solution to the problems they both care about. By giving people a voice and a platform for participation, companies can spark a movement more extraordinary than their brand.

Conversely, disappointed consumers will turn elsewhere, choosing not to buy at all rather than spend on a product that doesn't align with their values—or even worse, use the megaphones of social media to tear down a company that they believe is bad for the world.

Purpose-led companies will also need to listen to what their employees care about and respond accordingly. This inside-out approach will demonstrate that a company has the best interests of its employees at heart, engendering trust. In turn, these employees will create products and services that positively impact people and our planet.

And finally, purpose-driven companies will attract purpose-driven capital—those investors, both institutional and individual, looking for social and environmental impact alongside financial returns. Whether it's the $7.2 trillion behemoth that is BlackRock or the millennial and Gen Z investors wanting their 401(k)s to be invested in line with their values, these are important stakeholders for the modern-day CEO to understand and collaborate with.

The companies that will win in this new world will understand they are not solo actors. There are ever-expanding opportunities for brands to partner with various stakeholders, like nonprofits and community organizations, to develop purpose, tap external expertise, raise funds, and spur grassroots activism.

Powerhouse brands will make a long-term commitment to their purpose and be a North Star for all their stakeholders from consumers to employees to the community and the world.

We have spoken and worked with some of the best and most passionate leaders to understand how to build a purpose-led business. Here are the nine principles of purpose to stay true to along your journey, which we believe are essential to creating a truly purpose-driven organization.

HOW TO TRANSFORM INTO A PURPOSE-DRIVEN COMPANY

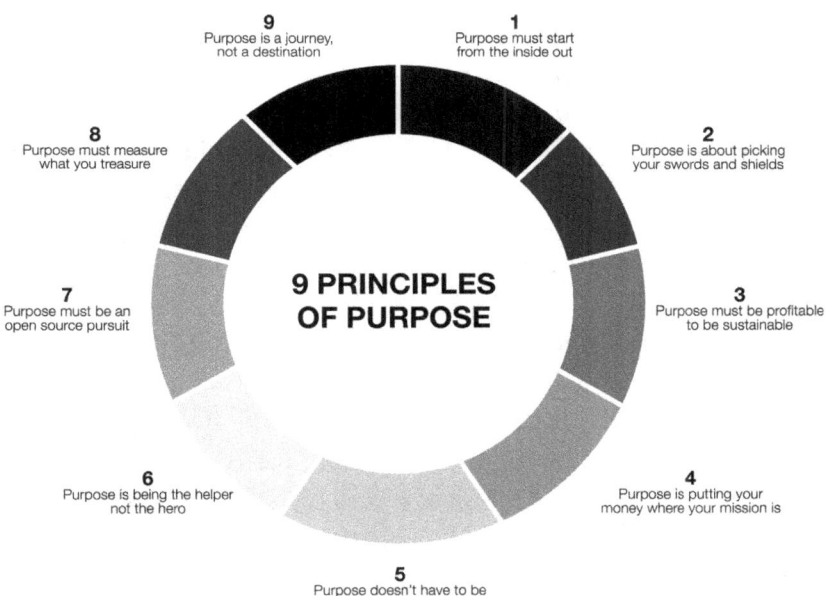

9
Purpose is a journey,
not a destination

1
Purpose must start
from the inside out

8
Purpose must measure
what you treasure

2
Purpose is about picking
your swords and shields

7
Purpose must be an
open source pursuit

**9 PRINCIPLES
OF PURPOSE**

3
Purpose must be profitable
to be sustainable

6
Purpose is being the helper
not the hero

4
Purpose is putting your
money where your mission is

5
Purpose doesn't have to be
political

Purpose Needs to Start Inside Out

Before a company starts preaching to the outside world about how it should behave, it must first get its house in order. It needs to take care of its employees, ensure that they are getting paid fairly, have benefits, and feel loved and cared for. It needs to ensure that it has gender balance, both in pay equity and in leadership positions. It needs to ensure that it has not just diversity but inclusion—the ability to empower people of all backgrounds to lead and have their voices heard. If a company is not doing well by its employees first, it cannot be indeed doing well for the world.

A caveat—it is important to realize that no company is perfect, just like no human being is perfect. Every company has made mistakes in the past; every company will continue to make mistakes as it attempts to evolve and grow. The important thing is that companies are transparent about their mistakes and use them as opportunities to do better. Companies should focus on building up their equity in their "purpose bank account". The more good they do, the more equity they earn in the eyes of their stakeholders.

Purpose Is about Picking Your Sword and Shields

Our good friend Sara Vaughan is an innovator, a creator of global brands with purpose, and a positive change maker. As the ex-VP of sustainable business at Unilever, she cites a phrase often quoted inside the company: "Brands must choose their swords and shields." Swords are a brand's crusade, the causes they want to lead and march forward with. Shields are what they use to help protect themselves from the attacks on their character by others. These are the values, actions, and truths that can help protect the brand's reputation even in the face of criticism.

Brands should then connect their sword with their core business. For example, Adidas makes products for athletes, so their belief that sport has the power to change lives is a natural fit. The North Face makes outdoor clothing, so it's only right that its focus should be on protecting the environment. Your territories for activation should ideally be consistent with previous efforts, connect to your core values, and feel like an obvious fit with who you are.

Some territories (for instance, sustainability) may be shields—defensive territories where there is an expectation that must be met as the price of entry

PICK YOUR
SWORDS AND
YOUR SHIELDS

Sarah Vaughan

into a category. However, finding the *sword*—that particular issue or cause that becomes a crusade for the company to focus on—is crucial to focus resources and differentiate yourself from the competition.

Purpose Must Be Profitable to Be Scalable

In the long term, your purpose must drive profitability. This is business, not philanthropy. Profit buys time and trust from your investors, employees, and other stakeholders, who all want the company to succeed. Society has a vested interest in helping businesses that are good for the world to do well. Profits allow for stable employment, investor returns, and solutions at scale that build resiliency to weather existential shocks. The more money a company can make from doing good, the more the good can scale. Adidas is now generating $2 billion from selling sneakers and apparel made out of waste ocean plastic, harnessing the engine of capitalism to solve one of the most pernicious problems in our seas. The UN estimates that succeeding in reaching all of their Sustainable Development Goals—the biggest challenges facing humanity and the planet—will create a staggering $12 trillion in unlocked value. As Peter Diamandis, founder of Singularity University and the X-Prize, says, "The world's biggest problems are the world's biggest business opportunities."

Purpose Is about Putting Your Money Where Your Mission Is

However, one of the most paradoxical aspects of purpose is that while in the long-run purpose needs to be profitable, sometimes companies need to risk short-term profits to maintain a long-term commitment to their beliefs. As advertising legend Bill Bernbach put it, 'a **principle** isn't a **principle** until it costs you money.'

Our friend Aaron Griffiths, a globally recognized creative leader, came up with the memorable phrase "Put Your Money Where Your Mission Is," which we thought nailed this fundamental principle. Truly authentic purpose-driven leadership sometimes means risking your profits to stand by your values. Patagonia made history as the first privately owned company to sue the president of the United States after Donald Trump signed legislation returning federally protected public lands to state ownership, making them vulnerable to

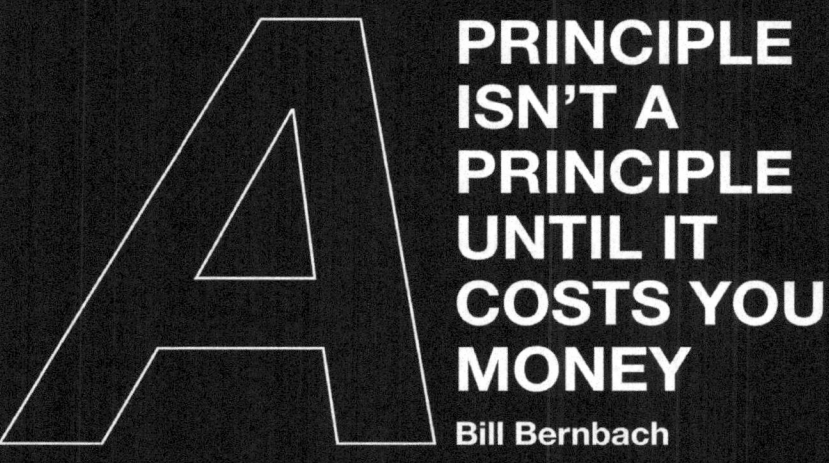

A PRINCIPLE
ISN'T A
PRINCIPLE
UNTIL IT
COSTS YOU
MONEY

Bill Bernbach

oil and gas mining. The decision generated a backlash and a record-breaking sales quarter as their consumers came out to support their decision.

Nike sparked controversy when it supported Colin Kaepernick in his protests against police brutality, a move that now looks prescient given the worldwide outrage after George Floyd—and which also led it to having a record quarter of sales. They proved the maxim from Nike founder Phil Knight, ': "It doesn't matter how many people hate your brand as long as enough people love it."

Delta cut ties with the NRA, leading to a potential loss of $40 million in tax subsidies from the Georgia State Legislature, with their CEO Ed Bastian saying, "Our values are not for sale."

Following the tragic Parkland school shooting, Dick's Sporting Goods lost an estimated $250 million in revenue by refusing to sell assault weapons and firearms to people under the age of twenty-one. That figure was dwarfed by the estimated $2 billion in lost revenue when CVS decided to stay true to its purpose of being a health-care company and forego selling cigarettes.

These actions win them true respect from their stakeholders as a test of their integrity, generating brand loyalty and advocacy that is invaluable in this day and age.

Purpose Doesn't Have to Be Political

However, despite living in an era of profound and troubling polarization, there are still issues people across political divides can agree on. Not every company needs to dabble in things that are politically charged. Some brands have such a broad and diverse customer set that choosing unifying causes is most prudent. There are plenty of areas to do good with bipartisan, broad-based support, such as feeding the hungry, improving schools, and creating more job opportunities.

It's also important to understand that purpose is relative. Even seemingly apolitical choices can be read in a political light. What Chick-fil-A and Hobby Lobby chose to do with their employees or their corporate donations with respect to their religious convictions can be read badly by those on the left, and what Oreo chooses to do by merely acknowledging someone's right to choose their gender pronoun on a pack can be read as hostile to the values of those

PUT your money where your mission is

Aaron Griffiths

on the right. In this day and age, some backlash is inevitable and should be planned for. The important thing is not to be paralyzed by indecision.

Purpose Should Be an Open Source Pursuit

As the adage goes, sharing is caring. Companies that genuinely care about solving our most critical problems understand that making innovative solutions accessible and replicable is the fastest way to impact change with scale.

Truly purpose-driven companies will give away their intellectual property to their competitors if they believe it can help improve the world. Tesla gave away patents for their technology like lithium-ion batteries to jump-start the electric car market. Volvo gave away decades of data on how car crashes affect the female body with their EVA project to improve all manufacturers' safety. We believe purpose-driven companies must collaborate on every level with others in their category (yes, even their competition) to create new models in service of our shared goal of creating a better world.

Purpose Is about Being the Helper, Not the Hero

Our friend Justin Dillon is the founder of Made in a Free World, an impressive enterprise software company dedicated to ending modern-day slavery. He tweeted this phrase, and it stuck in our heads as a fantastic way to think about a company's role in creating impact. This approach can help companies avoid making one of the biggest mistakes: casting themselves as the savior, riding in to solve the world's problems. This egocentric approach makes society recoil. When badly executed (see the Pepsi Kendall Jenner ad about Black Lives Matter as exhibit A), it can cause massive damage to your company reputation.

Your purpose is about service, so center it on people, not your brand, and help them see the power they already have. Involve customers and partners in your process and give them something meaningful and participatory to help the efforts succeed. Create platforms for participation ranging from lightweight (simply purchasing the product) to more engaged (collaborating with the brand, as Tieks did with their #SewTOGETHER campaign).

According to a groundbreaking study of Gen Z by DoSomething, **nearly 50 percent of respondents say it's important for a company or brand to have social change initiatives that consumers can be a part of.** Consumers are

It doesn't matter how many people **hate** your brand as long as enough people **love** it

Phil Knight

craving the opportunity to bring meaning to their lives. If you do that effectively, they will not only participate in droves but will also tell the story of what you did in ways that are more effective and credible than you ever could.

Purpose Must Measure What You Treasure

As the field of purpose grows, so too does the need to quantify and measure its effectiveness—the so-called return on purpose.

Part of the challenge of building a purpose-led organization is it requires a multidimensional model to measure the impacts across so many silos. These include the financial impacts (the ability to charge price premiums, the share price) and the brand impact (on reputation, advocacy, and loyalty, which lead to lower marketing costs). It also must measure the "employee brand" (the ability to attract and retain the best talent as people are drawn to the mission), the corporate citizenship reputation (leading to better engagement with governments and nonprofits), and ultimately the value of the social and environmental impact that is being generated.

Companies should create customized models of measurement that build in their bespoke goals and objectives in order to truly understand the multidimensional ways purpose can benefit them.

Purpose Is a Journey, Not a Destination

Finally, it is essential to realize that there will always be new frontiers of purpose that a company can achieve. Just as a company will never say that it is digital enough and stop innovating, so too every company can always find more ways to do good in the world. Even the most purpose-driven companies are still iterating new ways to refine and improve their operations continuously. TOMS created the legendary one-for-one model and has now chosen to discontinue it as it limits their abilities. Patagonia has made great strides in its materials and supply chain but still uses plastic, a problem it is grappling with solving. A clear purpose allows a company to stay true to its North Star and keep moving forward, even as expectations and context change.

The world's biggest problems weren't created overnight—and they won't be solved overnight either. Purpose-driven companies have the ability to evolve their thinking and contributions to keep pace with the changing world.

Be the helper, not the hero.

Justin Dillon

1.
PURPOSE NEEDS TO START INSIDE OUT

Often, we get asked the question, by companies seeking to become purpose led, Where should we start? Our answer is always, 'start within'.

The best purpose-led companies such as Tesla, Salesforce, Microsoft, and Patagonia have become the most successful and admired companies in the world. What do they all have in common? They all started with having a clear purpose—an aspirational reason for being that inspires action that benefits shareholders and stakeholders, as well as local and global society—which starts at the CEO and leadership level and permeates throughout the organization. Employees are invited to contribute their gifts and passions in service to a higher purpose, creating a greater sense of meaning and fulfillment in their work. This internal energy is then outwardly manifested through inspired innovation, authentic storytelling, and impactful marketing that attracts enthusiastic customers, investors, and employees. When these forces are aligned and working together out of genuine care for others' well-being, it forms a conspiracy of love that helps uplift business and humanity to its highest forms.

In this chapter you will meet some of the people and companies whom we believe embody this principle in inspiring ways. We will travel to Weybridge, England, and meet Sumaira Latif, the company accessibility leader at Procter & Gamble (P&G) and hear how P&G built a culture of inclusion that led to breakthrough innovations that are helping consumers with disabilities around the world. Then we will enter the magical land of LEGO and meet Loren Shuster, their chief people officer and head of corporate affairs to hear how LEGO created a company where playfulness has led to better leadership, a clearer purpose, and unrivaled commercial success. Lastly, we will hear from how Peter McGuinness, president and chief operating officer at Chobani, about how they have built a food-focused wellness company that uses food as a force of good.

Sam Latif, Procter & Gamble (P&G)

Sumaira "Sam" Latif, Procter & Gamble's company accessibility leader in the UK, helps create innovative breakthroughs to make P&G's products more accessible to more than 1 billion people living with disabilities. Sam's passion for this work comes from personal experience, and it's a great example of how employees' gifts and passions can be of service to a company's purpose, in ways that help the company become a force for growth and good.

* * *

If you were born a century ago with a disability, you most likely were sentenced to a life of invisibility and shame. Even someone who ascended to the height of the president of the United States of America could not escape the stigma attached to being physically impaired at that time. For example, President Franklin D. Roosevelt utilized a secret platform and elevator to ascend from the lower-level tracks of Grand Central Station directly up to the Waldorf-Astoria Hotel's presidential suite to hide his disability and wheelchair from the American public. Although Grand Central Station had ramps for carrying luggage and meeting other needs of disabled people, Roosevelt did not see ramps as a dignified means for a man with a physical limitation to move around. To be clear, the first physically impaired president was a great advocate for the rehabilitation of people with disabilities, yet he still operated under the notion that disability was an abnormal, shameful condition and should be medically cured or fixed, explains the Anti-Defamation League.

People with disabilities often went overlooked by society, and it wasn't until the 1940s and '50s that this sentiment began to change. After World War II, many of America's beloved sons returned home with mobility-related injuries. Decorated and applauded as heroes, these veterans still experienced many day-to-day hardships, from six-inch sidewalk curbs to buildings that lacked easy mobility. As the former abnormality of disability became common, what was previously acceptable became intolerable. Protesters took to the streets in the 1950s and '60s and smashed sidewalks as a way to make them more wheelchair accessible. Veterans and many others protested for accessible spaces for decades, and with the passing of the Americans with Disabilities Act (ADA) in 1990, businesses are now required to provide accommodations for people with disabilities.

Today, millions of people in America and around the world conveniently use ramps for wheelchairs, baby strollers, grocery carts, rollerblades, and activities unimaginable a hundred years ago, such as electric scooters and hoverboards. We have made great strides, since the 1900s, in learning how to build more inclusive societies, yet we still too often overlook a simple and perhaps the most powerful lesson history teaches us: when we solve problems for those most in need, we create solutions that can make life better for everyone.

Procter & Gamble is a company that has not only learned but applied this lesson to achieve business success. They touch the lives of five billion people around the world and see themselves not only as a force for growth but as a force for good. Their leadership has made a very deliberate decision to build things like sustainability and equality and inclusion into the business model to make it part of how brands grow. And, most important, they have built those values—particularly inclusivity—into their culture. An incredible example of this is Sam Latif.

Sumaira "Sam" Latif, Procter & Gamble's company accessibility leader in the UK, is one of the most inspiring people we've had the privilege to spend time with. Latif was born with a rare genetic condition known as retinitis pigmentosa (RP), which meant she could never see much through a narrow and blurry lens—until at the age of sixteen years old, she suddenly no longer could read anything anymore.

Passionate, positive, and engaging, Latif provides a perspective on how her experience fueled her career.

> My perseverance, resilience, and determination have helped me achieve anything I focus on in life. My aspiration always has been to lead what I thought I wanted: a "normal" life. But to do normal things was incredibly difficult as a young blind person. Simple things like reading a book, crossing a road, being able to see the latest fashion or film was impossible to do. I focused on the few big important things, like how to get through university; how I could work with others to become as independent and capable as possible for the things which really mattered like finding a job.

After a stint working for Arnold Clark, Scotland's largest car retailer (thanks to Mr. Clark himself, who offered her a job), she applied for a Procter & Gamble job. "I had previously got accustomed to the routine rejections from large companies who would outright tell me that although I interviewed well, they were not used to employing a blind person and wouldn't want me to fail in their organization. After all, there is no way a blind person can operate an XLS file—or so the decision-makers wrongly assumed."

Thanks to the efforts of Mike Bowden, an IT director who was actively recruiting disabled people into P&G, she was welcomed into the company, with

Bowden even taking the time to reassure Latif's parents that she would be safe in London on her own. Her current manager and P&G's chief supply officer, Julio Nemeth, has also been pivotal to encouraging and supporting her—and enabling her to explore accessibility for P&G: "Julio has championed and supported my work, not least with our CEO and his leadership team. He promoted me into a new role and position of Company Accessibility Leader, and I'm P&G's first blind, British Asian woman as an Associate Director."

Latif's perspective proved invaluable to P&G, as she began helping the company rethink its entire approach to inclusivity. Her personal struggles with products fueled her desire to fix problems for people with disabilities.

> Now that I was a mum, I used many of our products, some with ease and others with much difficulty. I could never independently read my Clearblue pregnancy test result, had a challenge reading the size of the Pampers diaper, differentiating between the Olay day and night cream, Herbal Essences shampoo and conditioners. I began evaluating our products in terms of accessibility. I had recently switched from using Ariel liquid detergent to Ariel Pods. I found the transition amazing, as I no longer was having challenges with measuring out or spilling the liquid detergent as I could pop a pod into the washing machine. We touch 5 billion consumers around the world, and 20 percent of these consumers will have some form of disability like me.

One area where Latif focused her attention was a common problem for many people.

> It dawned on me just how annoying it was to always try to find an elastic band to pop on my shampoo bottles to distinguish them from the conditioner bottles, and I started wondering what P&G could do, as I knew there were millions of people with low vision in the world who must also be struggling with this.

Latif's determination to solve this problem led her to focus on solving it with a simple design fix. "This year in the US and Canada, we implemented tactile stripes for shampoo and circles for conditioner on our Herbal Essences Bio Renew bottles, allowing people to be able to differentiate by touch shampoo from a conditioner."

Latif spoke to some of the other innovations that the company has made. "We've launched [Herbal Essences and Clearblue] on the Be My Eyes platform enabling low vision consumers to video call us for hair advice and pregnancy test readings." Latif's work led to her also convincing P&G chief brand officer Marc Pritchard of the need to make the company's advertising more inclusive. "We now include Audio Description on all of our TV advertising enabling blind and low vision consumers to be able to hear a description of the visual actions helping to paint a fuller picture of the action—the first advertiser to do this." Latif continued,

> More recently we have designed the Gillette TREO razor for assisted shaving, which allows a caregiver to shave the person they are taking care of so that it becomes easier for both. Mothers taking care of their sons, fathers taking care of their daughters, sons taking care of their elderly fathers, and wives taking care of their husbands. We've learned that caregivers like using TREO on both men and women, young and old, for those living with conditions ranging from Down syndrome to Alzheimer's and much more.

One of Latif's breakthrough ideas has been running disability challenges with senior leaders, helping them "walk in the shoes" of a consumer or employee with a disability: "This brings to life the challenges and the impact that small changes can make to making our products more accessible. Combining the stats with an immersive experience to actually experience firsthand what it is like to use one of our products with a disability has been extremely insightful for our businesses. It's a no-brainer now."

Latif is passionate about companies innovating to address the enormous potential of addressing this market.

> This is not just a moral or social obligation, it's the right thing to do, and it's using our brands to become a force for good and a force for growth. The data exists on the disability market. There are 1.7 billion people worldwide with a disability, and they have a disposable income

of over \$8 trillion. More than 20 percent of people have a disability, and this number is growing as people are living longer. By 2030, more households will be of people older than 50 than any other household group. The older you get, the more disabilities one develops. We want to ensure people keep using our products despite any disability. We recognize that disabled people have money to spend, so why not serve them better by focusing on their needs?

Latif has some parting wisdom for other leaders who may want to go on the same journey to make their brands more inclusive.

I think more and more leaders and companies can and will embark on this journey. It's a win-win-win if you do. A win for disabled consumers who often have been forgotten about. A win for business, by making products more accessible you increase the number of people who can use and buy your products. And a win for your organization, as employees love working on more meaningful products and services, where they see the real impact that it has on individuals. They become more passionate, engaged, and driven to a more successful outcome.

Why We Love This Example:

Procter & Gamble's purpose is to be a force for growth and good, which starts inside. By building an inclusive culture that welcomed diversity in all forms, they created a place where Sam felt cared for and where she could do great work. But beyond inclusion, P&G and Sam showed us in this chapter the power of compassion as a driver of business success. Many organizations encourage employees to understand and feel their customers' struggles. However, that is not enough. Sam didn't want only to feel her customers' problems; she wanted to help solve them. She used her deep understanding of the day-to-day experiences of disabled consumers to create compassionate solutions to the challenges they face to live a life that is "normal." The people of Procter & Gamble designed a work environment that made Sam feel recognized and cared for, and because of that, she was empowered to build products that did the same for others like her who had been overlooked for far too long.

Loren Schuster, LEGO

LEGO is one of the most beloved and iconic brands on the planet, yet not too long ago, the brand had lost its way. Loren Shuster tells the story of how, by refocusing on purpose, product, and people, LEGO has rebuilt a company from the inside out, showing humanity the power of playing well together.

* * *

LEGO has long been a company we have admired. The name "LEGO" is an abbreviation of the two Danish words *leg Iand godt*, meaning "play well"—which seems like an apt name for a toy company. But the company's ability to create and sustain a culture where its employees and stakeholders can play well together has made it a commercial powerhouse and creator of a better world.

Looking at LEGO's rebirth as a pop-cultural icon via the billion-dollar-plus grossing LEGO Movies and its ubiquitous presence in the lives of children around the world, it's easy to forget that not long ago, the company was on the brink of bankruptcy. Today the company is thriving, mainly by refocusing on its most valuable building blocks—purpose, product, and people. One of the leaders in this turnaround is Loren Shuster, EVP, chief people officer and head of corporate affairs. When talking about his work, Loren says, "I have the best job in the world." He is personable and positive, the type of person who seems born for his role at LEGO. When asked what else he could imagine himself doing if he didn't have this job, he says, "I would likely be found meditating on a mountain somewhere or coaching and supporting people's development."

We spoke with Loren about the brand's journey back to prominence and what they have learned along the way. "Our mission at the LEGO Group is simple: to inspire and develop the builders of tomorrow. We know that if we equip children with the right tools today, they'll have the critical skills necessary to thrive as adults tomorrow."

The company was founded in 1932 by Ole Kirk Kristiansen and has been passed from father to son and now to grandson Kjeld Kirk Kristiansen.

I think most people would agree that our values haven't changed since the first LEGO toy was made almost ninety years ago and that stems from being a family-owned company. So the issues back in 2005 weren't so much about purpose, but that we needed to get back to our core value proposition: the brick, learning through play, creativity, and our core fans.

But I think circling back to the brick was key. Almost every child finds joy and pride in building something that's challenging and then saying, "Hey, Mom/Dad, I built that." It's innate, and it's satisfying.

Toy trends change, but the brick is, and will always be, at the heart of everything we do. So reminding ourselves of this and returning to creativity was key. And again, our values and purpose have always been the guiding light for us: to "inspire and develop the builders of tomorrow."

Recentered on the brand's purpose and product, Loren and his team turned their attention to their people—starting with leadership—with the creation of the Leadership Playground.

At its core, The Leadership Playground is a psychologically safe place for colleagues to demonstrate bravery, focus, and curiosity. It's a metaphor on how children play: they're hands-on and fearless. I think this is something that should apply to learning and leadership.

We launched this initiative last year. Our first step was to empower a small, diverse team of employees from across the business, to decide what our future leadership approach should be. This group of colleagues came from all over the world, all levels, backgrounds, and tenure, some were people leaders, others were individual contributors. Once gathered together, we relied on this group to discuss and hammer out what leadership means to them. The Leadership Playground came out of those talks: the belief that leadership is for everyone. No matter where in the business or at what level, they said that people needed to feel safe to speak their mind and should truly care about the LEGO Group mission of inspiring the builders of tomorrow.

This safe space is critical to address the myriad of issues—(volatility, uncertainty, complexity, ambiguity) what they refer to as VUCA—that can affect a business.

In our VUCA world, we need to tap into the potential of every colleague and empower them to respond quickly to our consumers and shoppers. That means demonstrated agency and being able to self-correct and innovate. To do that requires all colleagues to be brave, focused, and curious. The Leadership Playground allows for this.

Loren spoke about the impact this has made on the organization.

I'm amazed by the results so far. When people are given the chance to speak up, without fear, all sorts of ideas, issues, and solutions are brought to light. This has also energized teams across the business. For example, in our LEGO Stores, employees set up daily challenges with each other to see who could concoct the best in-store experiences for shoppers and kids. And because we included factory workers in the creation and deployment of the Leadership Playground, they now feel more comfortable approaching their colleagues. To engage in a wide range of dialogues about what we can be doing better collectively. There is a greater sense of ownership for the wider agenda.

I recently learned of a global team who was struggling to collaborate and meet deadlines, but they managed to overcome these obstacles by putting the Leadership Playground behaviors into play. They had tough conversations and changed their processes. But this only worked because they involved everyone on the team, were vulnerable, and openly shared their mistakes. It was a journey.

This sense of empowerment has spread to its employees who want to extend the brand's purpose to impact its customers. "More than 3,000 colleagues volunteered in some capacity last year—at various STEAM events and building challenges—and because of their dedication, we were able to engage with 1.8 million kids across the globe. This type of involvement in local communities is hugely important to us." They famously engaged their superfans as designers who created a boost of energy and innovation into the product line.

LEGO ensures their purpose also extends as a through line to their commercial and philanthropic partnerships: "Our first partnership was with Star Wars more than twenty years ago, which was a tremendous success, and I think it spurred an interest in further partnerships. But we're thoughtful about these collaborations and always ensure the story and the message align with our core mission. Some of these partnerships are multiyear deals, so we want them to be mutually beneficial and sustainable."

LEGO recognizes the value of partnerships; they have become a source of excitement and a driver of growth.

> We have some amazing partnerships. I'm consistently blown away by the stuff these teams cook up. When you put a LEGO creative team in a room with a group from Disney or Warner Brothers, great things happen. And one of the true joys of working here is the number of iconic brands and companies that are not only interested in but truly excited by the prospect of creating something with us. This makes me really grateful for what I get to do every day!

But they are selective and only work with partners that share their values.

> If this means turning down a partnership when it doesn't align with our values, that's what we'll do. For example, because of the childhood obesity issue, we won't copromote with food companies. That's an internal policy choice we made fifteen years ago, and we've never wavered. So while it's sometimes difficult when you're launching a kid's movie not to do a Happy Meal or whatever, it's something we believe in.

The brand's rebirth as a pop-cultural icon via efforts like the billion-dollar-plus grossing Lego Movies is matched by its massive generosity. Its nonprofit arm, the Lego Foundation, owns 25 percent of the company, which has enabled it to give a $100 million (USD) grant to a consortium led by the International Rescue Committee (IRC). This grant promotes play-based, early-childhood learning solutions for preprimary and primary school-aged children impacted by the humanitarian crises in East Africa and living in Ethiopia and Uganda.

Most recently, the brand made headlines for its support of females impacted by the pandemic.

> As the COVID-19 situation worsened, we sat down with our colleagues from the LEGO Foundation to think through what we could do to help families and especially children through this unprecedented humanitarian, health, and economic crisis. One of our priorities in

the USA was to support charities who feed children because when schools closed, millions of kids stopped receiving free and/or subsidized lunches, which concerned us a great deal. So, a portion of the $50 million will go to food charities in the USA, including No Kid Hungry.

Another important priority for us is helping parents, who we know are juggling their jobs and trying to educate and entertain their kids from home. So, the bulk of the money will support charities who aid in remote learning tools and our "learning through play" philosophy. We will also donate 500,000 LEGO sets globally to families in need.

Finally, and separately from the donation, our designers put together a fantastic, free website called www.LEGO.com/letsbuildtogether and packed it with building instructions, video games, and activities that parents can trust, and kids can enjoy.

Loren spoke about the pride these efforts have created within the organization. When asked if he feels proud, he says,

Absolutely! And I believe that sentiment is true for my 18,000-plus colleagues. I'm incredibly proud to work for such a purpose- and values-driven company. The LEGO Group has been a toy company for almost ninety years, and its mission and our values have held steadfast. That's incredible. And to work for a brand with such timeless relevance is very motivating. Every day, I'm allowed, in fact, encouraged, to let my inner child show up at work. And I get to build fantastic LEGO sets whenever I choose. Who wouldn't love that?

As far as what's next, Loren shares, "As for the future? As the Chief People Officer and Head of Corporate Affairs I hope to create a culture where each employee feels integral, empowered, and heard as we approach our centennial."

Why We Love This Example:
LEGO's focus on purpose-led people, products, and partnerships has led to remarkable impact. They empowered their people to define what leadership

meant for them and the organization, spreading to its broader employee base, who want to extend its purpose to help its customers. They refocused the company's energy on creating great products that their fans would love and became evangelists. Once aligned on the values they shared as a company and the impact they wanted to make in children's lives, they remained disciplined in only working with companies who shared those values. LEGO's inside-out approach has led to initiatives that are seamlessly aligned and credibly connected, all working toward building for tomorrow.

Peter McGuinness, Chobani

Chobani is one of America's most admired companies. In many ways, it embodies the American dream—founded by an immigrant entrepreneur who built a company from the ground up to be the biggest yogurt brand in the country. But this only scratches the surface of what makes this company great. Peter McGuiness shares how Chobani built a billion-dollar business based on the values of inclusivity, respect, and genuine concern for others' well-being.

* * *

The Chobani story begins on a cold January day in 2005 on a quiet road in Upstate New York. Its founder, Hamdi Ulukaya, is driving down a nondescript street, past a street sign that reads Dead End, where he finds his destination, an old factory building that had recently been closed after eighty-five years. The structure is for sale, and the business is closing. The owners of the yogurt plant no longer saw any value in the building and were practically giving it away to anyone who would take it off their hands. But what struck Hamdi as he looked around the space was not the sight of an abandoned building; it was the sight of abandoned people. Fifty-five employees of the factory were losing their jobs. They had spent decades of their lives building this business, and their only remaining task was to ensure the plant was closed forever. Like the street's signpost warned, this was supposed to be the end of their road, which infuriated Hamdi.

He saw something in these people. He saw integrity, pride, worth, and a willingness to work to build a better life for themselves and others. He believed in them, and a few days later, he decided to borrow money to buy the building and start a yogurt business. He used the money to hire five of those employees, eventually hiring all of them. Their first order of business was to go to Ace Hardware and buy paint. Hamdi joked in his 2019 TED Talk that it was the only idea he had of what to do. Together, they painted the outside walls white, a clean slate for a new business that would always recognize and honor the value of people, especially those who have been given up on by others.

Since that day, Chobani has become the maker of America's number-one-selling Greek yogurt brand in the United States. *People* magazine recognized Chobani as one of the top "50 Companies That Care in 2018," and *Fortune* has recognized Chobani as one of the top fifty companies changing the world. It now employs thousands of employees, and for three consecutive years, Chobani has been a certified Great Place to Work. We wanted to learn how Chobani has grown from its humble beginnings to one of the most successful and respected American brands, so we spoke with Peter McGuinness, its president.

Passionate, provocative, and innovative, Peter is one of the leading voices championing the idea that business can be a force for good. Founded by the visionary Hamdi Ulukaya, the company starts with its employees: paying double the minimum wage in its factories and creating a shared-equity platform, which means employees own 10 percent of the $2 billion company. The goal,

Ulukaya says, is to pass along the wealth they have helped build in the decade since the company started. According to reports, at its $3 billion valuation, the average employee payout would be $150,000. The earliest employees, though, will most likely be given many more shares, possibly worth over $1 million.

Befitting a company started by an immigrant, Chobani is also hugely supportive of immigrants and refugees. It set up the Tent Foundation, which tries to mobilize the private sector to improve the livelihoods of the more than twenty-five million men and women forcibly displaced from their home countries, as well as numerous other initiatives around inclusivity, veterans, social justice, and sustainability. In doing so, it has become an iconic brand that rivals Ben & Jerry's in its authentic approach to doing good in the world.

McGuinness began by talking about the purpose of Chobani. "'Better Food for More People' is the founding mission and vision of the company. And this was based on an insight that people have good taste; they just need good options. Good food is a right, not a privilege. We thought that 'delicious, nutritious, natural, affordable' was the future of food."

But there's an inherent paradox embedded in that purpose statement that creates space for innovation and growth.

It's a little bit more of a loaded equation than you may think. It's hard from a profitability and supply chain perspective. That's a very tricky finance equation because our cost of goods is higher, our sourcing is better, and we're straining our yogurt (three cups of milk to one cup of yogurt). So we're not adding gelatin and thickeners; we're not adding artificial preservatives or cheap artificial sweeteners. We're using high-quality ingredients, but we don't want to price it out of the reach of everybody. So, I think it's a really noble mission to want to do "better food for more people," which is basically nutritional wellness. A "wellness company" is how we view ourselves, and we want "universal wellness" to happen sooner.

This rearticulation has led to the adoption of "universal wellness" as Chobani's North Star. "What we mean by making 'universal wellness' happen sooner is first, nutritional wellness—secondly, social wellness: immigration, equality, inclusion, our employees, our communities. And thirdly, environmental wellness. And so how we've distilled down our company is that we are a food-focused wellness company that uses food as a force of good."

Deep at the core of Chobani lies a set of core values that drive everything the company does.

> If it's just on a screen or on a piece of paper, that means absolutely nothing to me. You need to live it day in and day out. Deeds are louder than words, you know? At Chobani, it's very, very genuine; it's very, very natural. It doesn't look like we're being exploitative or commercial, because we've kind of always been about that. So it's not questioned; it doesn't look like a stunt. We're not trying to do this stuff to seem cool when we're not. We're not trying to do this stuff to seem like we have a heart, and we don't. This is how we live. This is how we work. This courses through our veins at Chobani.

This core belief naturally manifests so strongly in everything the company does that it doesn't even have a CSR department.

> We don't have a corporate responsibility department. I don't even know what the hell that is. That's our entire company, not a department. On all the good stuff we've done, we've never done anything paid behind it. A third of our workforce are refugees and immigrants. We don't do ads about that. If it's truly who you are at the core, you don't need to brag about it. If people find out organically, great, but we weren't doing it for that reason. I think that's the real difference.

McGuinness is thoughtful when he talks about how a brand can embody kindness and tolerance while also being a fierce competitor commercially. "I think you can be a warrior and a shepherd. 'Chobani' means 'shepherd' (in Turkish). And I think shepherds give the shirt off their back, and it's very unconditional. And then I think you can also be a fierce warrior and want to win in the marketplace. I think that the same company can want to do good

Be a warrior and a shepherd

Peter McGuinness

in the world and help humanity. I don't think that those are two divergent thoughts anymore."

McGuinness is also quick to admit that the brand has made some missteps along the way. "We've made some mistakes in the past where we're super righteous and called out our competition. We had the right to do it and had the science behind us, and you know what? Consumers didn't really like it if you're righteous and from the mountaintop. It's yogurt. So, I don't think you can take yourself too seriously." This lesson led to the realization that Chobani didn't have to wear its values on its sleeve.

> I think you can have packaging that's accessible and approachable and fun because so much of that's in the brand and almost goes without saying from a consumer perspective. You don't have to express all that in the packaging. We don't have to be uber-serious and have a million different claims about nutrition. And if you look at our core cup, it's just beautiful fruit. We don't talk about things like 'two billion probiotics' like it's a science experiment. We want our food to be good to eat, fun to eat.

McGuinness pauses as he thinks about what advice he'd give to other purpose-driven leaders in the space.

> I think everybody should have their own playbook and what works for Chobani may not work for many, many other companies. Find that one thing that is beautiful about your brand or your business, and double down on it. Every brand has something that's magical about it. Stop trying to search for the next thing. Stop trying to reinvent stuff, unearth something very magical that's there and authentic and real. And that could be a founder story, it could be a founding belief, a founding principle, it could be a cultural trait. Don't do it because it's on trend or because you think it could be exploited. Do it because it's something special and sincere and genuine about that brand. Champion it. Make everybody live it so that it becomes this prideful, galvanizing thing that later can manifest itself in the external world.

We asked McGuinness to summarize Chobani in one word.

Humanity. That's what we stand for. We're advocates of humanity in terms of how we treat our plant workers or employees. How we make our products, how we treat the planet in terms of the community, the disaster relief work we do, our hiring practices, our foundation work, our refugee and immigrant stances, our sexual and gender orientations stances. Just speak your values and views and have a point of view. If your culture is that, let it fly. Do the right thing, regardless of short-term impacts. By doing that, have we upset some people along the way that may have consumed yogurt? Yes. But that's what we believe. And we think it's the right thing to do.

Why We Love This Example:

In many ways, the story of Chobani's beginning tells you all you need to know about the values that guide it to this day. It's no surprise that a business started by an immigrant—and displaced employees forced to leave the company they called home—would build a business that employs refugees and champions causes such as immigration, equality, and inclusion. At the core of everything, Chobani does believe that people deserve better. They treated their first employees with dignity and care, and in turn, their employees built a multibillion-dollar business by providing better food for more people. They have proved that you can serve society like a shepherd and compete in the industry as a warrior, especially when that is who you most authentically are at your core.

2.
PURPOSE IS ABOUT PICKING OUR SWORD AND SHIELD

Swords and shields are both essential within a purpose-led company. Particularly in today's era of transparency, companies must ensure their practices in diversity and inclusion, ethical manufacturing, and equitable pay and opportunity are consistent with social expectations. These are the "shields": the processes, practices, and behavior that can help protect the brand's standing even in the face of criticism.

However, if your shield is your defense, your sword is your offense. It's the crusade that excites your stakeholders and ignites action that drives your business and society forward.

In this section, we are going to talk with three leaders who have found their swords. We will visit Dan Goldenberg at the Call of Duty Foundation to understand how they are harnessing the power of Call of Duty fans to put thousands of veterans back to work. Then we will meet Saquib Shaikh and hear his inspiring story of helping Microsoft see disability as an engine for innovation and growth. Lastly, we will meet Phaedra Ellis-Lamkins of Promise, whose passion for creating a more just incarceration system has attracted attention and investment from iconic artists from Prince to Jay-Z, leading to a critical change in our justice system.

Dan Goldenberg, Activision

Programs honoring veterans often are focused on symbolism, such as creating monuments and naming public parks. However, the Call of Duty Endowment believes that the best way to support veterans is to help ensure they have access to high-quality employment when they return home. Dan Goldenberg, the endowment's executive director shares how they are using the power of gaming to put over seventy thousand veterans back to work.

* * *

It is a Saturday evening during the COVID-19 pandemic, and millions of people around the world are restlessly obeying local and national stay-at-home orders. Many have been unable to leave their homes for weeks and some others, months. People are in desperate need of connection and distraction, and the biggest celebrities on the planet are more than willing to help fill the void. On television screens across America, Lady Gaga and John Legend lift our spirits with songs of hope, while raising dollars to feed the hungry. Movie stars like Tom Hanks and Will Smith express our universal appreciation for workers on the front lines of the pandemic, as Beyoncé and Ellen DeGeneres remind us that we are in it together.

While quarantined citizens accept the call to action from celebrities to join the battle against COVID-19, raising $128 million for relief efforts, there is another significant segment of society that is engaged in fighting enemies of a different kind. Across ages and geographies, massive numbers of people are battling in a fictional country of Urzikstan, combating Russian forces who have invaded the country. They are players in the video game world of Call of Duty. Although their world may be fantasy, the positive impact these players are making in the lives of other Americans through the game is as real as it gets.

The power of pop culture to do good is rich with examples when it comes to music, films, and TV helping to raise awareness of social issues and also drive active fundraising toward helping solve social and environmental problems. But often overlooked is the world of gaming, which is surprising given what a massive cultural and commercial force it is. Flagship gaming franchises like Call of Duty: Black Ops can make half a billion dollars on a three-day opening weekend (dwarfing even the biggest Hollywood blockbusters) and go on to make a billion dollars over two months. More people watch online gaming videos and live platforms like Twitch than the combined audiences of HBO, Netflix, and Hulu, and the numbers are increasing exponentially as global audiences come online.

One of the best examples of "gaming for good" is Activision Blizzard's Call of Duty Endowment, which recently reached a new milestone—it's now helped seventy thousand veterans find employment since 2009 (and has set an ambitious goal of getting one hundred thousand veterans back to work by 2024). The endowment has awarded more than $28 million in grants to date, and Activision has donated $31 million of its own money, much of it coming from in-game purchases by gamers supporting the cause. The Call of Duty Endowment was born in 2009 from a conversation between Activision Blizzard CEO Bobby Kotick and former VA Secretary Jim Nicholson. Kotick mentioned that a philanthropic foundation was planning on building a performing arts center on the grounds of the VA facility in West Los Angeles, to which Secretary Nicholson replied: "That's stupid. Our real priorities are finding jobs for veterans and improving their health care. I think if we could redirect people's energies and efforts for job creation, that would be a better use of capital and better for veterans."

Inspired by that insight, the Call of Duty Endowment was founded to provide grants to charities that prepare veterans for high-quality jobs and has a meticulous process for evaluating the highest performing nonprofits that meet its benchmarks. That has led to the endowment's average 2018 cost to get a vet a stable job being $516 per vet (versus $3,083 spent by the government). Leading the endowment today is our friend Dan Goldenberg, a retired Navy captain. Highlights of his military service include four tours as a commanding officer, carrier-based naval flight officer, and special assistant to four Secretaries of the Navy. He brings to the job twenty-four years of active and reserve military service and more than a decade of business experience. Enthusiastic and passionate, he talked about the importance of bringing a level of accountability and precision to the task of social impact.

> It's shocking to me, to be honest with you, how many companies check their business smarts at the door. They think when it comes to charity and philanthropy that if you're applying what made you successful as a business, somehow, you're not "charitable." And I'd argue that they are exactly wrong. If you apply what makes you successful in business and you apply it to a social realm where you can really add value, you actually do much more good.

Key to the success of their approach is a philosophy of extreme focus, which he expands upon.

> The approach that has made us really different is "Narrow and Deep," which means we try to do just a few things really well, better than

GO NARROW AND DEEP

Dan Goldenberg

everyone else. So rather than saying, "We are going to help veterans as a lot of companies do" we said, "No, we are just going to focus on veteran employment and are going to be so narrow, we're even going to rule out other worthy, adjacent areas like spouse employment and mentorship. We are just going to focus on vets and jobs." The thinking being if we do that, we can gain a deep understanding of what's working, what's not, and actually have some real impact.

Beyond the total numbers, another subject Goldenberg is passionate about is high-quality jobs, which is why the average 2018 starting salary for veterans placed by their partners is $57,850 (versus the national median, which is $30,240).

One of the trends—that you won't hear much talk about, but you will in the time ahead—is underemployment. It's a growing epidemic in our country. The US unemployment rate that we all rely upon as a major economic indicator is based on one question that the census asks every month, which is "last week did you do ANY work for pay?" So if I am a Reservist or Guardsman, and I drilled last weekend, but I don't have a civilian job, I'm counted as fully employed. If I work five hours a week as a barista? I'm counted as fully employed. If I cut my neighbor's lawn for twenty bucks? I'm seen as fully employed. That's the US unemployment rate. So when you see that number in a gig economy, in a world where people are working two or three jobs and have no benefits, what we see is a lot of underemployment. It hits vets particularly hard; it hits them 16 percent harder than the nonvets. And one in three veterans is underemployed. So to us it's not just that a vet got a job, it's really important to us that they got a good job.

One of the interesting side effects is that often the first in-game purchase a player makes is of a product like the Call of Duty Salute Pack, for example, which helps raise funds for the endowment. Those who have come into the economy by cause become excellent customers, often buying many multiples in non-cause items.

"Something interesting we've observed is that gamers really care about the cause. The support the endowment has gotten from Activision and the Call of Duty franchise stems from a deep desire to help veterans, period. But we've seen in-game charitable items bring cause-motivated consumers into the game. That was never the intent, but it's a nice by-product," said Goldenberg.

All of this had a profound impact on Goldenberg himself—as well as the employees of the company.

> I have no problem leaping out of bed every morning and coming to work. This is the longest I've ever worked anywhere, and I don't feel restless because the commitment from the company is real, and the people I work with are fantastic. I can't even think of a time when someone said, "Sorry I don't have enough time" or "I'm not interested." Activision Blizzard employees are deeply respectful of and engaged with the cause. There is not a function I can think of in the company— legal, marketing, PR, the developers in the studios, IT, HR, artists, sales—who have not found ways to add real value. It's people coming in and solving specific problems with a super high level of engagement.

Why We Love This Example:

By going narrow and deep on its sword, Call of Duty avoids the pitfalls of being spread too thin by causes to support and has learned to find a solution and stay focused on driving impact. They have identified an issue that their employees and their fans are both passionate about. Together, they are focused on their 'sword'; to create more equitable access to employment for veterans. Call of Duty has made an incredible impact on the lives of veterans with little attention or fanfare. Dan has been able to apply decades of experience to solve a problem affecting a community he is part of and cares deeply about. And for that, we salute him, his team, and those on the front lines, keeping us safe through their service.

Saqib Shaikh, Microsoft

Microsoft dedicates itself to empowering every person and every organization on the planet to achieve more. Next is the story of how one employee realized that by focusing on empowering people with physical challenges such as blindness, Microsoft could begin seeing disability as an engine of innovation and growth.

* * *

It's amazing how extraordinary a seemingly ordinary day can be.

It's a beautiful day in London. Andre Louis is at home enjoying a weekend, surrounded by the two most important things in his life—family and music. He's sitting in a makeshift studio enveloped by electric instruments and microphones, playing one of the many songs he has composed on his keyboard. He proudly proclaims he's a one-man band, and two of his biggest fans—his son, Jake, and daughter, Alice—are ready to rush the stage. He playfully picks Alice up and kisses them both goodbye as he carefully prepares to go outside by himself to run his errands for the afternoon.

The city's typical dreary clouds part like stage curtains for the blue sky and sunlight to take center stage. Andre walks through his neighborhood, navigating the people and vehicles whirling around him. He goes to Western Union to manage some finances and treats himself to lunch at one his favorite neighborhood cafés. After reading the menu, Andre decides on orange juice and a light entrée. He hops in the back of a cab and sits back, looking out of the window watching the buildings as he passes by on his way to shop at the outdoor fruit market. Andre visits a musician friend of his, a thirty-four-year-old drummer with a hipster beard and fisherman beanie. The friend gives him a twenty. Andre looks to make sure the money is right and heads home. As he sits down at the kitchen table, his kids greet him with a card they wrote. Jake's handwriting is getting better, every word becoming more legible. Alice's letter says, "I love you," bringing a big smile to his face.

On the surface, nothing about this day feels particularly remarkable—until you realize that Andre is blind, and everything he is "seeing" is made possible by the wonders of artificial intelligence (AI), via one of the most remarkable innovations for the 253 million people around the world with low or no vision: Microsoft's Seeing AI app (available for free on iOS). It is a veritable Swiss Army knife of a tool that narrates the world around you, using the power of AI to describe people, texts, and objects (e.g., currency bills or products using their barcodes).

We caught up with the architect of Seeing AI, the humble and soft-spoken Saqib Shaikh, to hear about how his journey helped fuel a new mindset at Microsoft, around seeing "disability as an engine of innovation," as he puts it.

Disability is an engine for INNOVATION

Saqib Shaikh

I lost my sight when I was seven, and after that, I started going to a school for the blind, and that opened up many opportunities. In fact, that's where I learned the power of technology to be an equalizer. We had talking computers and other gadgets, and that's where I learned to program, and that enabled me to go and study computer science at university and then on to do a master's in artificial intelligence. That led me to Microsoft almost fourteen years ago now. On that journey, I discovered that I enjoyed software engineering; I enjoyed making things. But I realized in addition to that, t was this idea that technology could really improve people's lives, and it was those two things together, which really drew me to this field.

Shaikh joined Microsoft as a general AI engineer, but after a decade, he realized that he was hungry for new challenges.

About ten years into my career, I think when I first joined as someone who is blind, I wanted to prove that I could be successful in the workplace, that despite being blind, I could do everything and be successful. And then after ten years in I was like, okay, I have achieved that, it's time to give back. So I started thinking about what were the opportunities to use my skill set to help other people. And I wasn't initially thinking of other people with disabilities. I was just thinking about "tech for good" in the broader sense until the hackathon came along.

The Hackathon Shaikh is referring to is Microsoft's annual event, the world's largest private hackathon, where more than eighteen thousand people across four hundred cities and seventy-five countries come together to bring world-changing ideas to life.

After Satya Nadella became CEO, we started having these one-week-long hackathons every summer where you're given permission to work on any of your interests. And I thought this was too good an opportunity to waste on just doing something small. So I thought, *What is the biggest thing I'd love to work on?* And very much driven by my personal experiences, I remembered this idea that I've probably had for so many years. What if there was a technology that could tell you who and what is around you and play the role, to some extent, a friend or a sighted guide or family member would play as you're walking along together, describing what's around you, and someone you can ask questions of.

The project launched at the 2014 Hackathon by Shaikh, but it really kicked into high gear in 2015 when other Microsoft employees, inspired by the project, came on board: "In the 2015 Hackathon, I was lucky enough to meet with some like-minded engineers and scientists from around the world, with over a dozen people contributing. And it was after that second hackathon that it became my job actually to do this. And then, 2017 is when Seeing AI entered the marketplace, and the rest is history."

Shaikh felt empowered by the new purpose-driven mindset in the company after Nadella arrived.

I love that term, *purpose*, because I think that is really, really important. I think I was seeing this switch before [I] starting working on the hackathon. This idea that it's not about doing the work; it's about what is the impact of your work. Some of the internal thinking I was having at that point in my career was, *What is my impact, and what is my purpose? What is it that I can do uniquely to improve people's lives?* So, I just feel in the company a lot of that shift in mind-set was happening.

Shaikh talked about the importance of the company celebrating individuality.

I remember this phrase from around that time of "bring your whole self to work." And that is something which was in my mind… during the very first hackathon. Because we are all individuals and if we bring our whole selves to work and follow our purpose, then actually the more diverse and inclusive workforce you have, the better you will represent our customers.

Shaikh believes other team members drawn to the project also felt the same way.

So many people have touched the project from around the company, and everyone has their own story on what gives them this purpose and makes them choose this to work on. But the common thread is this desire to have a positive impact on the world. Sometimes it's a relative who is blind or has low vision, or maybe sometimes it's just a more general desire to help. I think that's a common thread.

In developing the groundbreaking Seeing AI app, Saqib Shaikh and the team at Microsoft were driven by this simple but powerful reframing he articulated: "What if we could look at disability as an engine of innovation?" He added,

There's so many examples where the technologies we rely on today were inspired or influenced by disability, from speech recognition and text to speech to the touch screen itself. There's this terminology of inclusive design where if you focus in on one person's needs, then actually doing that can help you create solutions that benefit a broader population. With Seeing AI, we focus on the needs of people who are blind or low vision, but in doing that, I believe it also helps us make better products for all customers.

We spoke about the evolution of the platform and how the team approached adding new features. "We're always listening to our customers (the low or no vision community) and understanding what the challenges that they face are. And then we're talking to the scientists and engineers at Microsoft to see what are the emerging technologies we can leverage. And with each of these, we consider the type of task you can complete," said Shaikh.

These advancements led to a gradual ramping up of the functionality the app offers:

So we started with reading texts and identifying your friends and recognizing products based on barcodes (we used AI to help you find the barcode because you don't know where it's located), and a whole bunch of other things like that. And then we evolved into being able to recognize even handwriting and recognizing more objects, for example, currency bills. We started looking at different experiences that we can enable. So going from taking photos of what's around you to recognize the photos you already have on your phone.

Beyond the technology, what really inspires Shaikh is the impact it has on people:

I love these personal stories. There was a lady who was able to use the handwriting recognition to read a letter from her mother who had passed away. There was a father who was with his son and going to the zoo, and he was feeling a bit down because he couldn't explain what was around him. But then he used Seeing AI to read the signs, and suddenly for him that unlocked that father-son experience, and for him that was important. There's a teacher who's using face recognition to identify the pupils as they entered the classroom, and so for him, that unlocked a new level of interactivity.

He added,

We've heard from children that for them, it's not necessarily about task completion in the same way, but just about exploring and discovering the world. Sometimes it's easy to get focused on productivity and efficiency, and that joy of discovery is fun too. I love hearing these stories because everyone has their own. As we launch these new languages, I really think there will be cultural experiences brought to new people in different cultures, and I look forward to seeing what those new stories are like, too.

Shaikh believes he has really found his purpose through doing this work: "I was always looking for how you could use technology to improve people's lives. And I've got that, but then I've also found I've done that in a way that is deeply personal to me and so many of my friends and connections. So I do feel like I'm doing my life's work and found my purpose. I look forward to finding more and more ways for these emerging technologies to help people with disabilities over as well."

Why We Love This Example:

What Saqib and the team have created is much more than an app—it's an entire operating system, the beginnings of a platform on which it is possible to imagine a whole new ecosystem of cognitive technologies. It is a remarkable example of how business can indeed be a force for good by empowering their talented employees to show up with their whole selves and spark their purpose in a way that unleashes innovation, growth, and solutions to some of the world's biggest problems.

Phaedra Ellis-Lamkins, Promise

The United States has the highest prison population rate in the world. Phaedra Ellis-Lamkins is on a mission to change that through Promise, a "decarceration" start-up, using technology and policy to reduce the rate of imprisonment at the federal, state, and municipal level. If successful, Phaedra hopes to give millions of Americans a new chance at life.

* * *

After the untimely passing of the legendary artist Prince, there was an outpouring of love, tributes, and remembrances of his exceptional work as an artist. What also emerged, with less fanfare, was the indelible mark he made on people's lives as an activist. Black Lives Matter cofounder Alicia Garza said in a moving tribute, "He deeply wanted all of us to live in peace and harmony. He wanted us to be honest and truthful. He wanted us to pursue justice. He wanted all of us to be free."

One of Prince's most important legacies may be his deep and unwavering belief in the power of women, specifically women of color, to fight for and achieve justice and the liberation of all people. One of those women he entrusted and championed was Phaedra Ellis-Lamkins, a passionate advocate for human rights who is working to fix one of America's biggest problems—a broken criminal justice system.

According to the Prison Policy Initiative, America's mass incarceration system costs the government and families of criminal justice–involved people $182 billion each year. For companies profiting from services such as bail fees, health care, and private corrections, business is booming. But when Phaedra and her partner Diana had the opportunity to create a tech-based company, they eschewed the prison industry's high-performing market conditions to instead focus on a business that improved human conditions.

Promise is a decarceration start-up that was created by Phaedra Ellis-Lamkins and Diana Frappier to tackle the issue of mass incarceration, which raised over $3 million from partners as diverse as Jay Z's Roc Nation, First Round Capital, and Kapor Capital. There are close to 2.3 million people incarcerated in America overall, and approximately 4.5 million on probation or parole. Twelve million people cycle through local jails every year, more than 70 percent of whom are incarcerated pretrial, meaning they have not yet been convicted of the charge for which they were arrested. The vast majority of those remain in jail simply because they cannot afford to pay for their release.

Phaedra Ellis-Lamkins spent most of her professional life working on social justice issues—leading groups like the American Federation of Labor and Congress of Industrial Organizations (AFL-CIO) Labor Council, Working Partnerships USA, and the antipoverty organization Green for All. Diana Frappier worked in the criminal justice space for over twenty years, both as a defense attorney and as the cofounder of the Ella Baker Center for Human Rights. She has spent most of her career fighting against injustice and working to help people who have been harmed by the criminal justice system. After working together at the home-care start-up Honor, Ellis-Lamkins and Frappier wanted to harness the power of tech, human-centered design, and innovation to address an issue that has plagued their communities for decades—an overgrown criminal justice system known as mass incarceration.

Ellis-Lamkins said,

> We wanted to introduce tech solutions to the public sector with the overall goal of reducing the number of people who were incarcerated and empowering governments to make better decisions around public safety. Promise works with government agencies to support individuals released from custody, both pretrial and postconviction. Promise provides tools for the individuals being released, for the government workers interacting with those individuals, and for government leaders who need data to make better-informed decisions around incarceration and public safety.

Jay-Z has stated in a *Time* magazine op-ed, "When black and brown people are overpoliced and arrested and accused of crimes at higher rates than others, and then forced to pay for their freedom before they ever see trial, big bail companies prosper. This pre-incarceration conundrum is devastating to families. One in 9 black children has an incarcerated parent."

> He went on to say in a separate statement, "Money, time and lives are wasted with the current policies. It's time for an innovative and progressive technology that offers sustainable solutions to tough problems. Promise's team, led by cofounder and CEO Phaedra Ellis-Lamkins, is building an app that can help provide 'liberty and justice for all' to millions."

Frappier spoke about why focusing on bail reform was such a crucial part of dealing with the issue of mass incarceration.

There are problems with every aspect of the criminal justice system, and many forces are working to bring about change. As we were deciding what areas we wanted to focus on initially, the huge number of pretrial individuals being held in custody simply because they cannot pay for their release stood out to us as a necessary part of our work.

People who have been charged with crimes but not yet convicted should be released from custody in most instances. They should be able to return to their children, families, jobs, homes, and communities—regardless of their financial status. The current cash bail system keeps people locked in jail cells and subject to the many deeply destabilizing impacts of incarceration simply because they do not have enough money in their bank accounts. That is fundamentally flawed. It's un-American, and it's unjust. It's also completely ineffective at making our communities safe. And being held pretrial also has a dramatic, negative impact on outcomes, including being more likely to suffer a conviction, more likely to receive a longer sentence, and more likely to commit a future offense. There is a wave of litigation and legislation happening across the country that will eventually result in fewer individuals being unnecessarily incarcerated pretrial. Local public safety agencies will need to adapt to this new reality quickly. Promise can help them meet that need. We have met many public sector leaders who want to improve the status quo—both in reducing the number of people incarcerated unnecessarily and increasing public safety. The truth is, both can be done at the same time. In fact, we believe that public safety increases not when people are put in jail or prison cells needlessly, but when they have the support, services, and access to the treatment they need in the community to put themselves on a better path. Many agencies need tools and support to help implement these changes.

It was Ellis-Lamkins's work with the Prince that inspired her to create Promise. She became Prince's manager in 2014, where she was credited with winning his life long battle to secure ownership of his master recordings. During her tenure, Prince also performed a number of concerts to support social justice initiatives, after the tragic of Freddie Gray.. She said,

There is no way you can work with such a brilliant human and not be forever changed. He believed in women and, more specifically, in women of color in a way that I had never experienced before or since. I want to build a company that honors that faith. It was not just his music but his vision for the liberation of all people. We work every day to incorporate his values into our company, our product, and our team.

That led to the eclectic partnership between the various investors in Promise including Jay-Z and Roc Nation. Ellis-Lamkins said,

> We wanted investors who represented excellence and had made a specific commitment to improving the criminal justice system. Our investors needed to understand that we were not just building technology but that we are building technology that improves the system for those who we believe need it most. Kapor Capital and Roc Nation will hold us accountable to not just growth but mission, and that was critical for us as founders. We met Kapor Capital through Ben Jealous, who was leading the NAACP at the time and is now a partner at Kapor. We met Roc Nation through Prince, who believed that what Jay-Z and his team were building was the manifestation of a vision Prince had laid out many years before. They are both fundamentally committed to making the world a better place. While they use different strategies, I believe they measure outcomes in the same way.

The founders believe technology could help tackle the problem in new and innovative ways. Frappier said,

> Ultimately, digital technologies grant us the opportunity to scale quickly. New approaches in data science allow us to collect and analyze information more deeply than ever before. Our ability to build user-friendly systems while also making new connections between data that had been siloed will be critical to improving the criminal justice system. Our team brings that focus on user experience and scalable systems from their experience in the consumer space and applies

it to the civic arena where that has not typically been the norm. That said, it's not so much the technology by itself that will make the most impact but the intent and focus behind its creation—what and who we consider during the design process. This is a reflection of our belief that the movement toward a more equitable criminal justice system must view those currently marginalized as worthy of focus and civic, criminal justice systems as worthy of deep, thoughtful product strategy and service design. As developers of technology, our goal is to decrease the burden on everyone who has to navigate the criminal justice system. In a landscape where most of the conversation on new technologies focuses on replacing people, our focus is on augmenting and magnifying the value of human touch.

Ellis-Lamkins and Frappier believe brands could help advance solutions to the problem. Frappier elaborated,

We are definitely open to partnering with brands that fundamentally believe that the criminal justice system is broken and are committed to creating systemic change. There are many creative ways to partner, and interested companies should reach out to Promise. One important role companies can play is working to create a culture shift around formerly incarcerated/justice-involved individuals. We all need to promote the belief that people deserve second chances in life, especially given our flawed criminal justice system. A person may have taken a plea to a charge they were not guilty of to get out of jail because they couldn't afford to pay for their release and needed to get home to their kids or job. Or they may have committed a crime and served their sentence and returned to society. Whatever the case, individuals who have been convicted of crimes and were incarcerated or are on probation or parole still need to support themselves. They are part of our society, and they deserve to have jobs so that they can put a roof over their heads, provide for their families, and live their lives to their fullest potential. Brands who believe in this need to be willing to hire individuals who have convictions or who are on probation or parole. And they need to be public about it. They are in the best position to create the culture shift on the company side.

Why We Love This Example:

Embedded within the sobering and disheartening statistics on how unjust America's incarceration system is are the stories of real people with families, hopes, and dreams. Promise never loses sight of or focus on the people affected by these systems; they are diligently working to provide the support, services, and access to treatment incarcerated citizens need to get on a better path. Inspired by that intention, Ellis-Lamkins and Frappier have moved beyond human-designed thinking to a far higher ambition of justice-designed thinking. They are using their moral imaginations to envision a reform system that will finally fulfill America's promise of liberty and justice for all.

3.
PURPOSE MUST BE PROFITABLE TO BE SCALABLE

Purpose-driven businesses recognize that their ability to make profits expands their opportunities to make a change. That is why, as Blackrock CEO Larry Fink said, "Purpose and profits are inextricably linked."

In this section, you will meet Saul David, a senior director of enterprise systems at Zappos, who, by simply looking to help one grandmother in need, helped create a successful new business in adaptive clothing that makes life easier for families across America and beyond. We will then travel to Los Angeles to hear Sahm Jafari's journey to becoming a Tesla designer and how he is helping Tesla to accelerate the word's transition to sustainability while creating the most sought-after cars in the marketplace. And the inspiring Suzanne DiBianca will share the lessons learned leading social impact at the B2B tech giant Salesforce on how to turn business success into opportunities for enterprise and individual level impact.

Saul David, Zappos

Clothing, in general, is not made with the needs of the less able-bodied in mind. If you have limited mobility, getting dressed can be a real struggle. Although several companies have taken on this challenge to help people dress in adaptive clothing, those who seek it often struggle to find it. Saul shares how a customer call helped him realize the extent of the problem and the size of Zappos's opportunity to solve it, leading to a new business that is making life a little bit easier for those who need it.

If you are ever in Las Vegas, we highly recommend you call up and book a tour of Zappo's corporate headquarters, one of the quirkiest and most eclectic places we've ever visited, with employees encouraged to bring their whole selves to work in vibrant and fun ways. The fun only serves to encourage employees to be more human and empathic; Zappos's support center is renowned for the attention and assistance it provides its customers on a daily basis. Their team of employees processes millions of phone calls per year. Yet, it was one call in particular that transformed the life of an employee and inspired the creation of a multimillion-dollar business that is helping customers with special needs to feel seen, cared for, and empowered.

Saul David is in Las Vegas during the city's COVID-19 stay-at-home mandate. The city known for its bright lights and excessive indulgence has been quieted like a rambunctious youth on a time-out. He's relaxed, upbeat, and quick to smile. While others during this time have grown beards that hearken back to biblical times, Saul is clean shaven and seems undisturbed by the pandemic around him. He is South African and speaks with an accent that people typically mistake for being from New Zealand, Germany, or Holland.

He's a quick thinker and seems wired to be able to spot gaps and opportunities for improvement, which serves him well in his role as senior director of enterprise systems at Zappos. He's been with Zappos for eleven years and speaks about the company with great pride.

> 'Saul related to us how the story started'. Zappos is famous for its obsession with delivering *wow* moments through its customer service. As an example of the lengths it will go to, an employee once spent over ten hours helping a customer on the phone. The company has a rigorous training program that all employees must go through to learn the Zappos way, which it believes makes all the difference between success and failure.

So, after five years, they offered me a directorship at Zappos, and I'm not sure not how familiar you are with Zappos. But everyone in Zappos goes through new hire training. So, even though I'd been there for five years, now that I became a permanent employee, I had to go through one month of new hire training. And part of that new hire training is they take you through how to talk to customers and handle orders. You actually do live calls for two weeks on the phone.

One day, Saul took a call from a woman with a problem he couldn't solve:

So on one of those calls, this lady called in returning a pair of Puma shoes, and she said, "Do you have this other size? They are a bit small."

So I looked, and I said, "You know, we don't," and she sounded obviously upset.

So I asked, "What is so important about this shoe?" So she started talking about her grandson Gabriel, who at that time was ten or eleven years old, and he has autism, and he doesn't know how to tie his shoelaces. As he's getting older and his feet are getting bigger, she's finding it more and more difficult to find shoes without laces, like Velcro. So, I looked on our site, and we actually had nothing. So, I said, "Look, you don't have to return the shoes. Donate them to somebody who can use them. And I will make a note that we need to get bigger sizes of these shoes."

As Saul looked more in depth, he realized Zappos was not the only one without a solution. The problem and opportunity were much bigger.

So I put the phone down, and I just started doing some quick Google searches. I was Googling things like "special needs clothing" and all these things, and absolutely nothing was coming up. And the stuff that did come up just made you look like you have something wrong with you; it was just ugly stuff. And so I was thinking about it, and I spoke to a couple of execs about it. I said, "We've got all these customers, and I don't know how many who have kids that need adaptive clothes. And I think it's a good opportunity to have a look at catering to this market by finding fashionable products to help these customers."

Although the void was evident to David and others he spoke with, for months, nothing happened. During this time, David was invited on a golf trip to a tournament hosted by his fellow countryman and PGA golfer Ernie Els to raise awareness and funds for Els for Autism. Inspired by Ernie and his wife, Liezl's, autistic son, the organization is committed to helping people on the autism spectrum fulfill their potential to lead positive, productive, and rewarding lives. It was at that event that he learned that SAP, a company he works closely with at Zappos, had launched its Autism at Work program, which is aimed at recruiting and hiring adults on the autism spectrum. The initiative had been such a success, SAP announced a goal of having 1 percent of its total workforce—approximately 650 people—fall on the spectrum by 2020.

> I was like, wow! You know if they are busy doing something about this, I really need to get this going. And even throughout that year, I've never stopped talking about this idea of mine. You know, the ideas, I always find, are the easy piece. Getting them launched, that is the most difficult. You have to take that step. Literally, I flew home, and I went to see Scott Schaefer (who was senior director of finance and operations at the time), and I said to Scott, "I really want to start doing this thing for adaptive. It seems like there's a market; this isn't rocket science."
>
> Scott said, "Saul, just go and do it, don't ask us, just go and do it."
>
> And I did. And you know, I started off, trying to find the right people. It took a long time to get those people, and eventually, we put together a team of five people, and we moved forward. I had to get money, so I put together this whole pitch for this idea and went to everyone at Zappos to say, "Hey, you know, this is how much we need." And Tyler (Zappos's head of brand aura) really, really liked the idea. So he immediately gave us the money that we needed to start. And, you know, eventually after a slog of about fifteen months or eighteen months, we launched the website.

The team launched the site with one mission: to provide functional and fashionable clothing and shoes to make life easier for those who have trouble getting dressed. Now with the site born, the next big set was ensuring they had the best product. It turns out that brands were eager to be part of it. They started with smaller brands that were focused on this niche and needed a platform to sell.

Their biggest success story is BILLY footwear, the brainchild of two Seattle locals: Darin Donaldson and Billy Price. Billy broke his neck from a three-story fall in October 1996 and became paralyzed from the chest down. Not only did he suddenly face mobility challenges, but daily tasks that he took for granted, such as putting on shoes, became much more difficult. Billy and Darin launched the shoe company to fulfill Billy's personal needs, but the solution Billy was seeking for his own challenges grew into something bigger—it became a mission to create mainstream shoes that are functional, fashionable, and inclusive for everyone.

For BILLY, Zappos's adaptive fashion platform was a godsend, providing them with access to millions of customers who would not otherwise know they exist. David speaks with great pride about BILLY's growth. "They have become one of our biggest success stories. He's got a huge business now. He really inspired me to keep everything moving."

Zappos also started attracting the attention of the larger brands that would help drive growth and scale. "Nike contacted us and said, you know, we see you doing this. We've had this product for ages, we've got it on the website, and no one comes to it. So they actually gave us exclusive rights to their Nike FlyEase product. That was one of our big wows. Like man, Nike is coming and is joining us."

David's team has also inspired and helped show brands how to create an adaptive design. "We started influencing the bigger guys. For example, we are working with UGGs now. We had a workshop with them, and we brought people with varying types of disabilities, and they are adapting their shoes. They have given us an exclusive shoe. This is actually changing the way vendors are thinking, as well."

One of the most significant insights is how wide reaching the appeal of adaptive fashion is, even among those without physical limitations to getting dressed.

We call it adaptive, but a lot of the products are universal. So, for example, these Nike FlyEase will help people with some type of disability problems put on shoes, but other people wear them as well. They are actually fashionable shoes. If someone wears FlyEase, it's not like

Help one, help many.
Mick Ebeling

anyone's saying, oh, he's got autism or he's got a problem. It's a normal shoe that fits in, but it's also got the function.

David has adopted a mantra by his friend Mick Ebeling of Not Impossible Labs, which is "Help one, help many."–the idea that by solving a problem for one person, you can help many more.

"You know, so we always call Gabriel, you know, this ten-year-old kid with autism, he is our one. So if we solve for Gabriel, yes. Now we are going to solve for a whole host of our customers."

Zappos's adaptive business now generates about $6 to 8 million a year and continues to grow as this approach to design becomes more mainstream. It perfectly positions the company for the staggering global growth in adaptive clothing, which is estimated to be valued at $348 *billion* by 2024.[45] But for David, while the money makes it sustainable, it's not the main thing. What excites him is the impact Zappos Adaptive has made in the lives of those who need it most. "This one reporter wanted to do a story on us. We sent him boxes of products for his kids. He has a son, I also think with autism, and he wrote back and said, 'Let me just tell you, that's the first time in twelve years that I've seen my kid get dressed by himself.'" He has countless stories. "Jessica Kensky and Patrick Downes, who lost limbs in the Boston Marathon bombing, you know, they reached out to me on my birthday telling me how amazing they think this is."

In all of this, he discovered a sense of purpose in an area that he had no connection to previously. "To be honest, I didn't know anybody with autism until now. Even before then, I wasn't aware that somebody with autism couldn't tie their shoelaces. I just saw how upset [the grandmother] was, and that was something that seemed so simple that no one has looked at."

He reflects on how unexpected this journey has been.

I won't lie. At first, I was like, this is a new business opportunity for Zappos. If they can't find shoes on Zappos, they probably can't find

---

45 Tugba Sabanoglu, "Global adaptive apparel market size from 2019 to 2025 (in billion U.S. dollars)," *Statista* (Website), November 27, 2020, https://www.statista.com/statistics/875613/global-adaptive-apparel-market-size/, n.p.

shoes anywhere else. But once I started looking more and more about it, it's like, wow, it's so many people that need this product, and no one is looking at it, you know? I've got no personal thing with disabilities or anything like that. It was just something that, just the right time, right place, and I stayed with it. It looked for a while that it would never happen and ended up being successful.

Now, I stalk people. If they are walking with a guide dog, I'll go and ask them, what do they need? I was in Costco. And I said, you know, "I'm Saul from Zappos, and we are doing this thing, and do you mind if I just asked you a few questions?" And forty-five minutes later, I'm still talking to them. Anything with adaptive or disability, I immediately, you know, I'm looking, what else can we do with this?

David gives credit to the culture and coworkers who made it all possible:

Honestly, I give Zappos all the credit. It has to come from the top, and it started with a team of six people, but we will show you a map of who helped us, and half the company was behind this, you know. The whole company loved it, but we literally touched so many parts of the company to help us from web designers to marketing to you name it. There were so many people behind this initiative. I've worked at many companies, and I've never seen the extent that Zappos goes to do stuff for the community. It's mind-blowing, and it makes me feel 100 percent proud to be part of Zappos and what they're doing.

Why We Love This Example:

Saul's story shows us that the best way to discover purpose is often through service. By simply seeing a pain point that a grandmother was experiencing, he felt compelled to help. And in that process, he found a way not only to serve her needs but to help many others by connecting it to a business model that could make it scalable and impactful for many.

Sahm Jafari, Tesla

Tesla has become famous for its relentless commitment to accelerate the world's transition to sustainable energy. Yet, perhaps what has made Tesla the most valuable automaker in the world is its dedication to great design, delivering an experience that delights at every turn. Sahm Jafari, as a child, grew up dreaming of one day designing one of its cars. Today he is living his dream and shares why he feels so connected to the company's driving force, which is to prove to the world what's possible.

* * *

Sahm Jafari would describe himself as the product of a uniquely American mix of influences. He is the son of an Iranian immigrant father whose first business was fixing used cars and an Irish American mother who was a passionate eco-activist. He was also raised by an expressive aunt who used the power of her art to tell the stories of revolutionaries. Shaped by each of them in some way, Sahm has borrowed and blended the best of this eclectic trinity to build a dream-come-true career as a designer at Tesla that has helped change the world and made them all proud.

Sahm's mom, Diane, is an environmentalist who raised him to care genuinely for the earth's well-being. She also taught English to immigrants who were looking to start a life in America. It was in this role that she met her future husband, Masoud, Sahm's father, who came to the United States from Iran. As an American, his first business was a mechanic shop, where he would often bring Sahm when he was a child. "He would bring my brother and me in there when I was around five or six years old, and we were always looking at used cars. Not only was my dad a mechanic, but his brother-in-law was also a used car salesman and mechanic. So, we had a load of used cars around the garage."

This exposure sparked Sahm's love for automobiles at an early age. "I just really like cars. I had a group of friends when I was in elementary school where we would just go and point out each car and try to make a bet on who could name the most brands in a row."

Sahm's mom and dad were an eclectic combination, bringing different outlooks from both sides of the family, and parts of the world. He tells a story of how their varying world views could collide at times.

My dad bought a Hummer, a heavily modified used Hummer H1 when I was a kid, and my mom was furious. She was so pissed about it, she wouldn't give it up. He had the car for 18 months and would drive around every once in a while, and every time he'd get in the car, she would just be like, "Dude, you're killing the environment! What are you doing? Why would you ever want to do this to the world?" Eventually, she got him to sell it, and then I like to think that their lives were much happier because this gas-guzzler wasn't a point of contention. I think that story may be a good example of my mom. She can be very, very particular about how you can reduce your impact on the world, and calls people out on that. You might see a lot of these types of people in LA now—obsessed with their carbon footprint—but while it's quite common now, 15, 20 years ago, it was a little weird.

As a child, Sahm also spent a lot of time with an aunt on his father's side of the family, Manijeh, who was a fine artist with a garage studio a block away from where he grew up. "I would always go to her house, and just sit there and draw with her. She explores various mediums in her artwork, notably portraits and sculptures of people's faces. I believe that this desire to create was heavily influenced by experiences that she and her family endured during the Iranian revolution"

Sahm mostly grew up in Cupertino in Silicon Valley, where one day, he saw a store in his neighborhood that would change the course of his life. It was one of the first stores from a new company named Tesla that wanted to change the way people looked at automobiles, and the energy that powered them, forever.

As Sahm went to college, he became increasingly interested in illustration as a way to make a positive difference in the world.

I was really into children's books and how I could illustrate stories. I was having a great time, but about two years into school, I realized I wasn't going to be able to make a huge positive impact on anyone's daily life through a children's book, or an editorial illustration. I realized that I needed to go back and do something that was a little more physically oriented—it could be product design, entertainment design, or perhaps car design. But, just thinking back to my mom, it was significant for me to be able to create something that was going to shift people's perspectives on sustainability in the world. Maybe they could even use whatever it was to positively change the world. The advent of the electric car and the growing culture surrounding it are really great examples of something with potential like this.

He got his chance to apply his talents to cars as a student at the Art Center of Design, where during his education, he was able to spend a year working as an intern at the Guangzhou Automobile Group Co. Ltd. But while he was there, he knew his real goal was to work for this upstart company Tesla, which he was sure was going to be the future of transportation. He was persistent for years, pursuing opportunities to get in the door. One day, he received the message he had been hoping for.

> While I was in China, someone from Tesla reached out to me because I kept pinging them on LinkedIn and email, just trying to get their attention. I knew I wanted to work there, and then someone reached out to me and said, "Hey, we're looking for a full-time designer." And I was like, "I'm still a student, but I'm going to try to apply and see what happens." And of course, they fired back with "you're a student. I don't know how we accidentally put you on this list, and you're not applicable at all." But I kept in contact with them. So eventually, when the time was right, I reapplied and did get an internship about a year and a half later.

One of his first design projects was in response to a simple brief—design a cool electric truck—from Tesla founder Elon Musk.

> I got to present that to Elon, which was awesome, spontaneous, and vaguely terrifying, and I got to work with the team for a little while on that proposal. As an intern, this was mind-blowing to me. I had never felt so encouraged.

The project went away to focus on the Tesla Model 3, where Sahm was responsible for designing elements of the interior, often sleeping three to four hours a day for months until it launched in April 2016. The team was so impressed they offered him a job. "One day my manager just pulled me into a meeting room and said you're going to work here now. And I was like, f***ing awesome! I just started crying."

He also talked about what that job meant to his parents.

> They didn't think that I could make money doing this, and they didn't think that it was viable in the long-term. My dad is from

Iran, and he really found his groove in America and South America by working as hard as he possibly could, through trial and error in the pursuit of being able to support his family. My impression was that he thought art was just kind of a silly thing to do as a full-time thing. I'll tell you that initially when I went to art school, he questioned me for months. That was really difficult. So, you know, I think I've been able to prove to him that this isn't just art. This is not purely self-expression. You're creating things for people to use, and you can make good money doing it. And to him, that was important. Now that he has a deeper understanding of the craft and the goal behind it, he's proud of me.

His mom is not only now a proud parent but an owner of a Tesla as well. "She bought one of the first Model S cars that she could get her hands on, even prior to any involvement that I had with the company. We were both huge fans of the idea and the product, especially after the Santana Row store opened up nearby. She's a nerd about the car, still happy with it years later, and we talk about it all the time."

Turning skeptics into believers is not just part of Sahm's story; it's a mind-set ingrained into the DNA of Tesla.

The company's purpose—to accelerate the world's transition to sustainable energy—drives its culture. It was founded in 2003 by a group of engineers who wanted to prove to the world that people didn't need to compromise to drive electric—that electric vehicles can be better, quicker, and more fun to drive than gasoline cars. At the time, this idea seemed unachievable to even the most hopeful of environmentalists. Pursuing a goal so audacious requires people to have an unwavering belief in a vision that inspires them to do the impossible every day. It also requires resilience, persistence, and a great deal of optimism.

"What creates a deep sense of connection among employees here is a shared willingness to keep working diligently towards goals that will prove to the world what's possible. Even when things are tough, everyone knows in the back of their head that the reason they're here is that they want to change the world's perception of energy, through electric vehicles and energy consumption. I think that has to do with some sort of unrelenting optimism. They are optimistic about their ideals, and want to prove to themselves and others that they can do something, knowing that if what they are creating isn't right now, it will be right one day," explained Sahm.

This spirit of optimism and purpose is what draws people to Tesla and what they look for in employees.

> Some of the most talented people in the world have applied, and when the team is interviewing people and trying to figure out if they're a good fit, I feel like they are looking at two things. A friendly demeanor and the ability to work with one another and work with the team at large, that's one. The other thing is that applicants need to show real interest in wanting to help people. I think that willingness to help is what Elon has done a really good job of setting an expectation for it when it comes to hiring. Yes, you need to believe in the mission of the company, but at the end of the day, you're really trying to improve life as much as possible for the next generations of humanity. In a way, this unlocks my potential in a powerful way because everybody else here believes in the same goal. This makes us much stronger.

This resolute faith in a world not yet seen has inspired a deep devotion to the company's mission. "Yeah. It's almost like a weird religious sentiment. At Tesla, one could argue that it's a religion driven by data, right? That's what I was raised on and surrounded by growing up in northern California, and I think a lot of people at Tesla are raised on the same philosophy—a human-oriented hypothesis in regard to data and science driving your view of the world and how to help it. To me, that's what Tesla is."

That allegiance extends to its customers as well, evident by the fervent reaction of Tesla's fans to its newest groundbreaking vehicle, the Cybertruck— whose design is as brash, intentional, and uncompromising as the CEO who introduced it to the world. The truck was designed by Franz von Holzhausen, the brand's legendary design director; Ian Kettle, a British designer hired by Tesla two years ago; and Sahm. Driven by the purpose to make a truck with the most sustainable, low energy, low impact processes, they made a bold decision to throw out all the design language that they've used at Tesla so far and just

At Tesla,

it's religion, driven by data

Sahm Jafari

start afresh. It was the first project that Sahm was part of from start to finish, and from his perspective, it's the clearest expression of Tesla's personality and beliefs as a company.

For a self-described nerd, the truck's release event was a magical night.

> Being Cyberpunk-themed, I couldn't help but feel like "this is a perfect unveil." Like this is some sort of dream. I was able to be myself—be the biggest nerd on earth, and this project that I've been working on, on and off, for like two or three years was now finally being seen by people. And surprisingly, people thought that the Cyber-aspect of it was kind of cool, some showing up in complete Cyberpunk attire, some dressed as characters from Blade Runner. Definitely pretty surreal.

That excitement was reflected in the public's enthusiastic reaction as well. Within the first ninety days of the truck's reveal, 522,764 people deposited money with an intent to purchase, almost half of them within the first week. This success was the latest in a series of big wins that have made Tesla the most valuable automaker in the world (beating General Motors, Ford, Toyota, and Volkswagen) with a current market valuation of $700 billion. Perhaps even more remarkable, in March 2020, it became the most valuable industrial company in the United States (at the same time that the value of oil dropped to a historic low of minus $37 a barrel—a moment that couldn't be more symbolic if a Hollywood screenwriter had written it).

For a kid that was raised to love cars, people, and our planet, Sahm reflects on how lucky he's been to work at a company that is creating a world that previously only existed in his sketchpad.

> Well, I mean, you grow up, and you live next to this thing that's happening—a small company called Tesla—and you keep telling everyone how cool it is. And practically nobody gets it because an electric car didn't make any sense in the '90s, or even 2000s. Years later, things start to become clearer in that narrative. I knew that this advent of sustainability was something that had a place in the future, but now instead of speculating on it, I get to take part in it, and it's pretty emotional to

reflect on how that table has turned. As I said, I think that getting to this stage has been a combined product of everything that made me who I was when I was a child, and it's kind of a dream to end up at the culmination of that. I don't think it's going to last forever—I may not work at this company until I'm 80 years old—but it's just fantastic. It's everything I set my sights on, so I just feel really lucky that I get to do this.

Why We Love This Example:

Tesla has built one of the most valuable and remarkable companies on the planet with an obsessive pursuit to accelerate the world's transition to sustainable energy through innovations that inspire us to reimagine what's possible. From its first release, the Roadster, to its latest offering, the Cyber Truck, it has built a cult following of fans who have propelled the brand's sales to historic levels. It has also created a business that kids like Sahm dream of working for and contributing their talents to in order to transform the automotive industry and change the world in the process.

Suzanne DiBianca, Salesforce

Under Suzanne DiBianca's leadership, Salesforce has revolutionized corporate philanthropy through its Pledge 1% model, which reinvests 1 percent of Salesforce's equity, employee time, or product back into the community. The company has dedicated millions of dollars, hours, and technology to improve communities around the world. Suzanne shares how she created this model and what makes her most proud of the impact it's made.

* * *

Being at technology giant Salesforce's annual Dreamforce conference in San Francisco is a somewhat surreal experience. One hundred seventy-one thousand attendees roam the grounds dotted by giant inflatable animals with a parkland theme. There is a signpost listing a dizzying amount of inspiring talks by A-list speakers: Serena Williams, David Beckham, Steph Curry, Megan Rapinoe, and Apple CEO Tim Cook. We walk into the most highly anticipated event of the conference: President Obama in conversation with Salesforce's charismatic CEO and Founder, Marc Benioff. The two of them engage in what is most needed in the world. "If we can create a global platform for young people who want to do good, if we can harness that, the worlds going to be just fine," says President Obama. When asked for advice he has for young people, he pauses for a second and says, "Everything boils down to two things: be kind and be useful."

If you want a great example of how being kind and useful can drive innovation and impact on a massive scale, then look no further than Suzanne DiBianca, chief impact officer and EVP of corporate relations at Salesforce. Suzanne leads the company's stakeholder strategy—including all corporate giving, community relations, and sustainability efforts. DiBianca was previously cofounder and president of the Salesforce Foundation and Salesforce.org. Under her leadership, Salesforce pioneered the Pledge 1% model of integrated corporate philanthropy, which dedicates 1 percent of Salesforce's equity, employee time, or product back into the community. So far, it has generated more than $280 million, 3.8 million employee volunteer hours, and technology for 40,000 nonprofits and educational institutions around the world.

In addition, over 8,500 companies in one hundred countries (including companies like Box, Yelp, Docusign, Postmates, Twilio, Okta, Harry's, and General Assembly) participate in Pledge 1% (now a separate nonprofit run by Amy Lesnick), which in itself has donated a staggering amount: more than a $1 billion in volunteer hours, product licenses, pro bono resources, and philanthropic funding—making it the B2B equivalent of the TOMS one-for-one business-to-consumer (B2C) model in its simplicity and scale. We caught up with the frank and refreshingly unguarded Suzanne to find out more about the genesis of the program and how companies should be guided by their employees' passions as much as strategic goals.

BE KIND AND BE USEFUL

Barack Obama

Suzanne talked about her role at the beginning of the company.

I joined eighteen years ago. The company was about sixty people. I was actually hired to run the foundation. So Marc Benioff had a very unique vision of creating a new kind of company that took community service and baked it in really early on. He was trying to create sort of a new model of business from the very beginning. In the early days, we had no money and very little product. So, in the beginning, we were really focused on our employees and the volunteer part of it. And looking back, it was the right place to start. It became part of the hearts and minds of the people who work there.

Indeed Benioff has now become one of the most outspoken pioneers of purpose in business, even going so far as to say 'The business of business is improving the world'. Suzanne spoke about how that starting point created the genesis of the Pledge 1% model.

I was going out and doing a review of the industry landscape to look at what people were doing in this space that I really respected, like Levi's and Cisco. eBay was, I think, the first company that put a percentage of their pre-IPO equity into a foundation, and that fascinated me as it related to a business going public. The second part I looked at was the product donation programs, and Cisco was phenomenal at that. And Hasbro really stood out from the time perspective; they had an excellent employee engagement program. So we smashed them all together because what we realized was every company on the planet, no matter where you are, what you do, has those three assets.

She elaborated on how centralizing purpose also helped.

I think what we did uniquely about it was not only smash them all together and put a brand on it that could resonate with any company but also integrate it. At the time, many companies believed in philanthropy and had embedded it into their company, but it was disintermediated. They would give a product from one place, give their people's time somewhere else, and put their grants in a third area.

The business of business is improving the

Mark Benioff

There wasn't a lot of integration on how to focus those resources for maximum impact. So when we started working in after-school programs, for instance, we gave them a product, people, and funding that we directed centrally, which just made for a much better partnership and a way bigger impact.

Part of the success was picking the right partners from inception.

Google was one of the original Pledge 1% partners that made it to scale. So they were sort of the tipping point on the equity set-aside because of their IPO. I give a lot of credit to Atlassian, who are cofounders of the Pledge 1% with us and talked a lot about it because they saw the power of the movement. And then it really took off in our Salesforce ecosystem. We're a platform company, and we're a big believer in our ecosystem of AppExchange marketplace partners, who then began to pick it up. These are companies like Twilio, Okta, and others who have had successful IPOs. I think it's the simplicity and the holistic model that resonates, and because it's translatable across industry, region, and size.

When we ask her about the similarities with the TOMS one-for-one model, Suzanne points out one crucial difference: "I think the distinction is that it is much less scary than a one-for-one model because you can start anywhere on the continuum. You can just start with employee time, which doesn't cost you anything, so it takes the fear out of it."

She also revealed how she visualized the different areas of focus for Salesforce, which leverages its massive scale and allows customization down to an employee level.

When I draw it out for people, I draw a triangle that's divided into three. The top is "strategic philanthropy." For us right now that means education and workforce development and the work we do around ending family homelessness. The second part of it is "technology innovation," your core competency as your company, as the middle layer, like the nonprofit success pack that we built. The bottom is what I call "citizen philanthropy," which is, for instance, getting behind people who lost a loved one to a disease and they want to fight for that or someone who wants to foster animals. That is totally valid. So we tried to not put up a lot of guardrails and really let people's passions blossom. That's my mental model.

From her perspective, everything comes down to how purpose manifests itself in the company's core values.

It's about our core values and how they translate. And those core values are number one, trust: nothing is more important than trust. Trust with your customers, trust with your employees. The second is customer success: if our customers are not successful, we are not successful. And the third is around innovation; for human beings at work, for our product, for our lines of business, innovation is going to keep a company and a human being strong over time. Those values haven't changed in eighteen years. And recently, we added "equality," which has added to the further deepening of the notion of purpose; so we believe in equality of every human being: equal access, equal rights.

Developing Salesforce's unique approach involved a lot of innovation and experimentation. Suzanne said,

I think what we did really, really well was we listened to the needs of the community, and we listened to our employees and their passions, and we matched them up. It was not my agenda, or Marc's agenda, it was really driven from the grassroots. For a long time, we didn't have strategic grants; we just put our money behind our people. We're very committed to building what we call "citizen philanthropists" and "democratic philanthropy." So we took that principle, and we experimented with it: we like to say in our company that "tactics drive strategy," and as a former management consultant, I had a real big problem with that in the beginning. And yet I realized also (as an Italian!) "the spaghetti principle," where you throw stuff on the wall and you see what sticks? I began to see how it actually made for really robust, authentic programs. When you listen, and you experiment alongside people, you meet people where they are.

Suzanne is now focusing on even more ambitious way to harness Saleforce's immense resources for good; she recently announced its second Impact Fund from Salesforce Ventures, its global strategic investment arm. The new $100 million fund will accelerate the growth of cloud companies addressing some of today's most pressing needs including access to education and reskilling, climate action, diversity, equity and inclusion, and providing tech for nonprofits and foundations. She is fusing corporate venture and philanthropy in new and unique ways as befits a tireless pioneer in the space.

Why We Love This Example:

Suzanne shows us that caring starts with curiosity. Her journey began by asking communities where they needed help and seeking to understand how her employees' passions could help meet those needs, which created a culture of service. She was curious about how others in her industry-supported communities through philanthropy and employee engagement, which led her to discover how companies like eBay, Cisco, and Levi's were harnessing the power of their IPOs, revenue, offerings, and employee time to make a positive impact in the community. She asked how they were managing giving and impact and the barriers, which allowed her to build the Pledge 1% model that helps 8,500 companies give efficiently and effectively. By asking "How can I help?" Suzanne has made a career of purpose-led innovation and scaled it with a spirit of openness and sharing—which is something we should all care about doing.

4.
PURPOSE IS ABOUT PUTTING YOUR MONEY WHERE YOUR MISSION IS

As stated previously, genuinely authentic, purpose-driven leadership sometimes means risking your profits to stand by your values. It is often challenging for leaders to do but forsaking long-term trust and credibility for short-term sales is rarely a good idea.

In this section, you will meet some leaders who have made the brave choice to commit to their values even in the face of real or potential backlash. First, Kim Culmone, the designer behind Barbie's new diverse rebirth, will share how her team boldly made a gender-fluid doll. Amy Smith shares how TOMS's stance against gun violence grew the ire of some but the respect of many and contributed to real change. Then you will meet Justin Parnell and hear how America's favorite cookie, Oreo, is using the power of playful connections to help families with LGBTQI children come closer together.

Kim Culmone, Mattel

For centuries, dolls have been central to a child's development of empathy and identity. But they have been strictly divided into binary gender roles: more feminine dolls like Barbie for girls, and more male dolls like soldiers for boys. But in a new era where there is more accurate data on how gender is a fluid construct, Kim Culmone and her team at Mattel set out to create a brave new gender-inclusive offering for children that frees them to be who they want to be, despite the inevitable criticism and controversy.

* * *

Kim Culmone grew up playing Barbie dolls as a child. Although she described herself as an "equal opportunist" when it came to toys, Barbie was by far number one. Her office is adorned with reminders of her lifelong love for the dolls, including a framed picture of young Kim happily standing in front of a brand-new A-frame Barbie house on Christmas morning, apparently thrilled that Santa got the memo.

Yet, in 2012, when offered a dream job to be head of design of Barbie, after thirteen years at Mattel, Kim didn't immediately accept the offer. Instead, it made her pause and rethink everything. She went on what she calls "a purpose hunt" to decide what she wanted to do with her life and career. Kim spent a lot of time contemplating her "why" and asking if this was the right fit. "It [the job] is a lot of pressure, a huge responsibility. I wondered, am I the right person? Is this the right position? What was calling me to do this work? Was it perceived power or to move up in the organization?"

However, it turns out that it would be the questions asked by others that would ignite a sense of purpose in Kim that would spark a new chapter in the evolution of Barbie.

> I would walk into parties, and people would know me, but they would ask, "What do you do for a living?" I would say, "I work for Barbie," and sometimes I would get this sideways look. Like, really? Barbie with the skinny figure? I got tired of it because I know the purpose of the brand. But instead of being frustrated that people would not get our intentions, I asked, how can I turn this around, and look inward and ask ourselves, how do we do things differently?

The idea of turning a challenge into an opportunity to learn and reimagine the brand lit something inside of Kim, and she took the job. Since that decision, Kim and her team have led a remarkable transformation of the Barbie brand to become more inclusive and relevant to a new generation of children. There are now red-headed Barbies, disabled Barbies, even Barbies in hijabs (inspired by American Olympian Ibtihaj Muhammad). Representation matters: simply put, you cannot be what you cannot see. And creating positive representations of such a wide swathe of humanity, restored the brand back to being the

You

cannot

be

what you

cannot

see

You cannot be what you cannot see You cannot be what you cannot see You cannot be what you cannot see You cannot be what you cannot see You cannot be what you cannot see You cannot be what you cannot see You cannot be what you cannot see You cannot be what you cannot see You cannot be what you cannot see You cannot be what you cannot see You cannot be what you cannot see You cannot be what you cannot see You cannot be what you cannot see You cannot be what you cannot see You cannot financial powerhouse that it is. Barbie's worldwide gross sales reached over $1 billion in 2018, a 14 percent increase from 2017.

Kim (who was also recently named to the 2020 Out 100, recognizing groundbreaking members of the LGBTQ+ community) is now taking that spirit and those values to other brands throughout the parent company as senior vice president of Mattel fashion doll design—and tackling even more controversial topics. In one of the boldest moves in its seventy-five-year history, Mattel announced the launch of Creatable World, a customizable doll offering that invites kids to create characters free of gender norms. The Williams Institute in a new study found that, in addition to 0.6 percent of US adults (1.4 million individuals), around 0.7 percent of youth ages thirteen to seventeen identify as transgender. Studies have also shown that transgender kids already have a strong understanding of their own identity at an early age, supporting the need to have toys that allow them to explore nonbinary constructs in a supportive way. This can help avoid rejection, which the Human Rights Campaign points out can trigger issues like mental health crises, depression, and in some cases, suicide.

The statistics on suicide in particular are sobering. According to the American Academy of Pediatrics, "more than half of transgender male teens who participated in the survey reported attempting suicide in their lifetime, while 29.9 percent of transgender female teens said they attempted suicide. Among non-binary youth, 41.8 percent of respondents stated that they had attempted suicide at some point in their lives."[46]

Kim shared the insights and inspiration behind the launch.

Creatable World is the first doll kit that is gender inclusive. It allows all kids to see themselves in this product, and they can create characters that they want to create. Where it came from is a lot of analysis and observation; we spent a lot of time with kids just watching them play, not necessarily testing products, but just observing what they are doing with dolls and how they're playing. We do tons of research with

---

46 Russell B. Toomey, Amy K. Syvertsen and Maura Shramko, "Transgender Adolescent Suicide Behavior," *Pediatrics,* October 2018,142 (4), p.3.

parents and with kids, and what we observed, and what we heard specifically from kids, is they don't want rules and they don't want labels placed on how they play or what they play with. Parents are increasingly concerned about gendered toys as well.

Culmone has deep experience in understanding how cultural shifts require innovation in thinking. She and her team of product and graphic designers were responsible for the reinvention of Barbie (as outlined in the fantastic documentary *Tiny Shoulders* on Hulu) as the most ethnically and socially diverse doll line in the brand's history, leading to a *Time* magazine cover and record growth for the company.

We asked Culmone whether, in addition to the observational insights, Mattel was driven by these broader cultural shifts as well.

We absolutely see it in culture. We receive lots of trend data and interview data around how this generation of kids are perceiving themselves and the world, and there is no doubt that there is a difference between how children are viewing gender and how older adults are. There is definitely a shift. This product, in particular, started from the insight around "no labels and no rules." And so then we thought where do we go with that? And we've taken some of the research and data that you're talking about. We build prototypes, we do observational play, and this is how we got to Creatable World—where "all are welcome."

Culmone and her team took these insights about nongendered play and developed them into prototypes to test with kids. "When we started to get these dolls in particular in front of kids (I got to attend some of the in-home testings), it was incredible. It was so intuitive for them, they didn't need an explanation, and they sparked to it right away."

Culmone described what is in the actual product.

It is a fashion doll, but it's a gender-neutral body, and it's a kit that comes with about fourteen accessories, clothing, shoes, a long wig. The doll itself has short hair so the kids can put together all of these elements and build a doll and then rebuild it all again. It's about six kits, different ethnicities and all different accessories and clothing to put together in whatever expression they would like, and whatever character they would like to build. The target age for the product is five to eight, and the doll itself is prepubescent. So it's a body and an expression that's not a realistic rendering, but it's a stylized interpretation of a preteen child.

Culmone lights up when talking about how kids reacted.

What I see happening with the doll when kids play with it is character creation and the freedom to do it without defined character attributes of a personality or a scene or a theme or a life or a family. It is a bunch of parts in a box. One isn't a princess; one isn't a cowboy; there is no definition around any aspect other than that it is a youthful, gender-neutral body, reflective of a human being with clothing and accessories to facilitate self-expression. So when you put that in the hands of the kids, there is no explanation needed, which is what's so beautiful about it.

Culmone reflected on how this new launch was a manifestation of Mattel's purpose of "exploring the wonder of childhood and empowering kids to reach their full potential."

Our intention with this is that it helps facilitate a broader conversation around doll play. We know from testing what the benefits of doll play are: creativity, self-expression, storytelling—that is beneficial to all human beings. We also know that in our society, doll play has been defined and prescribed as perhaps "it's just for girls." The number of letters that I get from parents of boys who are into dolls, the number of guys I know who loved dolls, we would love for this line to create a dialogue and hopefully broaden the world's understanding of what doll play is, and who doll play is for. We can facilitate a larger our core consumer groups and create something that serves what they told us they were looking for—for kids, "no labels, no rules," and for parents toys that "my kids can just express themselves with a non-gender doll."

Something that is not put in a particular aisle or marketed in a particular way to a particular group of children.

Culmone ended by acknowledging that this product may not necessarily appeal to everyone.

"Not everyone may necessarily respond positively to it, and that's okay. We have a beautiful gigantic doll portfolio, and I'm sure we can find something else within the Mattel family that will delight the people that this may not be for!" By acknowledging the reality that exists today and celebrating inclusivity for all children, Mattel has taken a bold step forward, despite the criticism and backlash, which should be applauded.

Why We Love This Example:

For many centuries, dolls and action figures were strictly gender coded, However, in an era that sees gender as an identity, Kim realized that Mattel's purpose of exploring the wonder of childhood and empowering kids to reach their full potential requires that all young people see themselves and each other in the toys they play with. By asking young people to define themselves on their terms and giving them the space to imagine a world without limitations and boundaries, they help create a society where everyone is welcome, connected, and celebrated—and where no child should have to feel the need to contemplate suicide because of who they are at their core.

Amy Smith, TOMS

A mass shooting took place on November 7, 2018, in Thousand Oaks, California, killing thirteen people, sadly one of thousands of incidents that happen in America every year. One of the people affected was Blake Mycoskie, the Founder of TOMS, who immediately committed to pledging money and resources to end gun violence in the United States. Leading this initiative was Amy Smith, who admits it was no easy task. She shares with us the brand's evolution as a social impact company, what she has learned along the way, and the importance of allies when taking a courageous stand.

* * *

TOMS is steadfast in its pursuit of progress over perfection. They have been one of the trailblazers in the business-for-good space for over three years, pioneering the one-for-one model of giving, which has proved so successful that the company has now donated 93 million pairs of shoes since inception, not to mention giving millions of dollars to causes as well (the company donates between 40 and 50 percent of net profits, the highest percentage of any US company). We sat down with Amy Smith, Chief Strategy and Impact Officer at TOMS, to discuss the evolution of the company, the risks they have taken to stand up for what they believe is right, and what they have learned along their journey.

Amy is one of our favorite people. She is upbeat and optimistic, with a heart of gold. She's hosted hundreds of changemakers at our GOOD IS THE NEW COOL conference at the TOMS office and has always been generous with her time and wisdom, while at the same time being open to what TOMS is seeking to learn. Smith talked about how TOMS sees its role as proving that business and social impact can happen at scale.

> I feel incredibly grateful that my journey has brought me here. I'm so excited to see if a company like TOMS that gives at an unprecedented level can scale, can continue to give at that kind of a level. Because I think, then we can hopefully be kind of the inspiration (or at least guinea pig) for other companies that are trying to do this. And there's lots of small, amazing companies out there doing this. But I don't know if any of us have cracked the nut of going to scale.

The company expanded (some would say too quickly) beyond shoes into eyewear, coffee, water, backpacks, and watchbands (each tackling a different issue, like vision for eyewear, bullying for backpacks, and solar light for watchbands) in an attempt to create a truly socially conscious lifestyle brand for millennials. This led to a moment of internal self-reflection. "We really got to this point of, hold on: maybe having a new give and a new product every year, it might not make sense for us. And so we've since then been taking a pause to say, are we having as much impact as we possibly can have with this level of giving?"

After pioneering the one-for-one model (which was so successful that at one point, there were an estimated 1,800 companies who had adopted it as a giving model), TOMS reached an inflection point that led to the company for the first time exploring new models and issues. Smith recalled, "When I joined kind of the first question I asked was 'are there any sacred cows?' Like I assumed if I brought that question to Blake [Mycoskie, the founder], he would say, 'Don't touch one-for-one.' Right? And he didn't. He didn't because he's an incredibly self-aware, passionate, driven-by-the-impact person. And so that really opened the door for us to explore where else might we have an impact."

That first bold step came in the form of tackling gun violence—sparked by founder Blake Mycoskie's reaction to the Thousand Oaks shooting. Smith spoke passionately about the call to action and partnering with amazing organizations like the Black and Brown Gun Violence Prevention Consortium, Everytown for Gun Safety, Faith in Action, Giffords: Courage to Fight Gun Violence, March for Our Lives, Moms Demand Action, and Live Free. "If you know anything about the ending gun violence space, pretty much anyone and everyone you've talked to calls it 'the moment.' It's the moment where you say, 'That's enough. That's the end. I have to do something.' And for Blake and his family, that moment was the Thousand Oaks shooting."

The speed of the decision meant that the company had a steep learning curve. "It was a wild ride because it was quick. So the first ten days we talked to over forty partners. I literally would answer the phone to anyone that would call me back."

We asked Smith about what she learned from the process of onboarding a cause so quickly within a corporate environment.

So the first is, surround yourself with the experts, and do it really, really fast. We're not the experts, we will never be the experts in this, but we've got to learn as fast as we can. The second is be humble. The third is put your money where your mouth is. We invested $5 million in supporting ending gun violence, which is the largest corporate gift given to date. And then the last point was provide a place for your supporters to engage. And so along with the financial investment, we also invited our supporters to come to TOMS.com and to complete a postcard that we ultimately hand-delivered to the House of Representatives, urging them to pass HR8, which is the universal background check bill.

Over 730,000 people completed a postcard, which showed the appetite for action among the TOMS community, especially among younger millennials and Gen Z.

Smith is clear eyed about the pros and cons of taking on such a politically sensitive topic: "Ending gun violence, although it could be perceived as a real political issue, for us, it's a human issue. One hundred people in America die every single day because of gun violence. One hundred people. As we sit here chatting, we will have lost two or three people in the United States to gun violence. That's not okay. There's nothing about that that is okay. And there's nothing about that that's political. This is a public health crisis. And TOMS has stepped in to support."

Smith also has a perspective on which should come first—the purpose or the profitability:

> Authenticity is probably one of our biggest values, right? Ensuring that we're doing the right thing first—and then that it's right for business. And I think that that is where you see the most successful purpose-driven companies. I think when companies are doing it because it's on trend or doing it because it's a bandwagon or they think they might make one more sale? I think the savvy consumer sees right through it, and I don't think it's going to be successful for them. But purpose-driven companies also shouldn't be apologetic about the profit piece of this. That's what makes the engine work. Customers are voting with their wallets.

In keeping with its new approach, TOMS's new slogan is evolving from "One for one" to "Stand for tomorrow" (The word *TOM* actually symbolized "tomorrow" from the very beginning—not the name of some mythical founder).

> We started to say, "Let's explore a little more. Let's see what are the other issues, of course, driven by consumer insights and what we know this next generation of consumer cares about. And so we've chosen some new issue areas that we think we're going to be committed to over the long term."

One of them is mental health, which has so far way exceeded our expectation of where people's passions are. We'll stay with ending gun violence. We also have a category of equality, which is a broad category for us right now. We're still kind of working through where our people's passions are. But that can mean anything from LGBTQ rights to female empowerment to gender equality. And then homelessness, where that gap is becoming wider and wider as we know in the US here.

TOMS's approach is to "test and learn" as they explore these new territories.

So we're testing this in the United States. We're testing this with our e-commerce customers and our in-store customers at TOMS retail locations. And the response has been incredible. It's another way for the consumer to engage. It's another way for them to feel closer to it. And what we're excited about is we'll be able to now make meaningful investments in the issue areas that our teams are most passionate about.

Finally, we asked Smith for what advice she would give to other leaders engaged in the business for good space.

The three things I try to do every day [are to] stay hopeful, be humble, and try to understand the human components of all of this. Because I think it's really easy to become overwhelmed with how big some of these issues are. And so the three H's that I have written down and stuck at my desk [have] helped me through most days. I also think the other big one that I just continually try to help my team understand is progress, not perfection. I just think business is moving too fast now for perfect. If you're going for perfect, you're not in the game.

Why We Love This Example:

TOMS has consistently shown a willingness to listen, learn, and lead. They have always invested money in ways that were consistent with their values. When criticized, instead of treating their challengers as adversaries, they took time to understand the criticisms and do the work to determine which critiques were valid and which were not. They brought in the experts in the areas they wanted to impact, absorbing as much wisdom and knowledge as possible. And perhaps the noblest act is their willingness to be a pioneer, knowing that it comes with risks and pitfalls. But they believe that, even while taking hits along the way, they can create a path to a better tomorrow that will make the world better and others' journey easier.

Justin Parnell, Oreo

When iconic brands take a stand on social issues, they can have enormous impact on our culture. By using their position to champion ideas, they can actually move culture forward in progressive and optimistic new ways. Think about Coca-Cola and "America the Beautiful," which celebrated multiculturalism (which we explore in more detail in our interview with Jonathan Mildenhall on in the Purpose is About Being the Helper Not the Hero section) Absolut Vodka championing LGBTQ Rights with their iconic "Steve, Will You Marry Me" ad that celebrated marriage equality a decade before it became fashionable. Patagonia announcing "The President Stole Your Land" in the New York Times. Nike and Colin Kaepernick. The list goes on.

* * *

While we would be the first to agree that words must be backed by actions, let us not underestimate the awesome power that advertising alone can have to shape the cultural conversation. A brand that has mastered that has been Oreo (one of our favorite clients at Conspiracy of Love), one of Gen Z's most loved brands. In fact, in a recent survey of Gen Z, Oreo was the fifth most-loved brand (after Google, Netflix, YouTube, and Amazon, and beating PlayStation, Nike, Instagram, and Nintendo). It makes headlines with jaw-dropping cross-cultural collaborations, whether it's with HBO's *Game of Thrones* or streetwear juggernaut Supreme. Introduced in 1912, it has long been part of America's heritage. The simple ritual of a parent sitting down to have an Oreo and a glass of milk with their child is now as American as apple pie.

It's also been a brand that has been hugely creative on social media, winning it many legions of fans (a staggering 43 million on Facebook alone). When Oreo speaks, people listen. Which is why it has been so impressive to see the brand use its position to champion and celebrate social progress and the LGBTQIA+ community, despite the backlash it generates. We caught up with Justin Parnell, senior director of Oreo at Mondelēz International, to hear more about the journey the brand has taken. Justin related how he had long dreamt of working on Oreo.

> I joined Kraft Foods out of business school and before Mondelēz International came into being. My first assignment was on a tiny little business, Kraft Pasta Salads, and I dreamed at the time of one day leading OREO, our largest global brand. Over the years I worked up the ranks at Kraft then at Mondelēz International across various brand, innovation, and global assignments which ultimately led to where I am today leading the commercial business, marketing and innovation for OREO. I feel blessed to work on such an iconic brand that plays such a meaningful role in people's lives.

He shared his perspective on Oreo's deep heritage around playfulness—and the role it has to play in moving society forward.

> OREO is a brand that has brought families and communities together through playful moments for over 100 years. Playfulness opens our

hearts and minds to one another to create deeper connections and acceptance, and it is born out of our unique product experience. OREO is the only cookie that begs to be played with, and is rooted in our classic ritual of twist, lick, and dunk. While everyone has their own OREO eating ritual today, it's the shared experience and love for the brand that brings us closer.

What's special is how we activate playfulness in a way that connects with culture and especially the Gen Z audience. On one hand, we play with the cookie to spark playful conversation through collaborations like *Game of Thrones* and Supreme Limited editions. On the other hand, we have really leaned into our values of inclusivity and acceptance, which happen to be very important to Gen Z as well.

As Gen Z is the most diverse and liberated generation in history (*only two-thirds of Gen Z identify as exclusively heterosexual*), the brand understands that recognizing and celebrating identity is important. Oreo made its first foray into purpose back in 2012 when they showed their support for the LGBTQ community on Pride Day with a simple social post—an image of the iconic cookie with rainbow colored creme and the message "Proudly support love!"

Justin revealed, "That was at a time when the US was much more divided on gay rights and it was at the height of the debate around the legalization of gay marriage. It also was not common at that time for brands to step out and show their support. That simple post sparked a maelstrom of controversy, from the harshest critics declaring a boycott on our products to the most passionate fans expressing their love and support."

Justin pays tribute to the marketers who came before him who paved the way. "It's important to share that because it was the defining moment for us as a brand and possibly one that impacted the industry at large. The brave marketers who made that call helped set the stage for us today to live our purpose with conviction. In that regard, I don't take my role lightly for the influence I might have over future OREO brand leaders, who will continue to take the brand to new heights."

In 2019, Oreo made some waves when it decided to do limited edition pronoun packs at Pride in New York City, which said "Share Your Pronouns

With Pride," in a nod to the transgender community. The packs (in blue, pink, and purple packaging in a nod to the transgender flag) had "she/her," "he/him," and "they/them" on them. In the transgender community, the importance of being able to choose your own pronoun cannot be overstated: by doing this Oreo signaled a deep respect and empathy.

The accompanying social media post said "We're proud to celebrate inclusivity for all gender expressions and identities...encouraging everyone to share their pronouns with pride today and every day." The reaction was immediate on social media. "My beautiful 10 year old trans daughter who has forever been a fan of Oreo, would love a pack!" said one proud mom. "I love this! Time to hit the market and stock up on massive amounts of Oreos...Forever a supporter," said another. "Thank you, <u>OREO</u>!" another replied. "Representation matters. Normalizing asking what a person's preferred pronouns are matters. It's just plain human decency."

But equally swift was the visceral reaction against it. "And this is why I'm glad that my diet doesn't allow your cookies. You've lost a customer. Get woke, go broke," said one poster. "Oreo thinks it's smart to cater to 4% of the population while disgusting many more," said another. "Only 2 genders folks. Will always only scientifically be 2. Biology matters!" Conservative groups were outraged and right-wing media lit up at this supposed desecration of an American icon. The outpouring of dismay and disgust at this stance revealed how deeply divided America still is on the issue of transgender identity.

It also revealed the deeper truth that sometimes purpose is in the eye of the beholder; one person's joyful expression of values is a transgression of another's deeply help religious beliefs or social mores.

Justin shared the internal journey to that moment within Mondelēz, the parent company for Oreo.

When it came to the decision on pronoun packs, there was nothing but support across the organization. It was a natural way for us to continue to show our support for the LGBTQ community. We always ask ourselves how we can use our platform to support the issues that matter most to the community. One of those important issues today is to create broader awareness around the importance of pronouns.

It was a simple idea—to celebrate inclusivity for all gender identities and expressions. First and foremost, it was to inspire individuals to share their pronouns with pride and also for others to understand the importance of using the correct pronouns as it is one of the most basic ways to show your respect for an individual.

It's important at this stage to note that Mondelēz as a parent company itself is ranked 100 (the highest score) on the Human Rights Campaign's 2020 Corporate Equality Index, for its policies on workforce protections, inclusive benefits, and supporting an inclusive culture. Justin said, "Here in North America, we also have employee resource groups, such as our Rainbow Council, which is focused on building an open and inclusive environment at Mondelēz International for LGBTQ+ employees."

Despite the backlash over the pronoun packs, Oreo went even further in 2020. In celebration of LGBTQ+ History Month, Oreo created a #*ProudParent* platform and partnered with PFLAG (one of the country's leading gay rights organizations, whose name is an acronym for "Parents, Families, and Friends of Lesbians and Gays"). Oreo debuted a new film, titled *Proud Parent*, and released first-of-their-kind Limited Edition #ProudParent OREO Rainbow Cookies to reward acts of allyship for the LGBTQ+ community. Justin shared the thinking behind the partnership.

Our ambition this year was to go from showing support to truly making a difference. It was about driving the change we want to see in the world—fostering a more loving and accepting world. What we heard from our fans in the LGBTQ+ community is that feeling accepted starts at home. They often fear that the most important bond in their lives, that with their parents, is at-risk of breaking when they come out. However, when parents express their love and support it opens the door for greater self-acceptance. That inspired the idea of the #ProudParents campaign which encourages parents to come out in loud public support of their LGBTQ+ children, and has since expanded to celebrate allyship in all forms. PFLAG was the perfect partner as the country's leading ally organization committed to fostering greater LGBTQ+ acceptance.

The film itself is a beautiful and moving piece that shows a real-life couple, Jen and Amy, coming home to what they believe is a disapproving family member—only to see the love and acceptance revealed in the closing moments. We challenge you to watch it without tearing up. Justin shared more insights about the thinking behind the film.

> The film addresses the journey that many parents face after their child comes out of the closet. It shows the love between Jen and Amy, who are a real couple, and the challenges of bringing a partner home for the first time—especially for LGBTQ+ folks. Through the key campaign message, "A loving world starts with a loving home," the film aims to highlight the important role parental and community support plays in fostering greater LGBTQ+ acceptance. We hope this film is relatable to families of all kinds and, combined with the other elements of the #ProudParent program, inspires a new generation of proud parents and allies to come out in loud, public support of their LGBTQ+ loved ones.

As hard as it is to imagine someone being upset at this innocuous and loving idea, inevitably there was a backlash, with conservative outrage group One Million Moms demanding a boycott of Oreo and ranting that Oreo was "airing a gay pride commercial which has absolutely nothing to do with selling cookies" and "normalize[s] the LGBTQ lifestyle" and "brainwash[es] children and adults alike by desensitizing audiences."[47]

The tactic backfired spectacularly, with One Million Moms's social media feeds flooded with posts showing loving gay couples—and comments like "One Million Moms, I just bought a bag of Oreo's and donated to the Trevor Project (another fantastic LGBTQIA+ organization) in your name."

---

47 Rhuaridh Marr, "One Million Moms demands Oreo boycott over 'homosexual agenda' rainbow cookies," *MetroWeekly* (Website), October 20, 2020, https://www.metroweekly.com/2020/10/one-million-moms-demands-oreo-boycott-over-homosexual-agenda-rainbow-cookies/, n.p.

Justin also shared his personal feelings on how proud he is of this work and the impact that it has had on the wider Mondelēz community.

> The stories have poured in from suppliers, customers, employees, friends and family. In fact, it's had an unexpected and very personal impact on me. When I shared the video with one of my closest family members, she was in tears and revealed for the first time to me that she is a mother of an LGBTQ+ child and how hard it is. She told me "they seek signs of being loved at all times from their family because the world isn't always as kind." That hit home more than anything and reinforced the responsibility we have as brands to make a positive societal impact. It has been amazing to work on [a] campaign that has had such a profound impact on so many people.

Why We Love This Example:

It would have been very easy for this iconic global brand to shy away from controversy and just stick to creating fun and exciting campaigns. But by deliberately choosing to spend its cultural capital on advancing social causes, several generations of Oreo marketers have passed the baton to each other, to help celebrate ideas in society that move us forward in a loving and compassionate way. They understand that this comes with controversy and backlash and the loss of some fans. But by choosing to embrace it, they place the brand firmly on the right side of history—and giving its many fans reasons to love it even more for generations to come.

5.
PURPOSE DOESN'T HAVE TO BE POLITICAL

Companies often serve a diverse set of stakeholders—employees, customers, investors, and partners—with varying beliefs and political views. Thus, choosing a purpose sword can become a complicated process to avoid divisive territories. However, some issues can tap into shared values and passions and help us find common ground. This section will show how three companies have been able to do this effectively in vastly different ways.

You will meet the multitalented Tanya Sahanga from Adidas and learn how she and her team delivered a groundbreaking circular offering that is helping to reduce the waste from sneakers, one of the planet's biggest pollutants. Next, we will hear the story of Dawn Yancy and how Consumer Reports tirelessly fights to protect consumers' rights everywhere, particularly in an age of disinformation. Finally, you will meet Alicia Tillman, who uses SAP's power to help end the practices of modern-day slavery for good.

Tanyaradzwa Sahanga, Adidas

Adidas believes that through sport, they have the power to change lives. One of the most important ways it is doing so is reimagining how its shoes can be made—and remade. Tanyaradzwa was a central leader behind the groundbreaking Futurecraft.Loop, the world's first closed loop running shoes made to be remade by recycling to create new shoes. She shares how this product came to life and why it was the perfect fit for her unique mix of gifts.

* * *

Visiting Adidas global headquarters in Herzogenaurach, Germany, we see a temple that is dedicated to the idea of the future of sport. Walking around its giant campus, with futuristic cathedral-like buildings whose ceilings soar to the sky, you also see shrines to its incredible pop cultural heritage: the Keith Haring shoes worn by Madonna in 2008, Run-D.M.C's iconic shoes from the "My Adidas" video. But it's also filled with secret, playful touches, like a giant trampoline walking path on which you can literally bounce like Tigger on your way to a meeting. In one of the buildings, we're given a tour of the supersecret (no pictures allowed) Innovation lab, where among other things, cutting edge machines test shoes, apparel, and almost all sporting product imaginable to their limit—and where pioneers like Tanyaradzwa Sahanga, Technology Innovation Manager, are helping create the future of sustainability in all aspects of product creation.

We spoke with Tanyaradzwa (Tanya) about her work months later, after she had left the company to pursue other projects. Even amid the madness of COVID-19, Tanya's calmness and curiosity remain intact. She is in her home in Essex, which is located southeast of London. She is enjoying living in the moment with her family, away from the typical busyness of corporate life. But for us, she is more than willing to go back in time and share an exciting journey defined by clarity, creativity, and conviction.

Tanya knew from a young age that she had a creative mind and loved to solve problems. Although she would describe her interests as oxymoronic, it is her gift as a polymath that enables her to draw connections between diverse disciplines, such as chemistry, math, fashion, art, and literature, in ways very few can. It is a superpower that she has applied to become a renowned product creator, designer, and world-class problem solver, who, together with her team, has most recently realized one of the seemingly impossible ambitions of all sustainability visionaries for more than half a century—a fully circular product, in the form of a high-performance sneaker that can live again and again, by being recycled back into a new performance shoe.

Tanya found a deep sense of purpose very early in life to apply her creativity to solve problems. "I guess I've always been creative and hands-on. I was born in Zimbabwe and was raised in a creative environment, allowed and encouraged to explore and try things." As a child, Tanya had a wide range of interests and the smarts to choose any number of life paths.

I had (and still have) so many interests, somehow I saw a lot of symmetry and relationship between seemingly unrelated topics. I believe my purpose is almost independent of the career or discipline, I see the discipline simply as a medium of expression, the "how" to bring my purpose to life. So career-wise, I could have gone down the path to be a chemical engineer, and still [have] been perfectly within my purpose. I know that I love creating and I can create whether I'm a scientist or whether I'm a literary artist, it doesn't matter. For me it's all about solving problems, presenting logical and tangible solutions that genuinely improve lives, it just so happened I love expressing that purpose through product creation.

Ultimately it was fashion that drew her in and set her career course. "I think I made the decision around about fourteen to seriously go into fashion, and every choice I made from that age was serving me to meet my goal and to meet my target, which was to create products."

Tanya started her path in fashion by teaching herself the principles of sketching, designing, choosing fabrics, and making clothes. And it's during this process that she became increasingly curious about how fabrics are made and engineered. Having found purpose for study, she went on to interrogate this question at the University of Manchester. Yet, she discovered that even at the best of universities, finding a curriculum that matched her eclectic interests was not an easy task.

I wanted to do something that allowed me to design and engineer textiles whilst embracing a scientific approach. I liked it [the curriculum] because it was a cross-section of disciplines through a textile engineering lens. However there were limits to how much I could push the cross-sectional boundaries, I remember being regularly reminded of the limits by my supervisors and being actively discouraged from bringing in new angles and disciplines to my textile creation approach. My solution was to find ways to create as close to the edge of those boundaries as possible and then feed and push my interests outside the walls of academia.

Searching for her next challenge, she was drawn to Adidas as an international sporting goods company with a technical approach to product creation for elite athletes. It combined the art and science that she loves.

I was looking for a place to bring value, and ideally a place where I could be true to my product creation beliefs that the best product requires this marriage of function and aesthetic. For sporting goods a solid functional technical foundation is imperative for success. I was interested to see how a global player like this brand applied these principles to business, and how in turn the business of sports used science and design to solve athlete's problems. So I joined, and that was it.

Tanya immediately brought her intuitive sense of cross-functional thinking to her designs. One of her first projects was a running top that could be worn in multiple ways, looked good, and met technical needs. Although it was not the language she used, she later realized this approach was sustainable design and would inform her future work. "That top was sustainable. Why? Because you can wear it four or five different ways depending on how you put it together. It's using one fabric that has two distinct functions depending on which side you're wearing—really, really interesting methods of construction."

Her breakthrough innovation was Futurecraft Loop, a performance running shoe and recycling-technology platform that was first shared with the world in April 2019. This beta platform called on a few selected consumers to use and return their shoes to enable them to be recycled and made into new shoes. In many ways, it was the perfect project to combine her polymath mind with her purpose of creative problem-solving.

Managing the end of product life is, I believe, one of the biggest problems we face. This problem stems from our mindset and attitude as consumers. Everyone is a contributor to the problem and so everyone has a direct part to play in the solution. When we shift our mindsets and stop wasting "waste" and start valuing "waste" we can create new product and systems. I love this space because it calls on everyone and every discipline to collaborate and work together, success can only be achieved as whole.

Indeed, waste is one of our planet's biggest problems, and shoes are a significant contributor. Each year, billions of shoes are manufactured, worn until they start to fall apart, and chucked into landfills. Alternative, viable means to manage product end of life is a real need for the consumer goods industry as a whole. Current standard practice is incineration or landfill; both methods result in negative environmental impact. One 2012 study from researchers at the Massachusetts Institute of Technology found that a single running shoe can include sixty-five individual parts, all of which generally end up in landfills.

Extending product end life is something Tanya and others have been thinking about for a while. "I've always been attracted to the concept of multi-use products that can be reused in this way. In fact, this ambitious thought of product that can be made from one material to enable recycling and re-use has been a 'what if' for academics and experts alike for decades. This innovation goes beyond a single-brand story."

Futurecraft Loop stands out in how it's made—and remade; this is where the success comes from. This is a shoe made from one material without glue to enable 100 percent recyclability and zero waste. Tanya and her engineering team at Adidas have made the entire pair of shoes from one material: thermoplastic polyurethane (TPU). In comparison, industry-standard sneakers are made of at least twelve different materials. This innovation allows for the shoes to be ground into pellets, melted down, and applied into new running trainers.

It is a ground-breaking achievement that can revolutionize consumers' relationships with their shoes and the planet. The wider implications of this work cannot be underestimated. It heralds nothing less than the end of the supply chain as we know it. Imagine walking into a store in downtown Detroit and buying a shoe made from material that used to be another New Yorker's shoe the day before. It is a profoundly exciting idea, and one that we believe has the potential to be adopted by multiple industries in the world.

After the initial 2019 public trial of two hundred sneakers, which generated an enthusiastic response and buzz among environmentalists and sneakers heads alike, Adidas plans to introduce the shoe globally in Spring 2021 with hopes it inspires more in the footwear category to follow.

When asked what the keys to success were, Tanya points to a winning combination: her insight, talent, boldness, focus, and grounded hard work; a united, supportive, tenacious team; and timing.

"I genuinely do believe the difference was me taking it on. I think I was able to see different pieces that perhaps didn't make sense necessarily, bring them together and be able to say, guys, we're not that far away. The pivotal moment was in 2017, when I was able to put tangible evidence on the table (via an internal 50 pair Loop wear and recycling test). That led to having a bigger team that were committed to the concept and resources to realise the vision."

Tanya played many roles from the beginning.

I applied myself to do what was needed outside of prescriptive boundaries of job titles, knowing that they would restrict the ability to achieve the vision. I understood that I was leading a vision to create what had never been created, and I also knew that required an attitude and level of application that had never been defined. Much like when in a start-up you have to be hands on and prepared to do what's needed. I was literally on my hands and knees multiple times on factory, office and lab floors alike—cutting, counting, preparing textiles, prototypes, materials and sometimes leaving with blisters. Going from manual labour to presenting and chairing meetings with stakeholders and business partners was all part of my leadership role. All whilst managing and driving the project and leading teams across continents. As the team grew around the vision, this role shifted too to being more guiding and directive.

Tanya also speaks to the level of conviction that the vision required to not accept compromise along the way. "The vision was the standard and my job was to uphold that against every decision and you know, you need that sort of clarity and that focus in a team to be able to really deliver."

She is also quick to point out how vital the overall team was in this collective achievement. "We had a very strong shared understanding of the goal and that willingness to do what was necessary to achieve it developed into a team culture. So many people went above and beyond their job title to fulfil this vision. I called them the Amazing Loop Team: Amanda Verbeck, Ulisse Tanzini, Jason Xu, David Dai, Korbinian Berner & Andreas Thieret on the product team."

For many, the idea of this project coming together seemed impossible. But for Tanya, it felt like an inevitable outcome to a persistent approach: "I remember the inner elation and sense of victory I felt seeing the very first recycled material in production and the first early product prototypes well before they were "show ready," yet after those moments I wasn't surprised, I just knew it was coming. The rest followed and became history in the making."

Tanya is proud of what she and her team accomplished, and she actively celebrates the monumental milestones, experiences, learnings, and wins she has achieved.

As I think of shaping the path forward for myself, a big part of that is not stopping with today or yesterday's success, but striding boldly towards new problems to solve. It's very important.

The great thing is I am not restricted to one discipline to achieve my purpose. Being able to ask questions, explore and embrace unusual perspectives, has allowed me to walk in my purpose and serve. As I continue in the same vein that led me to this point, I am excited by the opportunities to solve problems that sustainability and product creation offer. The future is certainly bright.

Why We Love This Example:

As a society, we tend to be reductive to try to present ourselves, each other, and the issues we face in the most simplified terms. Often in that search for simplicity, we lose the complexity and nuance that we need to fully appreciate the people around us and the problems we seek to solve. Tanyaradzwa Sahanga reminds us of the need to resist that tendency. She is many things, and she holds on to all the aspects of herself that others may see as oxymoronic, disparate, or conflicting because she knows her ability to connect all those pieces makes her so extraordinary. She understands that eclecticism—selecting from various systems, influences, doctrines, or sources—is a secret weapon to innovation. By bringing a wide-ranging set of people and experiences, she and Adidas were able to tackle a complex problem that affects us all—the well-being of the planet—in ways that they would not have otherwise and, in the process, create something that can last forever.

Dawn Yancey, Consumer Reports

As our society becomes more focused on conscious consumption, having trusted resources to guide our buying decisions is more critical than ever. For over eighty years, the nonprofit Consumer Reports has been dedicated to ensuring all citizens can make informed choices on what to buy based on their budgets and values. Dawn Yancey talks about the role of Consumer Reports in today's marketplace and how, as a visionary, she imagines a future for the company as diverse as the society it serves.

* * *

When you think of inalienable rights in America, you will likely think of the well-known phrase "Life, Liberty, and the pursuit of Happiness" found in the country's Declaration of Independence. However, for nine decades, Consumer Reports has been on the front lines protecting another right it believes every American should have—the power to engage in fair and ethical trade. In many ways, Consumer Reports is to consumer rights what the American Civil Liberties Union (ACLU) is to human rights. It is a nonprofit, independent organization that works side by side with consumers to create a fairer, safer, healthier world. They are passionate, tireless advocates for the rights of citizens to get safe, quality products at a fair price. Each year, they provide millions of people with unbiased product testing, investigative journalism, consumer research, public education, and consumer advocacy.

For eighty-four years, they have been the most trusted resource for facts-based information on any product you can imagine. Reading one recent issue of their monthly report can help you get the best price for prescription drugs, select the most reliable car, shop for roofing shingles, and find the most nutritious food, as well as choose the best mattresses, pillows, and vacation time-shares. The breadth and depth of categories they report on require a tremendous amount of work done each day by hundreds of employees driven by a deep passion for consumer rights.

We spent a day at the Consumer Reports headquarters in Yonkers, New York. Walking into the office is like entering a shopper's paradise. Every product you can imagine is under one roof—each item purchased to avoid any sense of impropriety—from clothes and laptops to dishwashers and infant car seats. In designated rooms throughout the building, scientists and researchers put products through rigorous tests to measure their quality and durability against industry standards. The testers are focused and meticulous, paying attention to details that they know you and I never will.

Our host for the day is Dawn Yancey, an operations associate. We first met Dawn, a gracious African American lady, when she came up to us at a Good Is the New Cool book event in Brooklyn and firmly declared that we had to come and speak at Consumer Reports. When you meet Dawn, you can't help but be allured by her aura. She's warm, kind, and attentive and instantly makes you feel at home. She's been at Consumer Reports for over thirty years, which seems impossible given how young she looks, but her commitment to the company's mission and vision is as strong as ever.

Dawn has an encyclopedic knowledge of the company, which started in 1936 as a print publication created to serve as a source of information that consumers could use to assess the safety and performance of products. She shared how she got her start at Consumer Reports.

Back then, people found jobs in the newspaper; I don't think they do that now. So, I saw a position here in the executive office for an executive assistant. I sent in my résumé, and back then, the interview process was very open in that you might be interviewed by someone in HR, then followed by a director in another department. But I was interviewed by the president of Consumer Reports at the time, Rhoda Karpatkin. We had a lovely conversation, and she asked me, "Well, why did you choose [Consumer Reports]?"

I said, "I don't know if I'm going to choose Consumer Reports." I said, "I need to know more about what you do and why."

Rhoda, if you know anything about her, she's an attorney by trade, a trailblazer, and an amazing woman. And she said, "Okay, I'm going to sit down and tell you what we do and why we do it." I think she spoke for about a half an hour about Consumer Reports, the mission, and how Consumers Report would be "a voice for the voiceless." I was like, "Oh my gosh. That's just something I would like to do." So that literally, that is how I made it here. I did not know walking in the door that they did what they did. I mean, I know they've rated products; I was more aware of what they did, certainly with their autos but not the advocacy arm of their work, which they still do to this day.

We spoke about how that noble purpose—being "a voice for the voiceless"— sustained her and her teams over three decades: "Even when things are going not so smoothly, and there are hiccups and bumps in the road, I think what is constant is that we're all here for the purpose and well-being of others. I think that we try to inform the public, we inform consumers of what is available and so that they will make an educated or informed choice."

For Consumer Reports, making a positive impact on behalf of American families isn't as simple as it once was. There was a time when it wasn't so difficult to seek out expert information and confidently navigate the decisions of the day. Now, the unbelievable sophistication of products, the rise of powerful platforms that share information and options on their terms, and the fire hose of unvetted information at our fingertips have permanently changed our realities.

Consumer Reports' CEO, Marta L. Tellado, spoke about the urgent threat to consumer information.

> The quality, safety, and integrity of our products—from toys to appliances to cars—are increasingly determined by millions of lines of code we can't see or understand. More and more of our decisions are being made on digital platforms that narrow and filter our choices without our direct control, using complex algorithms that may not serve our best interests. And in an age of endless information, it has become harder than ever to know what and whom we can trust. If we can't learn the truth about products and services, then the supposedly free choices we make aren't free—and if our options are limited, then no amount of information will result in a fair exchange.

Consumer Reports continues to innovate to protect people's rights and help save lives even amid a tsunami of ads and misinformation. In 2019, it launched the groundbreaking Digital Lab. The lab represents a bold new approach to advancing and protecting consumer rights in the digital era, leveling the playing field for consumers in the face of Silicon Valley's extraordinary power. This effort will allow them to power up the digital testing and investigatory work they've embarked on in recent years—work that saw Consumer Reports uncover substantial consumer rights violations, such as algorithmic racial bias in car insurance premiums; expose inconsistencies in Facebook's facial recognition settings; identify security flaws in smart TVs and mobile payment apps; and secure landmark digital privacy laws in California and beyond.

Beyond addressing injustices, Consumer Reports' work also helps consumers prevent injuries and fatalities. In 2019, they led an investigation into the

Fisher-Price Rock 'n Play Sleeper that prompted congressional hearings and a major recall after a tragic number of infant deaths. Consumer Reports was also proud to work closely with Parents Against Tip-Overs, a group of mothers and fathers whose young children have been injured or killed by furniture tipping over unexpectedly. They brought their investigating, testing, and advocacy to bear to help pass Harper's law, a bill signed by the governor of New York in August. The law sets responsible new stability standards for the sale of furniture to reduce tip-over accidents, which have killed hundreds of children and which injure an American every seventeen minutes, on average. Most important, they expect that this state law will serve as a model for the country—bringing greater safety to an everyday part of our lives that once carried a hidden threat.

Dawn recognizes the importance of Consumer Reports' work. She's proud of what the company does and wants it to be more outspoken when it comes to its essential role in society. "We're not as bold as I hope we will be. It's okay to affirm that you're good and that it's cool to be good. We don't do enough of that here."

She is a go-getter and is actively contributing her gifts and passions to lead the organization to a bolder and more inclusive future. "I think that one of my gifts is that I am a visionary. I'm not only looking at what's in front of me, but I'm looking at what can be, and in looking at the possibilities, it's important for me to be able to make connections and to bring people together. And I do it through the lens of what's needed."

True to that approach, throughout her career, she's filled multiple roles, which has kept her engaged for three decades: "I stayed because I've been able to grow here. I started in the executive office, moved to editorial as a researcher, wrote for the magazine, moved into operations. And during that time, we discovered that the work in the area of inclusion was not strong enough in our products. Just somewhere along the line that has gotten lost or the focus was not what it needs to be, especially in the current climate."

As a passionate and persistent advocate for diversity and inclusion, she works to make the company as diverse as the country it serves. Dawn's push for the organization to become more reflective of society isn't just personal. It's also practical.

Just understanding the marketplace and just recognizing that as we continue to do business in the way that we have, we may not be relevant in another five years. I mean, you know, just that, that sixty-five-year-old white man, bless his heart, who has supported us well, maybe his second marriage was to an African American woman or an African American man or Latino man. So we have to start thinking about consumers in the way that they exist now.

As Consumer Reports prepares to celebrate its eighty-fifth anniversary in fighting for consumer rights, the issues of awareness and cultural relevance will be critical to address as it moves forward. It's the passion of employees like Dawn, who continue to help the organization fulfill its purpose, embodying its values from the inside out. We asked Dawn what she would say to others who are looking to effect internal change in purpose-led organizations.

Think about who you are before work because we all can be different things based on where we are. So who you are is most important. What do you find satisfying, gratifying, uplifting? What do you see that irks you enough that you would want to change it? What gets you? You know, anger is a great motivator. If you're in your community, if the kids are hanging out after school because they don't have anything to do, well, then maybe you're the one that needs to work with the school and start an after-school program. If you can do that each day, it is like, OK, we are doing something of value.

In the United States alone we all gave $400 billion to charities last year. That giving is critically important. But we all spent $13 *trillion* dollars buying stuff. The power we have as consumers is one of the biggest levers for change we have as citizens. For thirty years, Dawn has worked alongside many dedicated people to help protect Americans' right to engage in ethical trade to create a fairer, safer, healthier world. And she has also worked tirelessly to help ensure her company is as diverse as the society it serves, showing there are many way to effect change both inside and out of your company. She truly is a voice for the voiceless, and for that we salute her and all the employees at Consumer Reports.

Why We Love This Example:

Purpose is magnetic. When Dawn Yancey was considering if she wanted to work at Consumer Reports over thirty years ago, the first thing she said to the president was, "I need to know what you do and why." The president's answer communicated a mission and a sense of purpose that Dawn immediately realized she wanted to be part of and still works to help fulfill today. It is also why hundreds of her colleagues have joined and continue to serve so diligently to protect consumers' rights.

Alicia Tillman, SAP

Modern-day slavery, one of the biggest human rights issues globally, persists largely because we don't look hard enough at the products we buy and how they are made. Alicia Tilman is working to change that. Alongside Justin Dillon, founder and chief executive officer of Made in a Free World, Alicia uses the power of SAP to make the world run better by eliminating slavery.

* * *

If you were in any way contributing to the enslavement of humans around the world, would you want to know?

According to the International Labor Organization (ILO), 40.3 million people face slavery today—defined as being forced to work without pay, against one's own will under threat of coercion or violence, or through exploitation or bondage. Of these victims, 75 percent are women or girls, and 25 percent of them are young people, including eighty-five million children under the age of eleven who face hazardous child labor conditions every day in what the ILO calls the "worst forms of child labor." This labor is carried out in ways that severely jeopardize the physical, mental, or moral well-being of any child.

Justin Dillon, founder and chief executive officer of Made in a Free World, a San Francisco–based organization, is working to end the use of slave labor. Made in a Free World exclusively focuses on developing and implementing high-impact solutions to human trafficking by working with the most effective partners to rescue and care for victims worldwide.

Justin believes slavery persists in large part because it is usually hidden deep in supply chains where a company has little, if any, information. And unfortunately, companies are not looking hard enough at their supply chains to know if their profits are coming from the pain of others.

He shares a story to bring this point to life.

Seven years ago, I was sitting with our team, and someone asked, "Hey, do you think Steve Jobs knows if there's slavery in his iPhone?" Of course, we didn't know, so one of us wrote him the following email: "Steve, does my iPhone have tantalum mined by slave labor? I'm sitting in a boardroom in San Francisco with a group of tech guys who believe you are aware of this issue and because of your public company restrictions, will not respond to this email—prove them wrong."

Six hours go by, and an email pops up: "I have no idea. I'll look into it.—Steve," along with the email signature, "sent from my iPhone." No boilerplate corporate social responsibility report, no deflections. Just three vulnerable words: "I don't know." These three words were followed up with four equally powerful words: "I'll look into it."

Today, other business leaders also want to ensure that their supply chains are free of unethical practices that could be risks to their corporate reputations. And people like Alicia Tillman are partnering with Justin Dillon to let business leaders know once and for all whether forced labor is part of their supply chains. As CMO of enterprise software giant SAP, Tillman has been one of the boldest leaders in the business world championing purpose as a growth strategy. To that end, she wants to harness the power of SAP to help businesses run better, which means not just more efficiently but more ethically as well. Dillon's Made in a Free World software is now embedded into SAP's Ariba suite of enterprise products. Given that platforms like SAP Ariba connect over 3.5 million companies to exchange approximately $2.1 trillion in commerce, it presents a massive opportunity for corporations to drive both business and social impact, particularly in ensuring humane supply chain management. It allows chief procurement officers to become allies in solving the problem of modern-day slavery by helping them quickly identify and eliminate "suppliers of risk" in their supply chains at a speed and scale that has been impossible until now.

Alicia believes, in many ways, business is an expression of our humanity, and that purpose provides a way to bring our full selves to our work authentically.

My view is that there's this incredible convergence of our professional and our personal lives, as a result of which you see us as human beings unwilling to sacrifice. We are unwilling to compromise on our personal beliefs and our values. If, in our personal lives, we're very focused in our communities on things like economic prosperity or environmental change, when we come to our professional life, we don't all of a sudden forget about those values. And so we want that to be part of the employers that we choose to work for or the companies that we want to buy from.

Although purpose is often discussed as it relates to consumer-focused companies, Alicia believes business-to-business (B2B) brands can also be powerful forces for good that can deliver strong growth.

When I joined SAP about three and a half years ago, I saw a company that was founded with such a clear purpose forty-six years ago to "help the world run better and improve people's lives," and innovation that had been built to enable that. B2B companies are working in support of all the goals of the customers that they serve. And often, those goals are about cost-saving, transparency, control over spend—they work in support of their corporate goals.

The purpose-driven campaign that we established this year communicated our belief, which is to be a "best-run company," we believe that you have to give back, and you have to have a purpose in the marketplace. The majority of our previous campaigns were all very product-centric, which is not unusual for a technology company, but this one worked to start talking about a message of purpose when we showcased customer stories of how they are using SAP technology to help the world become a better place.

When we released our 2018 brand campaigns, our message was about solving the clean water challenge in India or saving the elephants and rhinos from poaching in South Africa. So it was a very different story than that of which a B2B marketer typically focused on.

The impact of telling a purpose-led story delivered immediate effect.

When you look at the overall contribution to the pipeline, over 65 percent of the pipeline [was] generated by marketing as a result of campaigns that we have run since April 2018 (when the new brand narrative and "best run" campaign launched). This campaign is our highest performing in the past five years. The other thing that we've seen is in both purchase consideration (willingness to buy) and customer advocacy. With the campaign being in the market for just three months, we saw over a 6 percent increase in each metric, which is quite good for a very short period of time. And so it is a beautiful demonstration of how much people are interested in how our technology is being used to help the world run better.

The power of SAP and their kindred values made them perfect allies for Made in a Free World to make the world run better by eliminating slavery. Alicia shares why the fit is so good.

So here's a company with a beautiful vision and technology being used to enable it. But I saw where we could expand our purpose even more and expand our ecosystem of partnerships to truly create something special to help solve a lot of these modern-day problems that we have—forced labor in the supply chain is one of them. Chief procurement officers and even CEOs are struggling to both gain transparency but also have the solutions to help solve it. And so what I saw was the increased opportunities for brands to come together. SAP and Made in a Free World could innovate together using the heat map created that shows forced labor conditions in the world combined with the millions of companies that transact on the SAP Ariba network to have the transparency necessary to know where these conditions existed and that companies can do something about it. To me, that's the action that I found so compelling.

Tillman shares why she believes it's so crucial for businesses that may have been part of the problem to begin to put purpose over profit for the betterment of their business and the world.

Companies have often been blamed for a lot of the challenges that we have in the world. And I believe that companies are the most equipped and have the incredible scale to be able to lead the change and offer the platform to be the voice for so much of what we've heard, this year in particular. I think it was a year of a lot of people finding their voices and speaking out on issues and opportunities of which we fundamentally need to change some things in our world...

I believe every company needs to spend time thinking about how you can take a stand and be at the forefront to drive the action that's needed on the issues that are plaguing the world in many ways.

We can start to position companies as having that ability and using their resources appropriately to solve the problems. I think how consumers base their decisions on not only where to spend their money but where they go to work too is only going to continue. How warm and inviting and diverse and inclusive workplaces are, I think, are going to be even more top of mind for people when they choose employers.

Why We Love This Example:

"I don't know." One sentence—three words—captured the heart of why one of the most horrific problems in humanity persists to this day. Awareness was the first step in compelling people to act to put an end to slavery, and SAP recognized they were uniquely positioned to be a catalyst of change in ways that aligned with their product and purpose. By focusing on educating people on the problem of forced labor, how they contribute to it, and what they can do to solve it, they allowed people to become allies of change as both employees and engaged customers and citizens, thus creating a way for all their stakeholders to fulfill their purpose and "help the world run better and improve people's lives."

6.
PURPOSE SHOULD BE AN OPEN-SOURCE PURSUIT

As the world faces massive threats to our well-being as a species and a planet, we see businesses dedicate more resources to help solve these problems. Companies also realize that making their solutions accessible and replicable is the fastest way to improve the world at scale. This open-source approach to innovation helps to radically accelerate transformation in categories and industries, helping companies become critical allies in change.

One of the best examples of this mindset is Patagonia. Wendy Savage, Patagonia's director, social responsibility and traceability, will talk about her passion for workers' and animals' ethical treatment and how they are making their best-in-class model accessible for all who want to adopt it. Next, we will hear from one of Gen Z's most prominent voices in environmental activism, Xiuhtezcatl Martinez, about how his organization NOW is turning this generation's passion into accessible action by leading with the cool. Finally, Paul Polman, one of the pioneers in purpose-led business during his tenure as CEO of Unilever, tells us how after a career battling with competing companies, he's now bringing competitors together to work together to address our biggest problems.

Wendy Savage, Patagonia

Patagonia has become the patron saint of purpose-led brands. Their commitment to ethical production, marketing, and sales of products is legendary among their legions of fans. Wendy, a lifelong activist for social justice, oversees the relationships with the workers in the brand's supply chain and shares how Patagonia has created an ethical model that it shares openly in hopes it will become a new norm for how to take care of workers and the planet.

* * *

It's 2019, an autumn afternoon in the Meatpacking section of Manhattan, New York. The trees are slowly beginning to turn a beautiful shade of orange, evoking feelings of excitement, enthusiasm, and warmth. Fall is a reawakening, a reminder to get back to reality after the escapism of summer.

The city has a buzz, and there is anticipation in the air—but not for the typical pageantry of Fashion Week that takes place during this time of year. This energy is different—it's youthful, electric, and urgent. Twenty-four hours from now, young people around the world—most notably, sixteen-year-old Greta Thunberg—will lead a massive coordinated strike from school to protest inaction on climate change. Over six million people across 150 countries, including tens of thousands of students in New York City, will participate. It will be the single biggest environmental protest in history, delivering a much-needed moral awakening to our world's leaders, who have been ignoring this reality for too long.

In the middle of this approaching whirlwind of activism sits Patagonia. Unlike their more upscale neighbors, their storefront windows are not adorned with beautifully put together models, expressing carefree calm. Rather, the windows' ads have the faces of young people intensely staring at you, unflinchingly, with the words "Facing Extinction" written across their faces. Although this is not the type of image that one would think is inviting, shoppers fill the store. Inside, walking toward the register with an armful of clothes is an older woman with gray hair and tanned skin—not the kind of tan you get spending too much time getting cocktails on a rooftop, more like the type of weathered skin one gets from years of living an adventurous life out in the world. There is a guy there wearing a buttoned-down shirt, khakis, and loafers with a blue Patagonia vest, which has become the de rigueur middle-aged executive uniform. Near the window is a young girl FaceTiming her friend. She's wearing a pair of perfectly worn-in Converse Chuck Taylor sneakers and a T-shirt that reads "There Is No Planet B."

The idea that this mix of people would be in the same fashion store seems odd. They in no way have a shared sense of style. Instead, what brings them there is a kindred set of values. The sign on the wall expresses Patagonia's purpose in its typical no-nonsense tone: "We are in the business of saving our home planet." And every customer in this store is their partner in this goal. As you exit, there is a sign that reads "We will be closed on Friday in support of Climate Strike." Well, of course they would be. The planet needs the company's full attention.

Patagonia vocally promotes anticonsumerism, environmental causes, and fair trade—traits that many would think could negatively impact their bottom line. Yet, these values, coupled with the fearless leadership of CEO Rose Marcario, have helped Patagonia to become a multibillion-dollar brand. Their success is rooted in their commitment to making the best product, and an open-source philosophy to help other manufactures—even their competitors—produce more ethical and sustainable clothing.

Yet, it is their moxie—their fighting spirit—that ignites the evangelism of their fans. Patagonia boldly joined a coalition of Native American and grassroots groups challenging the legality of President Trump's action to reduce public lands through the Antiquities Act. In this effort, the company invited and mobilized its customers to join them by petitioning and advocating online for the protection of public lands. Their passionate customers rose to the occasion and worked side by side with the tribes, climbers, canyoners, trail runners, and anglers that Patagonia has served for over a decade in its fight to save our home planet.

They have become the patron saint of purpose, an inspiring example of a brand that can achieve incredible business success by involving customers, employees, and societal stakeholders in their higher pursuit of creating a better world.

We wanted to better understand the passion of the people who make this company great. Months later, we are privileged to visit Patagonia's modest and friendly global headquarters in Ventura, California. We notice the little things: the laughter of children coming from the full-time day-care center right next to the reception, where childcare is free to all employees; the picnic tables outside where people are having meetings in nature, under shady trees; the solar panels throughout the entire campus, which provide clean energy to run it; the chalkboard that displays the day's weather and surf forecast—perfect for those who want to catch a little surf on their lunch break on the beach five minutes away by bike. Indeed, one of the rooms in the building jokingly is called "the board room" because—guess what—it's filled with surfboards.

This all adds up to a pretty attractive place to work, as exemplified by the young man who casually strolled into the reception while we were waiting and asked the easygoing receptionist if he could apply for a job on the spot.

"How often does that happen?" We asked the receptionist, curious.

"About two or three times a week," he said.

When you are one of the most loved and admired companies on the planet, this sort of thing seems par for the course.

We are there to talk with Wendy Savage, a longtime Patagonia employee who holds a very special role there. In her current position, Wendy is responsible for Patagonia's global supply chain compliance and commitment to upholding the company's Workplace Code of Conduct and Fair Labor Association (FLA) obligations. Wendy also heads Patagonia's Traceability Programs and spearheaded the development, implementation of, and switch to the Traceable Down Standard. Among her other responsibilities, Wendy leads the social compliance program implementation for Patagonia's food division, Patagonia Provisions, as the company embarks in working with food suppliers.

Warm and dedicated, she shared her journey to purpose, her role at Patagonia, and how her upbringing in Peru affected her perspective on social and environmental issues.

I think social and environmental issues always take me back to what I saw growing up. I didn't have a traditional childhood. It's a combination of where I was born and where my mom's journey took me, which allowed me to see and learn about multiple issues I now work to address. You see, my mom dedicated her life to social justice. From an early age, after my parents divorced, Mom and I traveled a lot to remote villages in the Peruvian jungle and the Andes where, as part of her Catholic mission, Mom taught the native communities, prepared them with first aid techniques and helped to procure food supplies for the villages. When I say "travel," I mean by car, bus, boat, and motorcycle.

Savage laughed and then explained,

As a baby, I traveled with her in an "ergo-baby" kind of thing my mom had sewn together. When I was old enough, Mom would tie me to her waist on the back of the motorcycle as we ventured out from town to town. She was nuts and really the definition of a badass single mom, and I saw it all through her eyes. Hardship, pollution, terrorism, poverty, injustice, hunger, lack of jobs, lack of education, inequality, discrimination, and the impact of government and religion, I saw all of it. It's all interconnected. I didn't know growing up, but I was in training from an early age.

Wendy continued,

Outside of work, Mom would come home many times with random homeless women and their kids. We would share dinner, let them wash, and send them with a bag of provisions, some toys, and clothes. She touched so many lives in her career, and to this day, she volunteers and helps the poor, but what I would often see her cry about was not being able to make a lasting change in these people's lives. I think this gives you an idea of how my upbringing connected me to the very issues I'm fighting for now and helped me look at a situation from multiple angles rather than only one. Social and environmental impacts go hand in hand. You can't fix one without the other, so we have to work on both.

We asked her how joining Patagonia had helped her translate that early childhood influence into action: "Patagonia helped take my calling to higher levels. My whole life, I knew I wanted to help make a difference, but I didn't know it would be in business, let alone supply chain. Patagonia has helped support ideas most other businesses would shy away from. I knew brands had the power to influence change, but I didn't know to what extent until I started working here and saw it with my own eyes."

We asked her how she found the culture at Patagonia when she joined: "Very interesting, very transparent, and very welcoming. One of the things that I really admire here at Patagonia is that over forty years, they've stayed true to the philosophy and the belief of protecting our environment—with the purpose of 'being in business to save our home planet.' You're continuously challenged to do better every day."

We can't be a brand without the hands behind our product.

Wendy Savage

One key area for her in social responsibility is looking at the welfare of the workers who make the product.

> We can't be a brand without the hands behind our product. We were founding members of the Fair Labor Association. We have a very strict way of looking at suppliers and selecting those who share our philosophy for continuous improvement. We have a fourfold approach to selecting them where business and quality have a say, but there's also an equal say for environmental and social responsibility. So that is very powerful for us to ensure that not only the environment is taken care of but human rights as well.

We asked Wendy what she was proudest of so far. "We implemented Fair Trade, and that's one of the proudest moments in my career—taking this program where a brand actually commits funds that go directly to the workers to help them improve their lives." We asked her to explain the process in a bit more detail.

> Fair Trade USA created a program specifically for factories where it doesn't matter what the product is, the brands pay a premium on each of the products that are made at that factory. And that premium goes directly into the workers' account. And the beauty of it is that the workers as a committee decide what they want to spend that money on. So, for instance, there could be 2,000 workers. There's an election, there's a committee, and they decide whether they want to use it for scholarships for their kids, day care, or just anything that they need. That's money that the factory doesn't control, Patagonia doesn't control. It's giving them the power and educating them to control those funds. It's incredible.

Workers in seventeen countries that Patagonia operates in have used these funds for day care, computers, stoves, and scholarships for secondary school. Wendy is quick to point out that this also has the potential to grow.

You'll hear the word *journey* a lot in Patagonia because it's always a journey. So, when we started, we started with one factory in very few styles, and we said, "we can make more of an impact; let's do it." At the same time, we've been talking to more brands working at those factories where we are making fair trade products. So, the impact can be higher for the workers if more brands join us and in fact, we have seen some brands joining the fair-trade movement. It's really, really exciting, and I'm hoping that this continues to grow.

Patagonia is focused on the next frontier, ensuring workers get paid a living wage—very different from a minimum wage.

In order to achieve living wages, which is a more sustainable way for the workers to have a better life, there needs to be more players than just the brand paying into a pot of money. Suppliers have to agree to do that. Governments have to get in the conversation. And consumers are a big piece of the puzzle because they need to start not supporting disposable goods that are cheaply made, and that at any point in the supply chain may be sacrificing human rights or environmental impacts. We're having issues here in implementing living wages in the United States. We know minimum wages are very, very low, and people cannot survive on it. So, it's a bigger conversation. But at Patagonia, we're trying to address that. We're working with the Fair Labor Association, we're working with MIT, and coming up with strategies on how we can make it work in our supply chain. And once we have a model, we can share that with the rest of the world.

Patagonia is also investing in regenerative agriculture, a way of growing crops that sequesters carbon and has massive potential to be a key driver in solving the climate crisis.

We are in a quest to reverse climate change, and we work with farmers to implement better farming practices, organic practices, and controlling the chemicals. All of that is great, but we want now to work with farmers so that the regenerative way of farming, how we used to do it in the past, where we can capture carbon back in the soil can be implemented again with industrial farming. All of those great practices from the past have been lost. And so, at Patagonia apparel, we're working with our organic cotton farmers right now. We're in a pilot. It's going to take some time because we're not only looking at the soil and capturing carbon and improving the practices there, we're also looking at how the farmers are being treated. Is there a fair price for the cotton? Because that's another very important part of the success of this. And then if there are animals on the farm, how are the animals treated? So, it's a trifecta that is going to help improve farm conditions. We can't do it alone. We need more brands to participate in this. We are seeing a lot of interest, and it will be a long journey, but I think together we can make more of an impact.

Wendy spoke about how they make decisions in balancing the environmental and social impact, and her answer was unequivocal: "If we want people in the places where climate change is affecting them the most to start worrying about the environment, we have to make sure that they're taken care of financially first. So, it's very, very important to make sure that we address all buckets at the same time. Not only the environment but also the financial and the social aspect of it all."

This philosophy also extends to animal welfare, another topic Wendy is very passionate about.

When I started here at Patagonia, we started looking at the down in our supply chain. We knew we had issues to remediate, and so we had to create standards; there were no standards for no force-feeding, no live-plucking…and a good environment for the welfare of the animals. So, after a few years of work, we were able to ensure to our customers that the down in our products came from geese that were not mistreated, that were protected, through animal rights. And now we're doing that with a responsible wool standard as well. It takes a lot of work because you have to map every single level of the supply chain, and you have to change hearts and minds at every single level of the supply chain. Because animal welfare is not a concept that is shared everywhere, right? So, in some cultures, you have to educate on "why you should care."

Transparency is a value that Patagonia also takes very seriously in its suppliers.

So, one of our requirements for all our suppliers at the beginning is transparency. We know there's no perfection. We know that there will be issues to work with. And, you know, if for instance, we are getting a new supplier, and their first thought is like, "We can't tell you where our stuff comes from," that's a red flag for us. We will not work with that supplier. We try to align with suppliers that are willing to be transparent, that are willing to work with us through the problems that they have and then eventually get to a solution.

Wendy talked about the need to help educate suppliers and bring them along on the journey. "It's very important for them to understand the reasons why we, as a brand, find things important. There's no changing hearts and minds by just imposing; it's very important to educate us and partner with them," she said.

Patagonia has also made its work open source to help others fast-track their journey.

On down, for instance, we started with an internal standard because it didn't exist. We gifted it to the industry, and now it's a global standard that is owned by another organization. And so, anybody can go and use those standards to look at their supply chain the same way. We also work with several brands, who call and say, "How do we create a responsible purchasing practices program?" And we say, "Here you go; here's how we're working with the Fair Labor Association on this" and share our tools. Because when you think about it in sustainability or social responsibility, we're not competing. We're all working together toward the same goal. And we know that working alone and creating islands of goodness is not the end goal for us. We can't make enough impact just by ourselves. So that's the message behind us making stuff open source.

In closing, Wendy shared where she feels most hopeful.

I think through the years, I see that the younger generations are more interested in moving the needle faster. When I started, nobody talked about these issues. The media is also helping a lot with that because the issues are much more tangible for people to see. That gives me hope. The growth of the B Corp movement gives me hope. We are living in a better place than before, despite the amount of work that we have to do. I think we're making progress.

Why We Love This Example:

Wendy's childhood and journey offer two lessons about the power of an open-source approach to purpose. The first is that our most urgent issues—environmental, social, and economic—are all interrelated. We cannot solve one without addressing the others. Patagonia's holistic approach ensures workers have livable wages and money to invest in improving their lives and drives the brand's commitment to treat animals and agriculture with care. They engage their suppliers, governments, and, perhaps most important, consumers as part of the solution. Although their values may reduce profit, they understand that it is necessary to replenish the planet and repair society's broken systems. Yet, the second lesson may be the most important: we—as humans—are all interconnected. How we live and what we buy impacts others. Wendy has a deep appreciation and respect for the people behind every product. And she fights to treat every worker with fairness, dignity, and love—just as her mother taught her.

Xiuhtezcatl Martinez, NOW

We have reached a planetary tipping point in awareness of the climate crisis, yet it has not resulted in the behavior change necessary to prevent the pending danger. Xiuhtezcatl (who pronounces his name "shoo-tez-cat") believes his generation, Gen Z—the largest generation on the planet—can make a difference on a massive scale. His initiative NOW is on a mission to accelerate a cultural shift to stop the climate crisis and build a radically different future and is combining the wisdom of indigenous communities with the passion of youth activism to create solutions that contribute to the climate justice fight.

* * *

Young people have repeatedly been told they are the future. As parents and teachers, we tell them that they will be leaders and change the world—someday. But this generation of young people is not waiting for tomorrow. They are rising up, speaking truth to power, and righting the world's wrongs, right now. One of this generation's most passionate leaders is Xiuhtezcatl Martinez, an eighteen-year-old environmental activist, author, and hip-hop artist at the forefront of a global youth-led movement to save the planet.

Recently named to the TIME 100 Next, Xiuhtezcatl has felt called to change the narrative on what it means to be an activist from an early age. He recalls, "When I turned six, I started asking, 'What kind of world is my generation being left with?'" Around the time when many kids are just learning to tie their shoes, Xiuhtezcatl began speaking on public stages about the urgent need to save the planet. Old VHS footage shows a passionate six-year-old addressing a large crowd at a national global warming event, demanding people open their eyes and educate their children to what's happening around them. "Most kids don't even know the world is sacred...Mother Earth is alive."

Since then, Xiuhtezcatl has continued to be a vocal advocate for the planet. He has spoken multiple times at the UN, sued the government, and spoken on panels with the likes of Bernie Sanders, Van Jones, and Pharrell Williams. He's won awards such as President Obama's 2013 US Community Service Award, the Nickelodeon Halo Award, and the Peace First Prize.

You could say defending the planet runs in his blood. His mother, Tamara, cofounded the original Earth Guardians as an experiential learning high school in Maui, focusing on environmental education and outreach. His father, Siri, is a proud member of the Mashika people (Aztecs from Mexico City), a tribe whose beliefs are rooted in the respect for and dignity of nature. The Aztec concept of "Teotl" describes the idea that there is a single force of sacred power that fuels the self-generation and regeneration of life. Xiuhtezcatl is a passionate believer in the power of young people to be leaders of change: "What I've seen personally traveling the world, talking more and more to my generation, young people are ready to use their art, their poetry, their passion for engaging with the world and being leaders today. Because, sure, we are a future generation, but we are here now, and we are not going to wait to make a difference."

Xiuhtezcatl has participated in the biggest protests and demonstrations in history, but he realizes that moments haven't turned into the necessary movements for sustainable change. "I have seen over and over again that no matter how big a march or protest is, no matter how good a climate conference or documentary is, that they never lead to a solution that meets the dire situation we are facing as a global community."

Xiuhtezcatl has a unique talent for connecting with fellow youth through popular culture. He wants to use that gift to marry the tenacity of young people with the traditions of indigenous people to tackle the most critical issue of our time—climate change—with a solution that is scalable and sustainable. His latest venture is named NOW, which captures the urgency to treat our climate crisis like the life-and-death situation it is.

He shared the impetus for starting NOW.

The vision for NOW came out of a culmination of twelve years of experience on the front lines of the climate movement. Witnessing firsthand how our climate crisis, since the age of six, was ravishing our planet and endangering our future, pushed me to look for a tangible solution that would give anyone anywhere the power to engage in stopping the climate crisis.

Cofounded by Xiuhtezcatl and his partner Eric Doak, NOW is a company with a clear mission: to accelerate a cultural shift to stop the climate crisis. It aims to remove CO_2 at scale and elevate a new generation of diverse leaders to bring about lasting change. They are creating a platform for engagement that ordinary citizens can participate in, using a monthly subscription for as little as $10 a month. Recently, they announced an ambitious new goal—to get to two hundred million pounds of carbon removed by Earth Day 2020, in collaboration with partners like DroneSeed, an innovative company using drones to plant trees at scale.

In addition to reducing carbon consumption by transitioning to a fossil-fuel-free economy, scientists have put forward a big idea that has sparked the public consciousness—planting a trillion trees to help with carbon sequestration (a thesis most prominently advocated by Crowther Lab in *Science* magazine). By some estimates, if we can reforest the world with one trillion trees, it may be possible to reduce two-thirds of human-made carbon emissions, restore vital ecosystems, and stabilize the climate to safe levels. It is terraforming on a scale more ambitious than anything attempted in the history of humanity—and may be one of the keys to tackling the most significant existential crisis of our lifetime.

Eric spoke to the massive size of the problem: "There are 1.4 trillion tons of excess CO_2 in our atmosphere threatening everything we love, much faster than we think, at a scale we can't imagine. NOW was built in response to the greatest crisis in human history with the intention to scale carbon removal solutions to meet the size of the problem, elevate a new generation of diverse leaders, and accelerate the climate movement exponentially through popular culture."

If you see a consistent theme around acceleration, it's because the reality is time is not on our side. Eric notes, "We acknowledge that yes, we need a massive political, policy, and a regulatory overhaul, we need to reduce global emissions at an unprecedented rate, we need to transition to a renewable energy infrastructure—but these things aren't happening fast enough. We need more time, and to have the time to make these transitions, we must remove massive amounts of CO_2 from the atmosphere."

Like Xiuhtezcatl, Eric believes we have reached a tipping point of awareness, but it has not led to action. They want to solve that problem.

Seventy-three percent of Americans now believe in the climate crisis; many want to help but feel stuck and don't know how to contribute. We felt called to create a platform that provides access to carbon removal and sequestration projects at a capacity that meets the urgency and scope of the crisis while providing our community with a clear path to measurable and transparent impact.

When it comes to carbon removal or sequestration, some believe that planting trees is the path, while others are betting on regenerating soil or innovative approaches like reforestation with drones or direct air capture—we provide digestible education on each project and empower our community to choose where to spend their dollars through a subscription service.

Xiuhtezcatl believes that the modern environmental movement lacks the knowledge of the past, specifically our ancestors' relationship with Mother Earth: "I feel like there is a huge gap that exists within the current climate movement that can be bridged if we are guided by indigenous wisdom. Any solutions that NOW partners with or proposes will need to be really guided by indigenous wisdom and the community relationships that we build with the peoples who are on the ground."

NOW is committed to a human-first, holistic approach to projects with which they engage. They believe in strong collaboration and taking guidance from the stewards of the land. They look for projects that create additional benefits to social, environmental, and economic ecosystems outside of just carbon removal.

They launched their first product in 2020, a subscription service to plant trees. According to Eric, early results are promising. "With nearly zero marketing spend, we've planted about 100,000 mangrove trees, with estimated survival rates accounted for, over twenty-five years, those trees will sequester 33,000 tons of CO_2."

NOW is expanding impact by funding planting in Mozambique and Madagascar with their planting partner Eden Reforestation Projects. In 2020, they will fund more planting partners around the globe and launch their planting projects. Their multipronged approach to carbon removal and sequestration at scale includes providing access to drone reforestation, direct air capture, soil regeneration, and hemp and kelp farms.

Another collaboration with DroneSeed can be summed up as "NOW funds planting projects, and DroneSeed executes the planting." Eric describes how groundbreaking the partnership is.

> Planting with drones provides an opportunity to scale reforestation for the first time in human history. Additionally, drones are capable of reforesting areas that are difficult for human planting efforts for myriad reasons. Often terrain that is too dangerous, too recently burned, or too remote is best planted via drones. As an example, drones can be activated thirty days after a wildfire [and] plant forty acres in a single day, about six times faster than humans can plant trees.

To my knowledge, NOW is the only platform in the world that provides the public access to funding drone reforestation projects directly.

They are committed to building a movement for engagement. Eric believes that "collective impact is the only way we can scale carbon removal, and we must come together in an unprecedented way. One way to build this collective impact is for individuals, brands, or organizations in our community to create their own team. Each subscriber has the ability to track their own impact as well as the collective impact of their entire team. It's time to turn influence and attention into impact and urgently mobilize around the solutions that give us a chance at the greatest comeback story in human history."

The duo believes to avert this crisis, they must engage and activate the masses by integrating climate impact into popular culture. Xiuhtezcatl says this idea is baked into the DNA of the brand: "From the start, Eric and I have had a clear vision to tap mainstream culture and use different levers—entertainment, fashion, music, sport—to create a monumental impact. We imagine a future where carbon removal becomes ubiquitous within culture. Whether you are attending a concert, game, or purchasing a product or service, we will help you understand the ecological impact of that decision and provide access to remove the equivalent of carbon."

To capture the minds and hearts of citizens, they must move beyond eco-friendly earnestness and do what others in the environmental world have not, which is "lead with the cool." Eric adds, "the bar for our design, our campaigns, our product collaborations, our video and visual storytelling must be at the level of the best and brightest creatives in the world. We live in an attention economy, and brilliant creativity that grabs attention gets rewarded with dollars. We want to channel those dollars into removing carbon at scale and stopping the climate crisis. In short, we believe art and creativity can save humanity."

As the name says, now is the time for action, and they are calling on everyone to get involved. Xiuhtezcatl leaves us with this powerful call to action. "We need students, artists, entrepreneurs, athletes, moms, warriors, and teachers, to reclaim our power to shape the future. We all have a part to play—regardless of who you are, where you're from, or what you do. In the face of a crisis that threatens everything we love, there has never been a more unifying moment."

Why We Love This Example

Climate change is the greatest threat to humanity, and we need behavior change to match the scale and urgency this crisis requires. Looking at the past one hundred years of powerful social movements—labor rights, women's suffrage, civil rights, marriage equality—they've almost always been led by young people and consistently had three components. There were stories of what is possible, leaders who embody these stories and are early adopters and influencers, and diverse, open, accessible invitations for people to join the community and take action. NOW's model has been designed to offer all of these. It is a youth-led effort that helps us imagine a world that deeply respects the earth, like our ancestors taught us, powered by those who shape culture and make the world move, and it provides us all with simple ways to be involved.

Paul Polman, Unilever/ IMAGINE

As the former CEO of Unilever, Paul Polman is one of the pioneers of purpose-led companies. He understands that CEOs set a company's tone and are the starting point to drive transformational change. In his new role as the chair of IMAGINE, Paul builds a collective of kindred and courageous leaders who are working collaboratively to transform entire industries, enabling impact at massive scales.

* * *

When Unilever CEO Paul Polman (now chair of the global business collective IMAGINE) turned up for a business dinner at the Taj Mahal Hotel in Mumbai in 2008, little could he predict that it would turn into what he calls "a crucible moment" in his life. Terrorists attacked the hotel, and he and his team were trapped there for hours. They were told to lie flat on the floor to avoid inhaling the smoke that was filling the room until the police rescued them in the early hours of the morning. In total, 172 people died in attacks across the city, a night of dread and loss that left many scars.

Polman reflected on that moment.

> During your life, you have these "crucible" moments that form you. It could be a death in the family or a tragedy around you. You find yourself in the Taj Mahal on that night. Thank God my wife had stayed home with our children—it was actually Thanksgiving (she is American, so we celebrate it), but I was there. And then you discover after you come out, not only how lucky you were, and that's obviously an important part of it, but you discover above all the goodness of people. I met many people that expressed the right qualities in humanity that night.

Months later, Polman and the other Unilever board members who had been trapped went back to thank the staff of the hotel for saving them. They held a dinner, scheduled for 9:36 p.m. (the time of the attack), but it wasn't a regular dinner. "The board did something unusual," Polman told *Vanity Fair*. "We served the staff. We needed closure, and we did not have it until that night. We made so many friends with one another and with the Taj staff. And we lived."

The experience made Polman realize the profound link between poverty and violence.

> What you then realize is that a lot of the violence in the world is driven by poverty and by exclusion, which religious fanatics seize upon and create these extreme forms of violence, which we should never give in to. And that helped me when we did the Unilever Sustainable Living plan. So many companies with purpose were on the side of the environment, which was very narrowly defined as trees and water and

conservation. But it runs much deeper. We need to fight for addressing these issues of exclusion and poverty, which are at the root of this violence. And so if you don't understand that human dimension, and that the crisis we face is one of humanity more so than anything else, you can't really properly solve it.

Of all the companies that embody purpose, alongside Patagonia, Unilever is one of the best examples, with iconic brands like Ben & Jerry's, Dove, and many more. Under Polman's stewardship as CEO for ten years, the company implemented its ambitious Sustainable Living Plan, which aimed to double its growth, halve its environmental impact, and triple its social impact. The plan succeeded, with Unilever's annual sales rising from $38 billion to more than $60 billion and the company becoming a beacon for those who wanted their work to matter.

Indeed, the achievement is all the more remarkable because unlike Patagonia, Unilever is a publicly traded company with shareholders. Though in true Polman fashion, on his first day as a CEO, he announced he would no longer be issuing quarterly share guidance and reports, to break free of the tyranny of short-termism (also somewhat cheekily reasoning that the board couldn't fire him on his very first day). Either way, the gamble paid off: Unilever delivered a total shareholder return of 290 percent over his tenure.

Polman spoke about the importance of attracting people who are purpose driven and attracted to the mission of the company. "If you want to have a purpose-driven business, it's very important that you have purpose-driven people. And to be a good leader, driven by purpose, you first and foremost have to be a good human being and understand yourself as well. What we were looking for was people that I call 'whole people' instead of 'half people.'"

He continued,

> The long-term success depends a little bit on what you're good at, your passion or your purpose, and then what the world needs. And if you can manage to achieve all three of them, you are in your sweet spot. That's what we found in Unilever, where despite the pressures of this industry, engagement was very high, and we became a recruiting

brand. I think part of that was really the secret sauce perhaps of how we recruited 75 percent of the people that came in, came in because of the Unilever Sustainable Living Plan. So a purpose is also driven by a strong desire to serve.

Today, Mr. Polman is the cofounder and chair of IMAGINE, a benefit corporation and foundation (led by Polman, Valerie Keller, Jeff Seabright, and Kees Kruythoff), which is focused on building collaboration between CEOs and companies across sectors to drive massive social and environmental change. Their early mission board includes an impressive list of global business leaders and humanitarians, such as Richard Branson, Suzy Amis Cameron, Arianna Huffington, Mo Ibrahim, Cherie Nursalim, Ngozi Okonjo-Iweala, and Sue Rockefeller.

We asked him how important it was for the CEO of the companies that IMAGINE worked with to have found their personal purpose to move things forward.

Well, we would say we are fortunate that we can work with the people we like to work with, and we don't really have time to do things in our lives that we don't enjoy. So the most important thing that we see now is that most of the people know what needs to be done. Big issues like climate change and inequality, obviously high on the agenda, but we are simply not moving fast enough. So we don't work with people that need to be convinced or are climate deniers. I think that train has left the station. We work with people that genuinely want to improve their companies by putting them in service of society by putting purpose, like your book *Good Is the New Cool* says, at the center of what we're doing.

Polman continued,

And we firmly believe that if you can put the entire value chain of an industry together, you can do more than if you only work with a part of it. And then you need to do it at the CEO level because if the tone is not set at the top, you will not get to where we want to be, which is truly transformative change. And so we select individual CEOs who could be drivers of a sector. Every sector (be it food and land use, be it fashion, be it tourism and travel), every one of these sectors has more forward-thinking CEOs. We like to work with them to set the pace and drive the sector higher, to show a little bit of courage. And then we bring the courageous collective of CEOs across the value chain together. And when we have 20 to 25 percent of that value chain together, you can create a tipping point, and that's what we're focused on.

One of the key ideas behind IMAGINE is that of bringing together corporations in what Polman calls "the precompetitive space."

So the precompetitive space, very simply, would be all the things that are not really important in the purchase decision of the consumer. For example, we brought Pepsi, Unilever, Coke, and Nestle together, and they are a critical mass, 20 percent plus, of companies that use these refrigerating cabinets. And if they have HFC or CFC gases in their engines, it's not good for this planet. Well, by putting this industry together, we were able to convert them to natural refrigerants. None of them have the critical mass to do that alone. Together, you can change and have a fundamental impact, in this case, on climate change, but nobody buys an ice cream or a Coke or Pepsi based on an engine in a cabinet. So, that's a typical example of what we mean by precompetitive.

He expanded on the thesis.

Another example of precompetitive is the things you cannot do alone but that will cause you all to collectively sink if you don't address it. For instance, plastic bottles and getting rid of the issue of plastic: No company can do that alone. But collectively, you can make an impact. In agriculture, everybody knows that you want to solve child labor or slave labor in the value chain. It's very difficult for individual companies to do so. If you are collectively together, you attract NGOs that

Purpose is
the growth
story of the
century

want to work with you. Governments are willing to put frameworks around it because they see a critical mass of responsible businesses. So get the right legislation (often less), you get NGOs working with you to make more robust plans, you attract innovation at a faster pace, and you bend the curve.

I asked Polman what advice he would give to the 181 CEOs (of companies like Amazon, Apple, Johnson & Johnson, and many more) who signed the Business Roundtable agreement on how to transform their companies into forces for good genuinely and what impediments he saw to their progress.

Many would argue that this short-termism of the market and the shareholder primacy is very much alive still, and that obviously gets in the way. The other thing is that simply, the CEOs, with their short tenures, lack the courage individually to address some of the issues where they can pioneer and take risks. And what we're trying to do is get to this collective courage by bringing them together. I would argue that many of the issues that need to be addressed today, be it climate change, be it income inequality, be it sustainable sourcing, could be done at the company level of any note, much better and much more than what we see happening if there was more courage.

He continued,

We're seeing some companies starting to lead because they see that the train has left the station and they want to be part of the future. And you get great commitments like Delta or Microsoft or others that we've seen, from Amazon around climate change, that we've just seen coming in in the last week. But there are still too many that haven't caught on that this is the growth story of the century, and that increasingly their employees expect it from them. The citizens of this world expect it from them, and increasingly the financial market as well. So what's the biggest obstacle? Willpower. Do we really care and do we have the right caliber of CEOs that can drive this change at mass?

Polman ended with a rallying cry for all CEOs to take courage and lead with the heart—especially relevant in these COVID-19 times, where societal expectations for corporations to get involved helping the world recover and rebuild have never been higher.

Courage comes from the French word *coeur*, which means heart. You cannot lead with the brain. We've distilled everything into numbers and calculations and costs and win and lose because we lead with the brain. It's always a binary approach and a very narrow definition. And if we bring a little bit more humanity, which actually is at the roots of purpose, back to business, I think we will be better equipped to lead in these uncertain volatile times. But we will also make better decisions for the longer-term multi-stakeholder models. And we will have stronger businesses, and we will all turn out to be so much the better for it.

Why We Love This Example:

Paul Polman understands the truth that the great poet Maya Angelou so eloquently stated: Courage is the most important of all the virtues because, without courage, you can't practice any of the other virtues consistently. For many of the problems we face as a global society—climate change, inequality, poverty—we already have the answers. We often lack bravery and a willingness to do the work we need to do to create the world we want, especially when it's difficult. Purpose demands courage. It has magic in it—it's contagious—and when harnessed by a collective, coupled with solutions that are openly shared, it can be transformative for businesses and society.

7.

PURPOSE IS ABOUT BEING THE HELPER, NOT THE HERO

Companies are accustomed to creating heroic narratives for themselves—the detergent that conquered the pesky stain, the refreshing water that quenched your thirst, the energy drink that gave you wings. It's easy for brands to want to do the same when expressing their role in purpose. However, it's necessary to recognize that the real heroes in social change are the people and organizations working on those critical issues every day. The brand's role is to be of service to them as their helpers.

As former CMO at Coca-Cola and Airbnb, Jonathan Midenhall understands this principle as well as anyone. He's built brands that have helped communities around the world to see and be their best selves. In this section, Jonathan shares what he's learned about being the helper. Kifr Gavreili, CEO of footwear brand Tieks, shares how COVID-19 showed the brand how they could help their community of women to find their power to help save lives. And we will meet Essence Smith and Justin Cunningham of Chicago's SocialWorks and see how, with their friend and partner, Chance the Rapper, they are creating opportunities for young people to use their passion and imagination to be the change they want to see in the world.

Jonathan Mildenhall, Airbnb/Twenty First Century Brand

Some of the most iconic campaigns of the twenty-first century have come out of the mind—or perhaps more accurately stated, have come from the heart of—Jonathan Mildenhall. From Coca-Cola and Airbnb to his consultancy TwentyFirstCenturyBrands, Jonathan has created stories that inspire us to be our best selves. In this chapter, he shares his approach to helping us to help the world.

* * *

Jonathan Mildenhall is one of our generation's most gifted marketers. But his journey to success didn't always come easy. Growing up young, poor, black, and gay on a council estate in Leeds during Thatcher's Britain, Jonathan had to overcome many obstacles.

After a long and distinguished career in the UK advertising world, he was handed the keys to Coca-Cola, finding ways to push this iconic brand into fresh territory, with spots like "America the Beautiful," which ran during the Super Bowl, and caused a huge furor with its optimistic, multicultural vision for the country.

As CMO of Airbnb, he created a uniquely innovative community brand, with a core purpose of "helping people to belong anywhere" and unleashing tremendous product and marketing innovation. In 2017, in an implicit rebuke to President Trump signing an executive order to temporarily refuse entry to all refugees and to citizens of seven predominantly Muslim countries, he lead a team that created a Super Bowl advertisement (in three days) showing a diverse group of people and text that read: "We believe no matter who you are, where you're from, who you love or who you worship, we all belong. The world is more beautiful the more you accept."

In his current role as Chairman of TwentyFirstCenturyBrand, one of the world's leading purpose consultancies, he works with his partner Neil Barrie to oversee strategic work for brands such as Headspace, Pinterest, and Uber. With an exuberant, roguish spirit and a twinkle in his eye, he sat down to talk to us one weekend in the middle of lockdown via Zoom from his home in the Bay Area, while his newborn children were taking a nap.

I was born in 1967. My mother, a white woman and my father, a black Nigerian guy, had an affair and I was the result of the affair. They were never married. And, honestly by the time I was born, that relationship was to all intents and purposes over. Then my mum, when I was four months old, my mom got pregnant again, to a different guy. When she was six months pregnant with the twins, she fell over and broke her leg. And so, I was put into foster care for a period whilst she had the twins and was nursing the twins and I came back into my household when I was about two years old. It was a very strange time for me because I was the only black child in that family. So my two elder siblings and my two younger (twin) brothers were white and my mom and my stepfather were white and I was being reintroduced to that family. And so, I have always felt like the black sheep of my own family because I was different, and I was put into foster care.

He continued,

I didn't really have a best friend in the family. My two younger twin brothers were best friends. My two older brothers were best friends and there was me in the middle, looked very different. And as I was growing up every evening, I'd come home, get my peanut butter sandwich for my dinner and then I'd be out on the streets knocking on the neighbors' doors, seeing if there was anybody else that could let me in to come and play or anybody else could give me a meal. And I share that story because I think that from a very early age, I was socialized to go out and meet people so that I could find my people when there wasn't necessarily an invitation inside my family.

He spoke movingly about his mother and the value she instilled in him.

I think what happened is that I'm a natural introvert that has taught himself how to be an extrovert so that I could find my people. Growing up in Leeds on the council estate, it was tough. There wasn't a great deal of anything. Except the values that my mom instilled in me which were about compassion and kindness and gratitude. And I knew that this manufactured extrovert, with this set of human values, would enable me to connect with people and build trusting honest relationships. And with a great education, I would be able to get a great career.

Jonathan's self-taught extroversion and his deep values led him to enter the privileged Oxbridge world of UK advertising, where he was one of the first black executives to rise through the ranks.

By the time I applied to the London advertising industry, I knew that in that year I was the best researched, most informed, creatively, most aware undergrad. And I was the first minority ever to be taken on by McCann Erickson London's official graduate training program. So, that was a pretty big start to my career. And already, you know, day one of my career in that London advertising agency was a million miles away, literally a million miles away from the poverty that I grew up in.

After a career working on some of the most iconic UK brands (like Nescafe Gold Blend and Virgin Airways) at agencies like TBWA and Mother, Jonathan realized that he wanted to be on the other side of the table—and be a client making decisions. His talent led to him being offered a job as Coca-Cola's head of advertising. The first thing he did was dive into the Coca-Cola archives, where he found inspiration in how the brand had always championed progressive ideas, including one of the first ads featuring black and white kids together, sitting on a park bench in Atlanta.

I had the creative keys to the creative fortunes of the Coca-Cola brand. At the time, it was the world's most valuable brand and I thought, "I am not going to leave this brand other than in its most glorious form, when it became a beacon of cultural relevance in a way that was really good for society." And that was my purpose. My purpose was to shift social mores forward in all markets in the world, like the people who presided over Coke before me had done. Coca-Cola was the first advertiser in the U.S. to put black and white people together in an ad. Coca-Cola was the first advertiser to put women in the workplace. Coke was the first advertiser (though it's kind of inappropriate now) to sexualize the male body, as opposed to the female body.

The "America the Beautiful" spot that Mildenhall and his team produced is a masterpiece: its simplicity lies in taking this well-known song and reinterpreting it, sung in multiple languages, including Spanish, Hindi, Arabic, and Tagalog. It is the perfect update to the iconic "I'd like to teach the world to sing" Coca Cola ad from 1971, relevant to our times and our reality.

Social media erupted when it ran during the Super Bowl in 2014, making it the most talked-about spot that year. Conservatives were outraged and threatened boycotts; liberals were overjoyed and rapturous at this paean to multiculturalism. Coke's answer? To run the spot again in the 2017 Super Bowl, after one of the most divisive elections in American history.

Jonathan's next gig was at Airbnb as chief marketing officer. His tenure there, as the consigliere to CEO Brian Chesky, was during a period of explosive growth for the company—which came with its fair share of growing pains. When the company began to get reports of discrimination against guests of color, it realized it was at odds with its stated purpose of "helping people belong anywhere" and made all of its hosts sign a nondiscrimination pledge.

We asked him the question, If we are living in the age of purpose, do CMOs have to help be almost the moral conscience of the company and have it translate into action and product—not just storytelling? Jonathan answered. "The role of a brand has evolved significantly over the last decade from being the extension of the company that presents itself publicly through the power of marketing. In the last decade we've seen the brand becoming the foundation of everything that the brand stands for; its narrative has to coalesce the investor agenda, the employee agenda, the supplier agenda, and the actual paying customer agenda, the CEO agenda and the company's role in society. It is now all singular."

This speaks to a deeper shift in the role of a chief marketing officer.

A CMO who isn't constantly thinking about not just storytelling but *story doing* is a CMO that is in a precarious position with the brands that they're stewarding, because storytelling is not enough. I can't say, this brand believes in equality and fairness and female empowerment when I haven't got a whole body of evidence to show that I'm actually acting as a brand in a way that shows that same female empowerment. So narrative and actions have never been more interdependent on one another. And sometimes the actions are much, much more important. If you haven't got budget to do both, I would always say, if you can evidence the brand values through actions, then start with that.

SHARE **OF MIND**
SHARE **OF HEART**
SHARE **OF SPIRIT**

We talked about how today it was no longer enough for a great brand to have a great product (which wins you "share of mind") with a great story (which wins you "share of heart"). Consumers were also seeking proof that the brand positively contributes to society so they can "vote with their wallet." Jonathan builds on the analogy.

I am at my best when I am stewarding community brands and I am shifting millions of people at the same time. What I like to do is I like to try and claim share of collective spirit. And if I can claim a share of humanity's collective spirit, if I can do that, then I know my work is important and I know my work will be remembered, in decades to come because it's actually shifted society. When I say shift society, I mean shift millions of people with the actions and the narrative of my brand. And so, I wonder what the world would look like if we were all battling for share of collective spirit.

This corresponded with the changing role of a CEO. Jonathan talked about his experience with Brian Chesky.

The role of the CEO, whether they like it or not, is so much more public and so much more politicized. The CEO has to be able to take and carry a very credible, authentic narrative on the social stands the company and brand must make to ensure fairness in the communities the company serves. When I was working with Brian Chesky, I was so inspired by his courage and his bravery as a young CEO to stand up publicly and fight for the things that he felt for. He's got a zero tolerance for any form of racism or bigotry on the Airbnb platform, because that's a compromise to the brand values of the Airbnb company. Brian will go up against the President of the United States when he signs a draconian order against immigration. And if he sees something in the world that's not right, then he feels that he now has an obligation to protect his community and protect his brand to make a very public stand. That was not the case for CEOs a decade ago, but it is the case for most CEOs now, as we've seen recently, especially with things like the Black Lives Matter movement.

To go beyond advertising, Airbnb went even further in its mission of a "belong anywhere" pledge, with its groundbreaking Open Homes program: a commitment to provide free short-term housing for one hundred thousand people in need over the next five years, including for refugees, victims of natural disasters, and aid workers. The idea is simple : hosts who want to donate their home for free can create a "zero-dollar listing" : Airbnb then makes these available to a vetted group of nonprofits who can use them to house individuals and families. In the wake of COVID-19, the program has also housed doctors and frontline workers who needed to be isolated from their families.

This idea didn't require a huge technological platform to execute it: it used the existing functionality of the platform. And neither did it require large investment from Airbnb—though the company has also donated travel credits to people in need, this particular program is primarily funded by the generosity of its hosts, who love the program for how it gives them an opportunity to serve others.

Airbnb's Open Homes platform does that beautifully. By helping its hosts become the "Heroes" of the moment, the company gives them a chance to do something meaningful to them—the ability to help fellow human beings in their time of need. In doing so, they helped someone without the "means"—a place to shelter—at times and moments when things seemed darkest. The value exchange that is created is priceless and the affinity that the brand builds—the share of spirit—is immeasurable.

Jonathan ends on an optimistic note.

I really believe that the currency of humankind is storytelling. The power of stories is that they move people. If you are a marketer and you have the privilege of marketing dollars, then if you invest them and you don't move people, then I just think it's a waste of investment. I think all brands have the opportunity through the power of story to expose the deep-seated human emotions and human values. And if you've got a great story and a simple execution, then you should move people to tears, or you should move people to laugh, or you should move people to act. Quite often, I think the reason my work moves people to tears [is] just because I shine a light on the beauty of humanity. And can you imagine what a beautiful world this would be? Honestly, if every single marketing dollar attempted to shine a light on the beauty of our existence on this planet? I think it would uplift the entire world.

Why We Love This Example:

A boy from Leeds who went door to door looking for connection found his purpose as the steward of some of the world's most iconic brands that connect us all through culture.

Jonathan's work shows us that it's no longer enough for great brands today to only have "share of mind" via a great product and "share of heart" (an emotional affinity). They must also win "share of spirit," showing how they can uplift the world through positive social impact. And to achieve that and truly move the cultural needle, there is a new expectation of how a company shows up in the world; great advertising is nothing if not backed by significant actions.

Kfir
Gavrieli, Tieks

Tieks understands the importance and power of the community. In 2020 alone, they empowered a passionate fanbase of women to serve frontline workers during COVID-19, that unleashed a tremendous of service and love and ended up creating 1 million face masks across the country.. Their CEO, Kfir, shares how they have found a way to support their customers' desires to serve.

* * *

Fashion brand Tieks has provided a remarkable example of how a brand can mobilize its community to do good. As a company that believes deeply in the power of women to change the world, they have invested millions of dollars in female entrepreneurs, mobilized women to help ensure the safety of medical workers on the front lines of COVID-19, and celebrated mothers with love.

We caught up with CEO and cofounder Kfir Gavrieli to learn more about their approach to building and activating an engaged community and to discover what other brands can learn from their experience. Gavrieli started by speaking to the origin of Tieks.

> We launched Tieks with little prior experience in fashion in 2008. We spent the first two years perfecting the Tieks shoe design. I wanted something that would be simultaneously comfortable, durable, fashionable, and portable—a combination of features that didn't exist in an industry that dates back millennia. Then, we invested heavily in building a formidable online presence at a time when e-commerce and social media advertising were in their infancy and became one of the first handful of digitally native vertically integrated brands.
>
> We also understood from the beginning that building a truly premium brand (especially online) meant delivering a premium customer experience. So we provided free shipping and returns before that was common, quality inspected 100 percent of orders shipped, and wrote a personal handwritten note thanking customers for each order. This meticulous attention to detail, combined with a product that was truly revolutionary, helped build our base of loyal customers. We are deeply invested in providing a best-in-class product while making a positive impact on the world.

Tieks's purpose starts with its product but extends far beyond to make a positive impact in women's lives.

> Our mission as a company is to empower women, and one way we do that is through a shoe designed to be uniquely versatile. Another way we advance that mission is by making loans through the Kiva platform

to women entrepreneurs living in poverty. I went to business school with Jessica Jackley, the cofounder of Kiva, and knew immediately that Kiva's mission dovetailed with our ethos at Tieks.

Through loans ranging in size from $25 to over $1000, Kiva allows us to provide much-needed working capital to women entrepreneurs in places where there is no easy access to small loans. This makes a huge difference in women's ability to start businesses, provide for their families, and in many cases, transform their communities. Through the Gavrieli Foundation, Tieks has become the largest single lender on Kiva. We have been fortunate enough to contribute more than $10,000,000 to thousands of women entrepreneurs in seventy countries, including the US.

Tieks understands that women multiply the impact on an investment made in their future by extending benefits to the world around them, creating a better life for their families and building a healthy hamlet. By delivering women access to capital, they are creating a ripple effect of impact. But in addition to money, Tieks recognizes that providing a supportive community is a key to unleashing women's power to help others in ways the brand never could.

An example of this is Tieks's efforts during COVID-19. After learning of the shortage of face masks, the premium brand challenged its community to #SewTOGETHER, a campaign that has lit up social media and helped generate six hundred thousand face masks for frontline medical workers (in return for which Tieks gave them gift cards).

Gavrieli shared what inspired him to get involved.

In March, a friend whose sister is a doctor told me that her hospital would be out of masks within a couple of weeks. I was shocked— and scrambled to figure out how I could help get personal protective equipment (PPE) into the hands of our frontline medical providers.

I partnered with some other entrepreneurs to try and purchase medical masks overseas, but the procurement proved very challenging. At the same time, we retooled our Los Angeles facility and retrained our staff to sew masks that we could donate. Quickly, we realized that we were sitting on a much bigger resource: our millions of customers and fans.

We launched Operation #SewTOGETHER to solicit mask donations from our customers for frontline heroes. Our website provides detailed instructions on how to make masks at home and offers up to $100 Tieks gift cards for fifty masks donated.

The response by the Tieks community was immediate and incredible.

Overnight, we saw thousands of dedicated volunteer sewers take up this cause across the country, producing more than 600,000 masks in living rooms, around kitchen tables, and [in] converted basements in only the first three weeks.

We've received masks from teachers who are working from home, sewing masks on their lunch break, and when they're off the clock. We've seen neighborhoods form sewing groups to encourage each other to join in the effort. We've received emotional emails from laid-off workers looking to do their part to fight the virus. Our social media channels are a continuous source of motivation, as thousands of medical providers have reached out to share just how much this effort means to them. It is humbling to be part of this nationwide, lifesaving effort.

Each day we have seen the rate of mask production and the number of participants in the #SewTOGETHER campaign grow exponentially.

What he found most remarkable is that women have continued sewing way beyond whatever the number of masks required for a gift card, because they deliver these masks to the hospital and see how grateful the doctors and nurses are. "They can't just go back home and sit on the couch and watch TV. They feel an obligation and also empowerment to help. That's the best thing I felt like we could do as a brand."

Customers are not the only ones who have been transformed by the outpouring of generosity. Gavrieli shared how the experience has made him rethink his role as CEO.

I believe that my number-one job as CEO of Tieks at this moment is to figure out how our company can make a difference in the fight against this pandemic. We plan to continue our #SewTOGETHER campaign as long as our hospitals and frontline facilities nationwide need protective equipment. Homemade masks are only becoming more essential as we transition to a new normal where everyone wears a mask.

Tieks is also a partner in a medical-procurement effort called the Emergency Supply Donor Group.

I was inspired to be there as we dropped off our first shipment of face shields and had the chance to meet the true heroes of this moment: the medical providers working to save lives. Tieks is also proud to be a partner in a new effort to create a public registry that will enable Southern California–area hospitals to ask for supplies and get direct donations. Finally, we are currently manufacturing masks that our customers will be able to purchase or receive for free with each order. We want to encourage the public to start wearing masks so that we reduce the spread of COVID-19.

Kfir is quick to deflect any recognition or praise for the brand.

The real heroes are the women sewing. The real heroes are the moms. The real heroes are the frontline workers. We as a brand really don't mind taking a backseat and just helping people do what we think is right during this time, and I think it's a reflection of the kind of values that are becoming more prominent during this time.

At a time when brands are struggling to find ways to engage customers meaningfully, Tieks has built a community that feels connected to the brand and each other. This approach is intentional and has been encoded in the DNA of the brand from the beginning.

It's something we take very seriously. I remember one of the first marketing books I ever read before starting Tieks was *The Culting of*

Brands. We created a real community around what some people might perceive as just a shoe, but we've always tried to be more than that. I think first and foremost, you have to stand for something more than only your product, and that's the ethos about empowering women.

And then beyond having that as a goal, you have to show that you're kind of in the trenches living up to what you say your values are, and that's something we've done throughout the years. We've seen manifestations of the actual community in everything from Facebook groups to women scheduling trips together with other lovers of Tieks, women they've never even met before. Our Facebook groups, the connection among women who know nothing about each other except that they all love our product—I think it is for me the purest form of being about more than just the product as a brand and creating a community and then being part of it, not trying to be the hero but empowering women to get what they want out of the community that we built.

Gavrieli thinks that this time presents a tremendous opportunity for us all to recognize the opportunity and responsibility to help each other. "More than ever, this is a moment that we need to come together—businesses, nonprofits, governments, and everyday people of all backgrounds—in which each of us asks, 'What can I do to help?'"

Why We Love This Example:

Tieks let people see the power they already had. By calling people to use the talents and resources they already have to make a positive impact in the world, they tapped into their community's hunger to be of service. And once they saw how they could make a positive impact, the strength of the community grew. The most influential brands will be those who understand how to harness the power of their people. Doing this might take a bit more creativity and investment by a brand, but it's where people can find their most profound sense of belonging.

Essence Smith and Justin Cunningham, Social Works

Social Works is all about youth. From programming in arts and sciences to resources for mental health and well-being, they have taken a youth-centered approach to design that is making a significant impact in Chicago's young people's lives. Essence and Justin share how they are helping youth rewrite the narrative of who they are and who they can be.

* * *

During his senior year of high school, a teenager named Chancelor Bennett was suspended for what he called "chiefin' a hundred blunts," or in layman's terms, smoking a lot of weed. The suspension lasted ten short days, but instead of remaining in a haze, the high schooler used that time to create an album—appropriately titled *10 Day*—kick-starting his transformation into a global music icon, humanitarian, and force for good named Chance the Rapper.

Inspired to pay his newfound fame and good fortune forward, in August 2016, Chance partnered with two of his high school friends, Justin Cunningham and Essence Smith, to create SocialWorks, which aims to empower the youth through the arts, education, and civic engagement. Together, they have built SocialWorks into one of the most groundbreaking and innovative nonprofits operating in the United States, empowering youth to use creativity and self-expression to change their community for the better.

We spoke with Essence Smith and Justin Cunningham about SocialWorks. We talked about their work to support Chicago Public Schools and solve social issues that affect Chicago's youth—such as education, homelessness, and mental health support—and how they create spaces for visibility to Chicago's artistic community.

Essence and Justin are both incredibly smart and passionate about their work to uplift and serve their hometowns. Smith received her sociology degree from the University of Illinois at Chicago, where she graduated with honors and became a member of Alpha Kappa Alpha Sorority Incorporated, Beta Chapter. As SocialWorks' director of communications, Smith works diligently to produce branding strategies, orchestrate favorable content surrounding SocialWorks' initiatives and events, and manage press relations, as well as maintaining the overall positive image of the organization.

Cunningham earned a degree in finance and a minor in leadership studies, graduating magna cum laude, and also held analyst positions with a nationwide food-service and facilities-management firm, a major convention center, and Chicago Public Schools. The desire to do work that impacted their community steered them to SocialWorks.

Essence talked about how their experience in high school shaped their desire to focus on youth.

We're all friends from high school, who were blessed to receive great mentorship and guidance from youth leaders at a young age. As we got older, we wanted to keep that same energy going for kids all over the city.

The purpose of SocialWorks is the youth! We aim to empower youth through the arts, education, and civic engagement. We use our human-centered initiatives within the sectors of mental health, artistic expression, childhood education and development, and homelessness, to respond to the community's needs and push for long-term solutions.

SocialWorks became an idea after almost two years of running an initiative now called Open Mike. Its origin is very personal to the founders. Chance named the series "Open Mike" after his mentor, poet Mike Hawkins, who passed away in December 2014. "Musically, from before he passed, he's just been a huge influence, and teacher, and molder of me [from] when I was 14 years old," Chance told Complex. He said, "I would think the open mic thing would be how he affected me musically, him building that space for me. And also, in his passing, taught me that's my job. I'm not a mentee anymore...[The] gratification of being donned a great rapper isn't as important as giving people the resources they need in order to make the statements they want to make."

A central theme of SocialWorks is drawing from their own experiences and passions as young people to create programming that provides the building blocks for holistically healthy people and communities. In addition to OpenMike, they have several programs that offer a wide range of youth engagement. For example, Kids of the Kingdom provides students ages five to thirteen with a spiritual environment that focuses on performing and literary arts.

Cunningham talks about some of their other programs and impact.

My State of Mind (MSOM) is a response to mental health access. With the help of local therapists and the state, county, and city mental health regulatory bodies, we've developed Cook County's first website to access clinical and nonclinical wellness providers. The New Chance Fund supports in-school enrichment through $100k grants.

We've supported fifty-one Chicago public schools through the city with a total of $5.1 million investment. Our New Chance students are experiencing new auditoriums, dance studios, state-of-the-art visual arts labs, and maker spaces, but most importantly, a renewed interest in learning. One of our New Chance Fund Schools, Michelle Clark, experienced a 100 percent graduation rate for the first time ever after our investment in their school! So exciting!

Warmest Winter aims to raise awareness and provide relief for individuals experiencing homelessness and extreme hardship through service, events, donations, and direct supports. Through Warmest Winter, SocialWorks offers communities both a chance to serve others and take care of themselves by providing direct access to resources through our events. Warmest Winters is executed with citizens and businesses who believe in taking care of each other!

Key to SocialWorks' success is forming brand partnerships that can expand and deepen their impact. They have partnered with Chicago Bulls, ConAgra, DTLR, Champion USA, Jordan Brand, Lyft, Goose Island, Postmates, Fat Tiger Workshop, and the Life Is Beautiful Festival. Essence shared, "We enjoy mission-focused brand partnerships that make charity a priority in a very intentional way. Though all of our collaborations are different, a common thread is beginning with a shared understanding that we are together to create a moment for our youth and the community."

Their recent partnership with Google is an excellent example of young people's power to imagine and implement new ideas with proper support.

The genesis of *SuperMe* goes back to 2017 when Google provided a $1.5 million grant to SocialWorks and the Chicago Public Schools (CPS) computer science initiative CS4ALL to provide twenty schools on the South Side with extra resources for computer science and STEM programs. Google representatives also announced an additional grant of $250,000 for SocialWorks on Monday.

As part of that initiative, four hundred students were enrolled in a ten-hour workshop to learn Scratch—a free coding platform for kids that teaches them how to make video games. The goal is to get kids interested in coding by letting them use code to create the types of things that are personally meaningful to them. The students created something unexpected, a video game called *SuperMe* that reimagined students as superheroes with unlimited powers and abilities to collect symbols of love.

SuperMe is composed of bits and pieces of dozens of games coded by students over the 2019 school year. The video opens with a description: "Superheroes come in all shapes and sizes. We all possess the power to be a hero. Take a journey with our Chicago Public School heroes." You play as a superhero (all digitized self-portraits of CPS students) whose job is to fly through a colorful, hand-drawn version of Chicago's skyline, which includes the John Hancock building as well as other landmarks. The goal is to collect as many floating hearts as you can in thirty seconds. The game's soundtrack is "I Love You So Much," Chance the Rapper's hit collaboration with DJ Khaled.

They "wanted the song in the game," said Cunningham. Chance "saw it, and he was like, 'Oh, wow. This should be the official video game for this song.' It's about celebrating the individual superheroes in our own lives, and there's nothing better to say to them than I love you." It's reportedly the first time a platinum artist has ever attached an online game to a single instead of the traditional music video treatment.

Chance excitedly tells the story in a Google blog post.

> In 2017, with CS4All, Scratch, and a little help from Google, we told hundreds of kids from the South Side of Chicago they could do anything with code. Since then, we've been busy with teacher training, hosting family creative coding nights, and getting the whole community excited about what's possible with code.
>
> Now the kids are coding. Seven elementary schools spent a bunch of time creating a game and drawing themselves as superheroes—that can fly! That can teleport! That collect hearts. All using code.

He continued, "A few weeks ago, I saw their incredible work and am so proud of them that I decided the entire world should see their projects…So today, the first day of Computer Science Education Week, I present you with—*SuperMe*, the official video game for 'I Love You So Much' (because anyone can make a music video)."

Smith leaves us with some words of advice for anyone looking to involve communities in the impact they want to create.

If you're trying to help someone, the best thing to do is ask, act, and ascertain. No matter the result, the process is the same. A lot of times, people get stuck in doing things the "right way," when usually, the work just needs to be done...or at least started! Honestly, as a body of people, we're better together. Community and collaboration are key. If someone is looking to help others, my first advice would be, what are you waiting for? It all begins with opening your heart, mind, and ears.

Why We Love This Example
The mission of SocialWorks, "To inspire creativity, to build dreams, to let you be you," is possible because they involve young people as active participants in the process. SocialWorks gives young people the tools to express their creative ideas and shows them how to apply their talents to create change. They move youth from passive recipients of services to active participants in creating better and healthier communities, proving that when you treat young people as capable of saving the world, they will see themselves as the superheroes they indeed are.

8.

PURPOSE SHOULD MEASURE WHAT YOU TREASURE

As businesses adopt a purpose-led philosophy, they must also effectively measure their business success and societal impact. In this section, we will visit the office of Hollywood's leader in social impact films, Participant Media, to talk with its chief impact officer Holly Gordon. Holly shares how they measure their films' performance across various metrics that have led to Oscar wins and lives improved. Next, we talk with Tracy Lawrence, who shares how childhood experiences with bullying led her to create a platform that ensures children don't have to eat alone. And in the land of Silicon Valley, we see how Aria Ashton of Google is helping to analyze critical data around incarnation rates to find lasting solutions that can lead to criminal justice reform.

Holly Gordon, Participant

In 2019, Participant received a company-record seventeen Academy Award nominations, including ten for Roma, five for Green Book, and two for RBG. Of those seventeen nominations, the company won six Oscars, including Best Picture for Green Book and Best Director and Best Foreign Language Film for Roma. It followed that success with winning the 2020 Oscar for Best Documentary Film for American Factory, produced by President Obama and the former first lady Michelle Obama. That level of success would be more than enough for any Hollywood studio, but Participant Media also wants to create entertainment that inspires and compels social change. Chief Impact Officer Holly Gordon shares their process of choosing content that combines the power of a good story with opportunities for real-world impact and awareness around the most pressing global issues of our time.

* * *

Walking into the offices of Participant Media as a film fan is a heady experience. The walls are lined with posters of some of the legendary pictures the company has created over its existence, since it was founded by Jeff Skoll in 2004. Searing documentaries like *He Named Me Malala*, *CITIZENFOUR*, *Food, Inc*, and the iconic *An Inconvenient Truth*. Emotional powerhouses like *Spotlight* (winner of the 2016 Academy Award for Best Picture), *The Help*, *Lincoln*, and many others.

Warm, funny, and wise, Participant's chief impact officer Holly Gordon has the enviable job of taking the cultural cachet generated by these films and TV programs and turning them into real, tangible social impact in the world, by orchestrating a coalition of brands, nonprofits, and governmental partners. We sat down with her to learn more about her journey and gain insights into how she does this groundbreaking work.

> "I've had one of those careers when you look back on it, it all makes sense. But never once did I wake up in the morning saying, 'I know exactly where I want to be in 25 years.'" After traveling the world (with a change of clothes and a manual typewriter) and working in broadcast news alongside the likes of Peter Jennings, her journey led her to something called "Girl Rising." "It was based on this fundamental truth that if you educate girls in the developing world, everything in your country will get better. I call it 'a global campaign for girls' education' with a film at the center. Our model was to show that great storytelling plus deep partnerships could create transformational change."

After three years of raising millions of dollars and building partnerships with foundations, nonprofit organizations, individual philanthropists, and companies, all of whom had the same belief that educating girls was the silver bullet to global development, Gordon was exhausted. "By the end, I was working 80 hours a week and on airplanes all over the world. It almost killed me. I was so exhausted. Living every day, not being sure that you're going to be able to raise enough to pay your team and being desperately afraid of failing were not small weights on my psyche."

Shortly after that, Participant came into her life. "I studied Participant when building 'Girl Rising' and the work they do around films. It is the one Hollywood production company that's creating stories at scale, all of which have a message of social good at heart. I was thrilled when they offered me the job, and I got in an RV with my dog and my two now teenage children and my husband and my mom (she got the best bed in the back of the RV!) and we drove to Los Angeles, and we haven't looked back."

Gordon talked about the importance of the role of being so senior in the organization. "We have both an opportunity and an obligation to try to lead the way in this kind of work. The fact that it's now at a C-suite level makes me think of it as a job where leadership and vision are important in terms of where we want to go." That seniority means she is also involved in evaluating what movies and TV Participant decide to make.

> I am 100% invited to the green light table, and I'm really careful about how I use that seat. My agenda is to support the vision of Jeff and the promise of the mission, which is "extraordinary content that will inspire social change." At the green light stage, what I'm looking for are traps, unseen risks that perhaps others don't have the same perspective on. I'm adding my perspective, but I'm not seeking to influence the content decisions. And here's why making content is such a difficult thing to do: Artists see things earlier than most people, and they see things in a nuanced way. Art is magic. I deeply believe in protecting the story coming first. That's the company we have here. The story is the product, and the impact is the byproduct. And if you don't focus on your product, you will not get your byproduct. The better the product, the better the byproduct's going to be.

So how does Participant Media bring a social impact campaign around a film or TV series to life? How does it choose which films to work on, and what partners to work with?

Gordon talked first about the process of evaluating what kind of stories Participant decides to tell. "We focus on human stories because human stories are at the center of everything we do. Our stories do fit into a set of categories; for instance, we consistently focus on the environment, health care, human rights, institutional responsibility. That's where you get a film like *Spotlight*—we see how institutional responsibility and journalism are linked to the preservation of democracy."

Gordon is also deeply aware of the intersectionality of many of the projects. "When you look at our recent projects, you have 'America To Me,' which is about race and equity and education. We have 'The Price Of Free,' which is about child labor. We have 'Roma,' which is about the rights of domestic workers. And we have 'When They See Us,' which is about race and equity in the justice system. And it turns out the more we learn about these issues, the more we understand how intersectional they all are."

However, Gordon is quick to point out that not every film gets a campaign. "You know, it depends where you are on an issue. Sometimes making the content is enough, right? We did a very small campaign around the film 'Wonder.' Why? Because the content itself gives you so much to talk about at the dinner table. And it really brought us the idea of what it's like to live with disfigurement and compassion to this fifth-grader who spends the beginning of the movie hiding in a helmet. So, we produce about ten films and episodic series a year, and we try to choose four around which to develop flagship campaigns."

Gordon also explains Participant's criteria for choosing a film.

We use six criteria to decide whether or not we choose a film to be a flagship. Number one is scale: how big is the issue? How many people are affected by the issue the film touches? The second is emotion: how does the film leave you feeling? When content goes into the world, it evokes a certain feeling. Compassion is an incredibly important feeling, but it's not an activating feeling. Inspiration is activating; fear (unfortunately) is activating. I think that inspiration and hope; those are transformational feelings, meaning they last a really long time. Fear and guilt, although activating short-term transactional feelings, you want to feel them and get through it fast. So, if you're trying to get someone to donate, for instance, fear or guilt are really good tactics. But if you're trying to get someone to change their behavior forever, go for inspiration and hope every time."

After scale and emotion, Gordon explains that timeliness is the next criteria—where each issue is in one of four stages of development.

There are four stages that move you from awareness of an issue to action, and you can't rush them. So those four stages are 1) Awareness of an issue 2) Understanding. I feel as though that's when you go from the external to the internal: you have an understanding of how it impacts you, and you've internalized it. 3) Engagement. You've internalized it so much that you now are seeking information, or you want to take your first step towards being involved in whatever this issue area is and finally 4) Action. Action is the furthest step along this continuum: you've been made aware, you understand it, you are engaged enough that all you need is a push and you're going to take action.

Clarity of the message is the fourth component of what Gordon and her team look at. "When you watch the piece of content, how clear is it, what we want you to do, how clear is the message around the issue? Obviously, with a narrative, the message is much more diffuse. In a documentary, it's usually much tighter and on the nose."

The fifth criterion is agency. "How easily or specifically can some regular person take action around the issue that the content has presented? Because if you give someone an issue where the action is not easy, clear, measurable, and makes them feel like they're really doing something, you break the agreement with them."

Gordon illustrates the problem using the example of the iconic Chinese artist Ai Wei-Wei's film about refugees *Human Flow*.

It is an enormously overwhelming film about the challenges refugees face around the world. It's so huge. And where it leaves you is "oh my gosh, I need to take a refugee into our home." That's how big the movie is. And so how can you think of ways that an individual can take action that's in the scope and scale of the content that you've seen. So, for us, we created an Amazon Wishlist where people could buy things for refugees, and I feel like that was valiant but not commensurate with the scale of the content. It felt small. When you watched the whole of "Human Flow," you understood that one box of diapers for a refugee family was not enough. And so, you know, you learn by doing.

The sixth and final element is "What can Participant Media bring to the table?" If Participant gets involved in this project from an impact perspective, how can we, because of who we are and because of the network that we're part of, add leverage and bring in the right partners. We're never the ones that provide the solution, and I really try to make this clear to my team. We are but a catalyst; we are a visitor to every space.

Gordon's journalistic background comes in useful in their approach.

What I encourage my team to do is to go into every conversation like a journalist. Our job is to really understand our partner's needs and our partners. And what we want to do is look at all of the different ways that this problem can be solved from different angles. What role can corporations play in solving a problem? What role can policymakers, government officials, nonprofit leaders play in solving the problem? We call those different entities, "sectoral leaders," and we say, what are you doing? How are you doing it? And how can a piece of hugely visible content accelerate your work? How can we create the right timing and the right formula so that when the distributor is spending millions of dollars on advertising for this piece of content, you are there with your engines running ready to put that fuel into the car and take your goals forward?

Gordon ends by talking about what she believes makes for a great partnership. "Partnership means learning the language of the person you're collaborating with. First of all, articulating clearly your shared goal because there are going to be bumps in the road when you're working with unexpected allies. And then learning and respecting the language of your partner and deepening engagement with your unexpected allies so that when your culture, when your art goes into the world, it is seeding change in ways that you could never have imagined."

Why We Love This Example:
Holly shares a critical lesson about creating a successful purpose-led business or initiative—it starts with the product. For Participant, the story is the

product, and the impact is the byproduct. Too often, to create change, brands lose their focus on creating a great offering to attract the attention and revenue needed to do good at the aspired levels. Participant's six criteria for choosing a film—scale, emotion, issue stage, clarity of message, agency, and Participant's value add—allow them to measure their ability to produce both a great product and byproduct. As a result, they make incredible films with passionate artists and spark action that changes the world.

Tracy Lawrence, CHEWSE

Most office-catered meals are nothing to write home about. Plastic wrapped sandwiches and unappetizing salads laid out on a folding table with cans of soda and water bottles. It's the antithesis of what one would associate with the care of a home-cooked meal. Tracy Lawrence has set out to change that through a purpose-based venture names Chewse. In this chapter, Tracy shares how Chewse bakes love and connection into every office dining experience.

* * *

San Francisco–based Chewse takes a purpose-driven approach to tackle the problem of office-based catering. There are over seven hundred thousand plus enterprise customers who feed their employees, which is increasingly becoming one of the perks of the job, especially in sectors like technology, and catering is estimated to be a $55 billion industry with rapid growth. But instead of the usual sad shrink-wrapped sandwiches often eaten alone in someone's cubicle, Chewse curates family-style meals that bring employees together to create a sense of community around food. We caught up with one of the cofounders, Tracy Lawrence (who started the company in 2011 with Jeff Schenck), to find out more about how her personal experience of being bullied at school led her to create a solution where "nobody ever has to eat lunch alone."

Funny and self-deprecating, yet insightful and highly self-aware, the Asian American Lawrence represents a new breed of start-up CEOs—ones who aren't afraid to embrace vulnerability as a superpower. We asked her to define the purpose of Chewse and how it connected with her own personal story. "Our purpose is to make sure nobody ever eats lunch alone. I went to a small school with about 40 students in total. I found myself being friends with the girls who were outsiders, often from other countries and with different backgrounds. But doing this actually made me an outsider myself. The 'in' girl group bullied me so hard, I used to eat lunch alone in the bathroom."

Lawrence continued,

As I grew older, I told myself that I had to move on. That remembering it wasn't helpful. But the opposite of "remembering" isn't "forgetting"—it's "dismembering." I took an important part of me, my past, and I tried to throw it out of my identity. As if I could actually do that. The desire to bring people together to authentically connect became my job. When I was in undergraduate business school at The University of Southern California, I became an event planner and started planning large scale events on the side. It was in my blood to bring people together. And that's when an office manager came to me begging for a better restaurant than Subway to feed her team of 30 for an all-hands meeting.

It was at that moment that Lawrence had a stroke of insight.

I saw a market opportunity, right? I did. And it came back to my history. My coach asked me at one point about my history, and as I shared about being bullied, he asked, "What does your company do?" I replied, "We ensure that no one eats lunch alone." In that moment, it felt like 30,000 volts of electricity went through my body. I had never put the two things together. It was as if that "dismembered" part of me was being re-introduced to the present so that I could walk forward fully into my vision of the future: a more authentically connected world.

Lawrence has also spoken publicly about the idea of Chewse being a "love company," again driven by her own experiences dealing with the investor community when raising money for her start-up.

We had an investor who was at the final stages of diligence to potentially invest in our company. He had interviewed customers, I had spoken with his business partner, and he was about to visit the team. He called me up that day and said, "I interviewed your customers, and they love the service. They said it's the best thing that's ever happened to them at work. Unfortunately, we can't invest."

I was floored. "Why not?" I asked. "This is a tough market that requires a ton of hand-to-hand combat. And we don't have conviction in the team because we don't think you're out for blood." I hung up the phone, lay down on the floor of my San Francisco studio, and I cried for what felt like hours. And I questioned everything. What am I doing in the tech world? Should I be out for blood? Do I fit in? Can I be successful in any other way? It took me a few days to email him back. In that email, I told him he was right—I'm not out for blood! I'm out to build a service that our customers love, which is why we stand apart from our competition.

This became the rallying cry for Chewse as a "love company."

I came back to the company and I shared the story of how being bullied made me want a world with more love and connection. And the company rallied around this. Not the stories of destroying our competition, but rather moving towards bringing more authentic connection into the world. Our company has two pillars: love and excellence. Each has three values under them. I believe that you can't have one without the other. You can't care about someone without holding them to their highest potential, and you can't expect someone to meet those expectations without them knowing that you care. We decided it wasn't about love or excellence, but rather love *and* excellence.

Chewse has now raised over $30 million in funding from investors including Foundry Group, 500 Start-ups, and Gingerbread Capital, showing that their integrity-driven approach has paid off.

Chewse takes the idea of "Love and Excellence" and applies it not just to their customers but also to their own internal operating system.

Our focus is on community impact. That means we donate unwanted food to local shelters, we make our delivery drivers employees instead of contractors, and we source our food from mom and pop restaurants instead of national chains to drive revenue back into the cities we operate in. And within our culture, we have initiatives geared towards inclusion. For example, we have Transparent Salaries—this means that we decide compensation based on actual performance, not on negotiation ability. I launched this because I saw women and engineers not negotiate hard enough for their compensation, and I decided that I wanted us to be part of the solution instead of the problem.

The company is currently focused on San Francisco and Los Angeles, and we asked Lawrence what the future held for Chewse.

Our vision is to transform the drop off delivery experience into an onsite dining experience—nationwide. The future will see the expansion of Chewse across the U.S. and abroad. We also aim to take our unique love culture and codify it into a playbook to share with other companies who want to use love as an operating model. Love may feel out of place in business, but I actually think this is the key ingredient that businesses need. As the modern workforce starts to put expectations of authenticity and community on their companies, love is a key ingredient that companies can use to differentiate their cultures and attract the next crop of amazing talent.

Why We Love this Example:

"Love is the key ingredient." We couldn't agree more. Too often, companies demand love from their customers or employees. "We want to be the best-loved brand." "We want to be the best-loved place to work." But too often, companies never give the love they want to receive. By focusing on giving love, measuring it and codifying it, Tracy and Chewse are pioneering an admirable approach to business that we wish more companies would emulate.

Aria Ashton, Google.org Fellow

Google's Fellowship program supports employees' passions by offering them the ability to volunteer their time to serve important causes. Aria has used that time to work on an issue close to her heart, prison reform. She shares why she is so connected to this issue and the measurable impact she seeks to make through her work.

* * *

Google has always been famous for its program that allowed employees to use 20 percent of their time to work on whatever they wanted—an initiative that famously produced Gmail, Google Maps, Google News, and even AdSense.

Extending that idea even further but now focusing on social impact, Google.org has just celebrated the one-year anniversary of its Fellowship program, which enables Googlers to apply to do full-time pro bono work for up to six months with grantees working in areas like education, criminal justice, or economic opportunity. The Fellowship program is a key part of Google.org's approach to philanthropy, as fellows and nonprofits work as a team to build solutions that have a lasting impact.

The approach is rooted in Google's purpose, which is "to organize the world's information and make it universally accessible and useful." While Google has had its fair share of controversies (from anti-trust violations to issues with workplace culture), we believe that this program was still worth lifting up as an example of how to help employees work with purpose.

Thanks to the help of its fellows, the Vera Institute of Justice released People in Jails 2019, a first of its kind look at real-time jail data, which includes surface trends and draws actionable insights about US jail populations.

The statistics on mass incarceration in the United States are almost surreal. According to the Brennan Center For Justice, "America now houses roughly the same number people with criminal records as it does four-year college graduates. Nearly half of black males and almost 40 percent of white males are arrested by the age twenty-three. If all arrested Americans were a nation, they would be the world's eighteenth largest. Larger than Canada. Larger than France. More than three times the size of Australia." [48]

We sat down with Google.org fellow Aria Ashton, who participated in the Fellowship with Vera, to find out more about her journey. With her long, curly hair, Aria is one of those people who have a quiet determination about them,

---

48 Matthew Friedman, "Just Facts: As Many Americans Have Criminal Records as College Diplomas," *Brennan Center for Justice* (Website), November 17, 2015, https://www. brennancenter.org/our-work/analysis-opinion/just-facts-many-americans-have-criminal-records-college-diplomas, n.p.

but with a warm, friendly personality. The issue of criminal justice reform is something Ashton was passionate about for personal reasons.

> I've seen firsthand some of the failures within our criminal justice system as my brother cycled in and out of lock-ups from a young age. With a history of mental illness and substance use disorder, his behavior was regularly criminalized. My community's solution for getting him off the streets was to lock him up, rather than provide an opportunity for medical intervention. Using detention facilities in this way not only harms individuals and their families but ultimately contributes to a cycle of poverty in our society which goes largely unchecked. In my work with Vera, I learned that county jails are often filled with people arrested on charges related to substance use (which often goes hand in hand with mental illness). If our work eventually contributes to a decline in this trend, it would benefit a lot of people like my brother.

We asked her how the program first caught her attention. She said,

> Volunteering in my community has always been an important part of my life and I'm usually looking for ways to help folks in need. I learned that Google.org runs a Fellowship program that enables Googlers to do pro bono work full-time for up to six months, to help nonprofits solve some of their toughest challenges by filling in gaps that Google technology and expertise can help address. I was fortunate to learn that they were seeking a Program Manager for a project with Vera Institute of Justice—an organization working to improve justice systems—to bring transparency to jail data nationwide. It was the perfect fit—not only was this an opportunity to apply my own set of skills to an urgent problem, but I was already personally connected to the issue of criminal justice reform. It's incredible, really, to be given the opportunity to put your normal day job on hold for a period of six months in order to work full-time on a project with an enormous potential for positive impact.

Aria elaborated on the experience of working with Vera and what they were able to achieve.

It was humbling to work with an organization like Vera, which has been doing really important work in the criminal justice space for a long time. As volunteers, the other 11 Fellows and I were bringing our skills to the table, but most of us had never worked on this type of problem before. By working with the Vera team, we were able to build a tool to ingest anonymized up-to-date jail data to help surface trends and draw actionable insights for Vera to use in their work. This is meaningful because the most recent jail data from the Bureau of Justice Statistics is usually at least a couple of years old, which is eons in the dynamic environment of criminal justice reform. Gaps in data are a big issue for advocates—if you don't have data showing how jail populations are changing over time, it's tough to convince anyone that things need to change. When you can point to data, you have a much more powerful tool for enacting change.

We asked her what some of the key insights worth sharing were.

The data revealed that there has been an overall increase in the nation-wide jail population; an increase due to larger jail populations in rural counties as well as small and mid-sized metropolitan areas. For me, the most important thing to remember is that the majority of people in jail are pre-trial. This means that our local jails are primarily used to incarcerate legally innocent people. These are folks who have not been convicted of the charges they are facing; many of whom are being detained in civil matters, which can include people incarcerated pre-trial for immigration cases, or for something as banal as unpaid fines and fees. The difference between being in jail and being free is often a question of what resources a person has available to them at the time.

Finally, we asked her whether this had sparked a desire in her to do more work in this field.

Working alongside folks who have devoted their lives to this kind of work was incredibly rewarding and it has inspired me to do more. I am particularly passionate about the kinds of structural shifts that need to happen in order to welcome masses of people back into our communities as we continue the work of decarceration in the United States. These populations will need housing, access to work, and affordable health care, so I'm hoping to continue to work on projects in the future which look to solve these kinds of problems. Ultimately, there is an important investment to be made in formerly incarcerated communities, so that these vast stores of human potential don't go untapped.

Why We Love This Example:

Aria's love for her brother and her empathy for what he went through had a profound impact on her life. Google gave her a chance to apply that passion in alignment with the company's goals around "organizing the world's information" in a way that generated new insights that can help the crucial work of decarceration and help so many people caught in a system that robs America of so much potential. What must be healed must first be revealed; Aria's work and that of the Vera Institute is crucial in helping us build a society driven by love, compassion, and forgiveness.

WHAT WE
CAN REVEAL
WE CAN
HEAL

9.
PURPOSE IS A JOURNEY, NOT A DESTINATION

Building a purpose-driven company is a marathon, not a sprint. It requires patience, persistence, and perspective to overcome the temptation to resort to short-term gains that contribute to many long term problems. In this section, Dr. Kate Ringvall of IKEA shares how IKEA learned to build a circular business model, after years of trial and error, that is setting new standards in manufacturing. Michelle Cirocco of Televerde how she went from an incarcerated mom to a corporate executive who now trains women in prison to be business leaders. Finally, we end our journey in the village of Mannya in Uganda with Dianah Diamond, who shares how her life's story has inspired her life's work with the Cotton On Foundation.

Dr. Kate
Ringvall, IKEA

IKEA's approach to being a circular-driven company is something to marvel at. Every aspect of the cycle is purposefully thought out, thoroughly measured, and carefully implemented to ensure it aligns with their equitable access and environmental-sustainability values. In this chapter, we visit Dr. Kate in Australia to talk about her decades-long work in building a circular economy and why IKEA was the right place to bring all of her experience together under one roof.

* * *

For someone who has an intimidating list of academic achievements (a BA in population resources and technology, a master's in public policy, and a PhD in city and urban community and regional planning), Dr Kate Ringvall, with her colorfully dyed hair and red glasses, is surprisingly warm and down to earth. We met her when we invited her to speak at our GOOD IS THE NEW COOL conference (GOODCON) in Sydney about IKEA's incredible journey to become a truly circular economy company.

Growing up in Perth in Western Australia in the seventies and eighties, she established a real connection to nature. She's worked for governments at all levels, and universities, before finally arriving at IKEA, where she led the circular economy, renewable energy, zero waste, mobility, and accessibility strategies for Australia. She spoke to what it was about the topic that drew her to it.

> I think it was this idea that we could design better. That if we really knew how people lived and existed in cities and if we designed them well, everyone could thrive. And that really appealed to me, I think, because I've always had this belief that everyone is equal. We all deserve the same kind of opportunities, no matter race, creed, whatever. And that's always been my guiding principle, I suppose. For me, it was about making sure that everyone was lifted up at the same time.

She couldn't have found a better home than the resolutely egalitarian Swedish company. But she almost never got the job. "I applied on a whim thinking they're not going to call me in a million years. You know, I'm in Western Australia, in Perth. I don't have any management experience and I was not sure that I really wanted any at that point. And they called me, and I almost didn't answer the phone because it was a random number!"

Fortunately, she did answer the phone call, and her first day on the job made her feel like she was in the right place. "When I walked in, nobody was wearing a suit, no ties, nothing. Everyone looked, neat and tidy, and there were no offices, nobody had their own office. So, it was like this kind of multi-layered sort of inspiring experience.

IKEA's purpose has famously been "to create a better everyday life for the many people." Buried in that purpose is a tension similar to Chobani's: making better quality products but at as democratically low a price as possible. Kate explained the core philosophy that enabled them to achieve this goal: "So essentially the design process starts from democratic design and that's an Ikea focus on sustainability, form, function, quality and cost consciousness. And those five things are the drivers for everything that they do within IKEA. They've got to exist all together. An enormous amount of testing that goes into meet that criteria and a product won't be produced unless it meets those criteria."

The surprising thing is that the prices are the starting point of the design process. "The thing that really stood out for me about IKEA designers is that they start with the price first. What is the lowest price that the most amount of people can afford for this item in the majority of the markets that we exist in? It's kind of a Swedish egalitarianism that everyone deserves access to good design, but your income level shouldn't determine that you get the crap."

However, even more startling is the fact that the price has to also take into account the pay of the workers who *make* the product.

So, if that's the price that the most people can afford, how can we make it for that price and still be caring for climate and planet, caring for the population, caring for the people who are going to make it. Can we do all of that for this price, in a way they are supported and properly housed and paid and all of that kind of stuff to make that item? That's the kind of stuff that people want to know when buying something today.

Taking cost-conscious design approaches like this especially makes sense when you think about the massive populations around the world moving into the middle class. "When you start to look at the 'bottom billion' the people at the bottom end of the 7 billion people on the planet, you know you're going to have to find a way of scaling furniture to meet their needs, offering something that's light and cheap and extremely portable, as well."

This two-sided equation is the starting point for a design process that is laser focused on efficiency. "Very early on IKEA said, 'we will not ship air.' Okay, well, what does that mean? It means when they design the product, there's as little waste in the first layer of kind of design, in cutting it out or whatever it might be. Second is when it's packed. It's packed in such a way that there's the least amount of air both inside the product, as well as in the packaging," said Kate. This simple idea leads to massive reductions in carbon emissions when products are shipped to stores, and people take them home.

IKEA Australia was also the first to experiment with a buyback service that allowed people to return their secondhand products for a gift card. "So, the buyback service at IKEA has really transformed the way how brands take responsibility for their products. They've literally said we will buy your product back as long as it's in good enough condition that it can be bought a second time. We will take that item back. We will check it out. We'll make sure that it's safe and then we'll sell it in the 'Used' section. This is not a profit-making exercise. This is about brand responsibility for our products and a recognition that we need to be part of the solution, not the problem," said Kate.

This circular economy model is also in response to understanding that some people are in hard economic straits.

> I think it's a recognition that people are struggling. And IKEA said well, if we can provide the platform for our customers to bring back their stuff that is still good, that they don't want anymore and us to buy it from them for up to 50% of its original value, then we can also allow a whole other branch of customers to have access to products that maybe they couldn't afford at the original price." And it seems to be working. "The last I heard people were bringing stuff in at record numbers and then those items were selling on that foot, on that shop floor within 24 hours."

In fact, it seems that the idea worked so well it is being adopted globally. At the time this book was going to print, IKEA had announced that the buyback program will begin in twenty-six other countries, including Britain, Ireland, Canada, France, Germany, Italy, Japan, and Russia. It shows the power of a simple idea to help people responsibly return furniture when they no longer need it (instead of it ending up in a landfill) and giving access to another group of people in need. We hope it is an idea that more retailers try and adopt.

Globally, IKEA has announced an ambitious agenda that includes designing all IKEA products with new circular principles, with the goal to only use renewable and recycled materials; offering services that make it easier for people to bring home, care for, and pass on products; removing all single-use plastic products from the IKEA range globally and from customer and co-worker restaurants in stores* by 2020; becoming climate positive* and reducing the total IKEA climate footprint by an average of 70 percent per product; and achieving zero emissions home deliveries by 2025.*

Kate spoke to the attraction she had to the size of the ambition.

> A hundred percent circular really for me spoke to everything. Once you're talking about circular, you're talking about transport, you're talking about energy, you're talking about food and products and textiles and it's not just zero waste. It's actually about regenerating the systems that we use every day to live. And that's really what open cities is about. It's driving the agenda for circularity in our infrastructure and planning that currently doesn't exist.

IKEA Australia has also pioneered becoming energy independent at a scale most other retailers would balk at. For instance, the Adelaide store is installing 3,025 solar panels on the roof of the retailer's Adelaide store, linked to a 3.4MWh on-site battery. The solar panels, due to be installed by the end of December, are capable of generating 1,650 MWh per year of energy, sufficient to provide 70 percent of the store's annual electricity consumption.

In the second stage of the project, IKEA will also build shade structures across the store carpark with additional solar panels, increasing energy produced to about 2,600 MWh per year. This not only satisfies 100 percent of the store's annual needs, it also enables surplus energy to be sold into the grid. When the microgrid is complete, the IKEA Adelaide store will save 2MWh in the first year, or about $600,000 in energy costs.

In the third and most ambitious stage, IKEA and its partners hope to use the solar energy to produce hydrogen, which would then be used to power hydrogen-fueled buses traveling to and from Adelaide airport. If this experiment works, IKEA plans to install solar panels and batteries in all Australian stores, and by doing so, hopes to encourage other IKEA stores overseas to join them in decarbonizing their stores with the goal to get to net-zero emissions by 2030. Again, we hope this is a move many other retailers chose to take, especially in an era when due to the climate crisis, the energy grid is vulnerable to increasing natural disasters.

In closing, Kate reflected on how she felt a perfect alignment between her own purpose and that of the company. "People have asked me; how did I get there? And I think really for me, it's because I have always followed that inner call to a purpose higher than me, without really understanding that's what I was doing. To create a better everyday life for the many people, not just a few. For me, that's the light, that's what I want to be following."

Why We Love This Example:
Dr. Kate Ringvall is in "alignment with her assignment." She's found a place where her unique skill sets meet her deeply held values of inclusivity and equality. IKEA has embarked on an inspiring journey to show us what a truly circular economy company should look like in the twenty-first century: innovative, humane, profitable, and never resting on its laurels—always seeking to find ways to serve even more people—while respecting and honoring the planet at the same time.

Michelle Cirocco, Televerde

Bryan Stephenson—a widely acclaimed public interest lawyer who has dedicated his career to helping the poor, the incarcerated, and the condemned—has said, "Each of us is more than the worst thing we've ever done." We often forget that truth and banish people who have committed crimes by never providing them the opportunity to be more than criminals. But Michelle's story shows the redemptive power of opportunity and how Televerde is building a thriving business by offering incarcerated women the chance to find meaningful employment and a renewed sense of purpose through their work.

* * *

Valerie Ochoa is impossible to ignore. She's confident and charismatic and has a lightness about her that you want to be around—the type of woman who would be everyone's favorite coworker at the office. She's funny, and she knows it. Almost every sentence out of her mouth is accompanied by a smile, and without realizing it, you find yourself smiling along with her. But today, as she holds court in front of a packed room, she's all business.

Ochoa's dressed in a suit, her hair is pulled back, and she's presenting a compelling business case that would make any CEO proud. She's here to talk about ROI, passionately making her points with textbook terms like "trends," "innovation," and "bottom line." But this isn't a corporate boardroom in an office building. Valerie is delivering this talk at Perryville Correctional facility at a TEDx event. The suit she is wearing isn't from a fancy designer. Instead, she is styled head to toe in an orange state-issued prison uniform.

Valerie entered Perryville with no prior business acumen and zero experience in the sales and marketing industry. She never imagined that the future ahead of her included being a successful sales leader from behind bars. Valerie found solace in Televerde, a company partnered with the Arizona Department of Corrections, which offers employment and skill building to incarcerated women. It was at Televerde that she discovered her natural ability to sell. Valerie is a showman, and today, she has the crowd in the palm of her hand.

She leads an enterprise sales development team, and onstage, she's making the business case for why investing in Televerde's model is not just good for society but good for business as well. "According to a recent study, 50 percent of sales operations outsourced some function as a part of their strategies. And I bet you didn't know that one of the world's largest telecommunications giants recently outsourced a number of their sales and marketing functions to a company that has 56 percent of its workforce in the correctional facility. I bet you didn't know that this disenfranchised workforce delivered a 60 percent increase in forecasted revenue, all the while reducing a sixteen-month sales cycle down to six months all in less than one year."

As any great saleswoman would, she outlines the undeniable benefits of hiring Televerde's workers. "So think about it: companies can have access to a super hyperfocused workforce that has nothing but time to use towards their growth. And the benefit, I mean come on: employees, they're never stuck in traffic; the security policies here are so tight the FBI gives us a thumbs-up; turnover, it's nonexistent, and company dress code—well let's just say there's no issue but state issue." The crowd can't help but laugh.

This event was organized by Michelle Cirocco, chief responsibility officer of Televerde, who not that long ago was also in a correctional facility. When we catch up with her, she is having a particularly good week. She's just returned from the White House, where she attended an event celebrating the First Step Act, focused on easing employment barriers for formerly incarcerated people.

Televerde, one of the leading B2B demand generation companies in the world (working with companies such as SAP, Adobe, Microsoft, and Dell), is on fire, generating more than $8 billion in revenue for its customers. What makes the company so unique is its focus on hiring women who are currently incarcerated, giving them sales training, education, and jobs, which help them transition to life outside. The company also recently announced it was expanding the number of positions in Arizona and opening up a new facility in Indiana.

And if the visit to the White House wasn't enough of a cause for celebration, when we speak to Cirocco one Friday afternoon, she is about to head to Las Vegas for the marriage of her son. But, when I ask about the beginning of her journey to get to this point, she laughs and offers a frank and honest story.

"I started my career with Televerde in 1996 when I was sentenced to prison for bad decisions I made. I made some foolish choices and had some foolish friends, and I like to refer to it as 'a misguided sense of entrepreneurialism' that led me down a path doing some illegal things that took me to prison. And when I got there, my counselor said to me, 'I'm sure you didn't grow up expecting to go to prison, but here you are. What are you going to do about it?' I decided that I was going to use it as an opportunity to change the trajectory of my life. And that's how I then heard about this little company called Televerde, that wasn't even in the prison I was in at the time. But I heard that if you were really good, you got a job in prison. If you were really good, you could get a job at the corporate office when you got out," she said.

She continued,

"And that's all I cared about at that moment. I had two small kids. They were four and seven, and I now had a felony conviction, and I had lost custody of my kids. I wanted my kids back and I knew I needed to get a job and the only job I'd ever had in my life was bartending. I didn't want to grow up to be a 40 year old bartender. I knew that it wasn't going to be a healthy option for me when I got out of prison. And so I focused my efforts on getting this job at Televerde while I was in prison, and then getting the job at the corporate office when I got out."

Cirocco's determination and focus paid off. "And so then from then, I was very goal-oriented, very future-focused. I just worked my way up the corporate ladder. Once I was released, I was offered a job in sales and literally just made it by my career path. I ran sales for a while, I restructured the company, created our Client Success department, ran that for seven years, and then was Chief Marketing Officer for a couple of years."

Her current role as chief social responsibility officer has given Cirocco a unique opportunity to advocate on behalf of the women she represents.

"Somewhere along the way, I really found my purpose, and I found passion. When I went to the White House on April 1st, I came back and everybody was congratulating me and thanking me, and the women in the prison were so grateful I'd given them a voice. And I realized that morning that I never set out to change the world and I never set out to be anybody's role model. I didn't set out to do any of the things that I do today. I just was a girl who wanted a job, and wanted a better life, and Televerde provided me with that opportunity. So that was a long answer to your simple question!" She laughed.

At first, Televerde didn't really highlight its unique workforce, preferring to downplay it to prospective clients. "I knew from my experience in Client Success that our clients viewed our prison model as the business model is our biggest differentiator. That was our secret sauce. That's what made us good at what we do. And so I decided to turn our marketing approach upside down a little bit and start telling the story boldly and loudly because it was my story too." Cirocco started by organizing a TEDxPerryville event to showcase some of the profound journeys of change that are taking place at the Perryville Correctional Facility, where Televerde has a significant base of operations.

The arrival of a new CEO who heartily encouraged this approach galvanized the company. "She said, let's turn this whole thing on its head. We really don't need as much traditional marketing as we've had. We need to be leading with our purpose. We need to be out there shouting from the rooftops about what we're doing and how it's impacting the women and how it's impacting the community and how other businesses can get involved and 'do well while doing good.'"

Cirocco talked about how the women of Televerde go through extensive training, including an eighty-hour boot camp of classroom training where they learn about the technology they are representing, the proven demand generation strategies, and martech platforms such as Marketo, Eloqua, and Salesforce. "We provide them with job training and education and the opportunity to learn and grow and have a better life. And while they're here, they can see hundreds of examples like myself, of women who were there, had that job and got out and now have a career and now have a better life. So it's what gives us this loyal, dedicated, engaged, committed workforce that you can't replicate. It's the best workforce in the world because they love their job, and they're so goal-oriented, and future-focused, that they just deliver better results than anybody else will."

Cirocco truly believes that this deep drive to have a better life is the secret sauce that helps Televerde outperform its competition. It perfectly syncs up to the stated purpose of the company, which is "to optimize business results for our clients while improving the lives of disempowered communities across the globe." The company has set itself the goal of providing ten-thousand life-changing opportunities over the next decade and has now expanded its international footprint to Scotland, Australia, and Argentina. So far, the company has helped over three thousand women in twenty-five years and has a remarkably low recidivism rate of just 7 percent. Cirocco points out an equally compelling statistic. "Of the 200 people that work for the company that are not in prison, almost half of them started their career on the inside—people at every department, every level of the organization, including 30% of the leadership team. In fact, we have more Televerde graduates on the leadership team than there are men."

But what is perhaps as equally important as the training the women get is the focus on values such as respect: something that takes on quite a different meaning in prison compared to a regular workplace. Cirocco framed it beautifully. "Respect is like air, right? As long as you have it, you don't even think about it. But the minute you take it away, it's the only thing that you think about. That's one of the things that makes our model so successful, you have to think about the juxtaposition between what's happening on the prison yard and working for Televerde."

Cirocco continued. "You're now getting called by 'Ms.' or by your first name and you're communicating with people in a way that is the total contrast to what's happening on a prison yard. We invest so heavily in their training, the coaching, the development, ongoing education, and provide people the opportunity to learn and grow. And when they make mistakes, it's a place that's safe to make mistakes, to say, 'I don't know how,' and the person next to you will show you, and help you, and enable you. That's what true respect is about." A lesson that leaders in all workplaces would do well to remember and practice.

This approach has paid enormous dividends for Televerde's clients. "One of our biggest customers is one of the most massive global enterprise software companies in the world. They've been a client of ours for ten years. We have delivered them over 30,000 qualified sales opportunities, from which they have gotten $825 million in revenue and a 14-to-one return on their investment. Companies like that [are] not going to just buy from us because we have a cool business model. They can just give money to charity if that was the case. And we're not a charity, so they buy from us because we're the best at what we do," explained Cirocco.

Cirocco believes that part of the changing attitudes of companies is driven by the astounding fact that one in two Americans has a family member who is formerly or currently incarcerated (based on a study by Cornell University and FWD.us). "This is an American problem. There are other numbers which are even more shocking. 70 million people (or as many people who have college degrees) in our country have criminal records. It's caused a softening in the hearts of people, and it's forcing people to open their minds to the problem because now suddenly they've experienced it firsthand." Cirocco is a passionate advocate of "Banning the Box," the movement to remove the question about past criminal convictions from job applications.

Finally, I ask Cirocco what it felt like to be invited to the White House. "Actually, even just getting the invitation to the White House I thought was an April fool's joke because the event was on April 1st! I thought 'ha, how does a girl like me get invited to the White House?' And we went there and it's cherry blossom season in Washington, it smells wonderful. And we're going through more security checkpoints and metal detectors than at Perryville!" She laughed.

She reflected on the moment.

"Do you know what the biggest personal takeaway was for me? The most surprising thing for me when I was there was how comfortable and how natural I felt, and how I felt like this is absolutely where I belonged. I never once had that moment of fear, doubt, or insecurity about my position in life, or where I've been, or anything. It just felt right for me to be standing in the room with all of these incredibly powerful and important people. I felt like their peer. At the end of the day, when I thought about it, I realized that I've actually made the complete journey. That no longer do I think or feel that my background has any bearing on who I am or where I belong."

Why We Love This Example:

What we admire so much about Michelle Cirocco and the women of Televerde is that they prove the maxim "Your history is not your destiny." For twenty-five years, they have been showing the world that it is possible to have a measurable business impact and social impact, profoundly changing lives for the better in line with their purpose. They deserve to be recognized as pioneers and trailblazers in this global business movement for social impact, and their model, values, and approach are a shining example of how all businesses should aspire to behave, driving ROI for business and people.

YOUR ◀◀◀ HISTORY IS NOT YOUR DESTINY ▶▶▶

Dianah Diamond, Cotton On Foundation

Our final story takes us to Africa, the motherland, to visit Uganda. The Cotton Foundation, over the past decade, has helped over one hundred thousand young people to change their world through education, career support, health care, and skill development. Dianah Diamond is one of the young people whose lives have been transformed with this work. We talk with Dianah to hear her story and work with the foundation to help other Ugandan youths fulfill their dreams.

* * *

It is a peaceful morning in the beautiful village of Mannya, Uganda. We are staying in a parish guesthouse on a mountain with a picturesque view of a sprawling primary and secondary school campus. Although it is considered the rainy season, the sun is out, and basking under its light are hundreds of young scholars surrounded by their families, teachers, priests, and employees of the Cotton On Foundation. It is Career Day, and the community is here to celebrate a future filled with possibilities that not too long ago seemed unimaginable.

In November 2007, Cotton On arrived in Mannya Village, Uganda. Known to be an area rife with HIV/AIDS and deemed "Mission Impossible" by its local diocese, Mannya was a community in need of help. A lack of education, basic infrastructure, and health-care facilities had led to a village in desperate need of a helping hand. The call for help came from Father Nestus Mugisha, a local parish priest desperate to find a way to help a community ravaged by HIV/AIDS, which in the 1980s had wiped out nearly an entire generation in Southern Uganda. The priest contacted Father Greg Foley, from Geelong, Australia, who, in turn, reached out to someone he knew—Nigel Austin, the bold, charismatic founder of Cotton On Group, now the biggest Australian fashion retailer with over 1,400 stores in eighteen countries, employing twenty-two thousand workers globally.

Nigel recalls his first conversation with Father Mugisha. "He said we have this health center in Uganda, and we need some money for it. So, no trouble at all, we wrote a check, and that was fine. And I said I'm keen to go over and have a look. And that's how it all started from there. We jumped on the back of a ute (pick-up truck) and went on an eight-hour ride through Southern Uganda on all the back roads and dirt roads and landed in Mannya."

From that simple conversation came a commitment from Cotton On to helping communities like Mannya and others around the world. They have cumulatively raised over $100 million (AUS) and helped thousands of children in Uganda, South Africa, Thailand, and Australia gain opportunities for a better life. Nigel put its simply and powerfully:

"We realized that we could break the cycle through empowering the kids and the women, through education and giving them the best chance in life that we have for our kids here in Australia. That's where we would win. Every cent that

we raise, we are custodians, and we want to make sure it goes to the right place."
Today, we are going to visit another place that Cotton has invested in, a school in
Kalyamenvu, one of the most remote communities they have ever worked with.
The brand-new school accounts for five hundred quality educational places. Our
driver is Dennis, who is a former soldier in the Ugandan Army. A natural-born
protector, he is tall and commanding, with a coffee-like complexion and lively
laugh. His copilot in our ride is Jade Slater, Cotton On's commercial manager, a
native Australian with a vivacious spirit that just pours out of her petite frame.

On our way to Kalyamenvu, we drive down the dirt roads to the Cotton On
office to pick up Dianah Diamond, who can't seem to control her excitement.
Today is her first day on the job as a sponsorship coordinator, and she knows
perhaps better than anyone how important her work is to the community.

Dianah is lovely and illuminating. She radiates gratitude and joy in ways
that are contagious and even more remarkable considering the pain and loss
she has experienced in her life.

> I grew up in south Mannya. Life wasn't easy before Cotton On. My
> parents both died when I was in the early stages. My mother died
> when I was nine. And then, my father died when I was eleven out
> of AIDS. Life was not that easy those years. My grandmother had
> to struggle to take good care of us. So there were many, five of us.
> She took everything possible to see us growing and living a better life,
> which was not okay.

Dianah was one of the first children to go through Cotton On Foundation's
internal sponsorship program, which allows Cotton On Group staff to sponsor
children in the foundation schools who need help with their fees. Her sponsor was Tim Diamond, Cotton On's general manager. Described by Father
Mugisha as compassionate, courageous, and someone who gives hope to others, Tim looks the part of a Hollywood leading man whom you would expect
to save the day in a summer blockbuster. But he didn't need to be an actor to
play a heroic role in Dianah's life story.

She credits Tim and the Cotton On Foundation with changing her life,
supporting her journey from primary school through completing her bachelor's

degree in adult and community education, a moment of great pride. "Wow, it was amazing! I didn't believe in myself all that time. Cotton On paid for each and every thing, so that's how I stayed in school. It wasn't that easy. My grand[mother] had no source of income to support us. But to me, when I joined the group, I was the lucky one. I was the first to graduate in my family. It was a time of happiness. My grandma was happy. I was happy. Tim was happy. And the Foundation at large."

She adds, "I'm now admired in the community. I grew [up] to be someone with a degree. I can now support myself, my family, and even the community members. Because I am born of Mannya, many students at the schools say, 'I want to be like Dianah!'"

The Cotton On Foundation has been able to support thousands of young people like Dianah through a simple giving model. Cotton On team associates in stores around the world offer shoppers at checkout a chance to buy additional products (like tote bags, tissues, hand sanitizer, face wipes, and mints) where 100 percent of the proceeds go to the causes. Just to give you an idea of scale—one of these items is sold at the staggering rate of every 1.5 seconds in thousands of stores around the world.

Cotton On Foundation (COF), the internal "nonprofit," then takes 100 percent of the money and utilizes it in development projects focusing on education (and also health care, infrastructure, and more). What started with the commitment to one community has grown to a beautiful network of robust schools. It has been gradual, but in the last couple of years, they have proved that their model works and can now implement it at scale. Today, the foundation supports 12,500 students across twenty-three COF-supported schools and has, for instance, delivered seventeen million meals to students and given 46,000 children access to health care. The foundation sees the students, teachers, and communities as a global family connected by a vision to provide quality education to every child in the world.

As we drive down the dirt road toward the Kalyamenvu school, the windshield is covered with a constant stream of rain. But through the raindrops, the most wonderful sight begins to emerge. For as far as our eyes can see, there is a parade of beautiful Ugandan children walking up the road to greet us. Smartly dressed in their green school uniforms, they walk toward us with open arms and hearts, serenading us with love. Their voices reverberate throughout the village as they sing, "You are welcome! You are welcome! You are welcome, our visitors!" As the rain comes down, it becomes more evident than ever what unconditional joy really means. Regardless of condition or circumstance, these young people choose to shine their light and love into the world, reminding us of who we all can be, at our best.

We walk with the students toward their school, singing along. They proudly show us their classrooms and what they are learning in math, science, grammar, and ethics. The gratitude of the students and teachers is abundant and clear. But it is Dianah and Jade who are the most thankful for the honor to help provide them with the education they deserve. Together, we dance and celebrate a day that every single person in that school helped make possible.

For the Cotton On Foundation, the best is yet to come. Tim Diamond talks about what the future holds for their work beyond education. "We want to create more practical pathways. Not only [offer] more university and vocational opportunities for these students but help develop real jobs. Drive better agriculture, develop amazing farming support, build farmer cooperatives, fund ways to build trade that are efficient and rewarding for these individuals and communities to really thrive."

He continues, "When you think about the vast areas that we operate in Uganda, Thailand, and South Africa—we can really affect the tide of poverty in those specific areas by 2030. I want to walk back into those regions at that time and see real change. Meet the people we have worked with and really see a measurable difference, a thriving community, and the world. It's going to be an exciting journey."

For Dianah, it's clear her journey has come full circle. Her new job is to bring in more sponsors to support children who need a helping hand as she and her grandmother did over a decade ago. She recalls another experience.

In Kamunuku, one of our outreach schools, we had a community engagement meeting. So parents had to share their views about how they can keep pupils at school. There was a lady, she had six children, and unfortunately, she lost all those children. She ended up with one boy.

He is now in upper primary seven. But the lady had no source of support for that adopted child so that he can continue with his studies. So when she stood up talking about herself, [and] she cried, I was so much attached. I felt like she was my grandmother. I committed myself to help that boy to complete primary school. So after I did that, the lady keeps on calling me, "My Dianah, thank you. Thank you, Cotton On, for coming to my place. Thank you so much."

To be able to help caregivers like her grandmother to create opportunities for their children, the way Father Nestus Mugisha and the Cotton On Foundation did for her, is an incredible gift. She says there is no way she can thank Cotton On enough for what they have done for her, but in her new role, she is committed to paying it forward. "I'm working hard. I'm believing in my best to help many more to be like me, be better than me."

From what we have seen, she's off to a terrific start.

It was a wonderful experience to travel with the Cotton On Foundation to spend time with these beautiful, brave, and brilliant Ugandan children. They are joyful, curious, loving, and powerful young kings and queens. Their resilience and strength blow us away. It's been incredible to see firsthand the work that the Cotton On Foundation and this community—together in partnership—are doing to empower these young people with the multigenerational support they need to get the education they deserve. Cotton On is showing a path for all businesses where integrity and dedication to making the world better can go hand in hand with business success and growth. We can't wait to see what this fantastic company does next.

Why We Love This Example:

As we leave Uganda, we cannot stop thinking about our time with the Kalyamenvu students who welcomed us that morning. Despite the rain, despite our jet lag, and the reality of our humble surroundings, their unconditional joy, pride, and confidence were so overflowing that we couldn't help but sing along. We could not have imagined that our lives and our journey would take us here to this moment. We are marching together down this dirt lane in the rain to their school in the middle of Africa, built by the generosity of total strangers in another continent who never knew them, and how much their simple actions could transform their lives forever. If anything shows us the enormously transformational power of how business can be a force for good, it is this moment.

And together, we are singing.
We are singing.
We are singing.

PART IV
IN CLOSING

FINAL THOUGHTS

The fourteenth-century Persian poet Hafiz wrote, "I felt in need of a great pilgrimage, so I sat still for three days."

For decades, we as a species have been running faster and faster as we chased some target that was forever out of reach. We never collectively stopped to pause and think about what we were chasing—and whether it was worth achieving in the first place. And in the process, we created a system that has yielded monstrous inequity and a planet damaged almost beyond repair.

But now, because of the devastation of COVID-19, we have paused. We are all sitting still. Life has a way of creating space to look at what is truly important, not just urgent. And in that space, there is a growing realization of what matters—family, community, human connection, being there for each other. There is a crack in the universe. And inside that crack, we can see the beginnings of a new approach to life.

The Great Pause caused by COVID-19 has led to many sudden changes in the way we work. One of the most underappreciated (but perhaps the most profound) is the way it has broken down the barriers between our work selves and our home selves. Without the ritual of the daily commute, when we could put on our corporate masks and assume our business personas, we live a more integrated life, with our families all around us all the time.

The lines between our two sets of values—corporate and familial—are blurring, making us see not only how our lives affect our work—but how our labor affects our lives. We are beginning to awaken to the horrible realization that the same job that puts food on our tables for our children may be inadvertently creating a world that is too toxic and unstable for them to live in.

In our 2016 book *Good is the New Cool: Market Like You Give A Damn*, we issued a stark warning to business leaders: "If we don't deal with income inequality, no one is going to be able to afford our products. If we don't deal with climate change, there's not going to be anybody left to buy them."

These are the two existential threats that capitalism, in its current form, has created. They seem to be intractable and unsolvable because of the lack of consensus to do something about it.

The statistics around income inequality seem surreal. According to Oxfam's 2020 report *Time to Care*, the world's 2,153 billionaires have more wealth than the 4.6 billion people who make up 60 percent of the planet's population. And the problem is only accelerating. The report also states between 2009 and 2018, the number of billionaires it took to equal the wealth of the world's poorest 50 percent fell from 380 to 26.

The disproportionate effect on women is even more troubling. The twenty-two richest men in the world have more wealth than all the women in Africa.[49] Women and girls put in 12.5 billion hours of unpaid care work every day—a contribution to the global economy of at least $10.8 trillion a year, more than three times the global tech industry's size.[50]

We are in a new age of feudalism; except this time our overlords are billionaires who have created a system that supports their perpetual dominance. Enabling this scheme are tax evasion policies, insistence on outsourcing jobs, refusal to pay living wages, and the relentless drive to automation, among other tactics.

The idea of a universal basic income, or a "citizens' dividend," where every person, regardless of age, income level, or work capacity, would receive a minimum level of financial support for the government (usually in return for some form of national service or community volunteering) has been proposed as a radical yet practical solution to income inequality.

By giving every citizen financial support, we would lift the poor above the poverty line and provide redress to the middle-class in case of illness or job loss (now more real than ever because of the specter of AI and automation) and create a social safety net for everyone. Critics have long dismissed it as being dangerously "socialist" and impossible to execute.

But look at what happened during COVID-19. The governments of fourteen major economies started issuing their citizens direct payments, replacing their salaries, and providing relief in many ways. The UK and Danish

---

49 Oxfam, "The 22 richest men in the world have more wealth than all the women in Africa," *Oxfam America* (Website), January 20, 2020, https://www.oxfamamerica.org/explore/stories/22-richest-men-world-have-more-wealth-all-women-africa/.

50 Oxfam, 2020, n.p.

governments stepped in to pay 80 percent of workers' wages, and the Hong Kong government paid 50 percent of workers' salaries for six months. The United States sent many Americans $1,200 stimulus checks, France offered self-employed workers $1,600, and every Japanese citizen got $930. Spain announced that they would set up a permanent basic income for lower-income residents. The list goes on and on.

The genie is out of the bottle, and we are all now involved in a real time experiment to see if universal basic income works.[51]

Here is another startling fact, this time to do with the climate crisis. The UN stated that we need a decrease in carbon emissions of 7.6 percent every year until 2030 to avoid climate and ecological disaster. For a long time, we thought this was an impossible goal to hit, given the rapid pace of growth in the global economy and the relatively slow transition to decarbonizing it.

However, according to recent calculations by scientists published in *Nature*, the pause during lockdown created by the pandemic will produce an estimated 8.8 percent decrease in global emissions in the first half of 2020 alone.

We did it. We did it under extremely tragic and challenging circumstances, but we did it, nonetheless. It shows that we, as humanity, can radically change economic behavior and still survive.

Now the question is how we replicate it more constructively and sustainably through modest but sustainable changes in our lifestyle and behavior so that we can ward off the biggest existential threat of our lifetimes.

So, to summarize what we think are two of the greatest existential threats to civilization, income inequality and the climate crisis, humanity, albeit under extreme duress, seems to have found ways to tackle both.

We did the unthinkable. Therefore, it is no longer impossible. Everything is on the table.

Disruption is a necessary precondition for innovation. And we have just had it on a massive and unprecedented scale. The question is, "What kind of

---

51 Juliana Kaplan, "14 countries that are paying their workers during quarantine and how they compare to America's $1,200 stimulus checks," *Business Insider* (Website), May 8, 2020, https://www.businessinsider.com/countries-offering-direct-payments-or-basic-income-in-corona-crisis-2020-4

innovation will fill that space?" Will it be innovation that continues to drive income inequality to even greater heights, returning those essential workers that we now hold up as heroes back to the bottom of society where we ignored them before?

Or innovation that starts to pollute our clearing skies again, pushing back against the cautiously returning biodiversity—the signs that our planet can heal itself, given enough love and support?

Can we ignite the type of innovation that allows us to create a new vision of the future? One of a circular, regenerative economy that serves the many, not the few, and aims to restore and repair what we broke? Where we can rebuild with a new commitment to the needs of society and the planet in a way that allows for balance, not just growth, for us to thrive, not just survive? As Patagonia founder Yvon Chouinard wisely said 'There's no business to be done on a dead planet'.

We have a once-in-a-lifetime chance to tip the scales toward justice and prosperity for all. The question is, Do we have the will to use the energy of this moment to make these solutions permanent?

We must reject the false narrative that we have a binary choice: between capitalism and that tired old bogeyman, socialism. Instead, we have a choice between capitalism as we know it, with its systemic failures, and what we can for now call 'capitalism rebooted'; a regenerative, restorative approach that balances the needs of humanity and the planet to help us thrive, not just survive. We need a system that takes the best of capitalism (its innovation, drive, and scalability)—and tempers its worst (greed, selfishness, shortsightedness) to harness it for humanity.

As we look ahead to what lies after COVID, we have the opportunity to "Build Back Better"—to help society evolve to deal with these fundamental social and environmental issues and make things better than they were before. We hope this book shows you how purpose is the key to understanding how businesses can help transform themselves to serve the world best—and how you and your company have a vital role to play in helping shape the agenda and be part of the solution.

The problems we are talking about may be so gigantic as to make you feel helpless about your role in solving them. We understand that they have

There's no business to be done on a dead planet

Yvon Chouinard

been caused over hundreds of years, so we won't be able to change them in months, days, or a few years. We must be patient; even though we cannot stress enough, some problems, like the coming climate apocalypse and biodiversity loss, require immediate and urgent action. We cannot change an entire system overnight. It would be like trying to stop a massive ocean cargo ship moving at full speed by throwing a tiny anchor overboard and expecting it to stop immediately.

The reason we decided to use stories of everyday people to describe this purpose revolution is twofold. We believe that purpose is best served by story: it is best explained through people's experiences to see how the human ladders up to the corporate. And two, it is so you could see how their journeys, with all their insecurities and vulnerabilities, are not so dissimilar to your own. We are all ordinary people. But like the individuals in this book, we can choose to do extraordinary things to find our greatness through service to others and the planet.

As Brene Brown said, 'You can choose courage, or you can choose comfort, but you can't have both.' So, what is your role in all of this? We'll leave you with one final story.

In a 1971 interview with *Playboy* magazine, the famous American architect and designer Buckminster Fuller offered a wonderful metaphor on how we can all play a role: the trim tab. The trim tab is the tiny rudder on the much bigger main rudder that turns an enormous ship. Fuller said:

Something hit me very hard once, thinking about what one little man could do. Think of the Queen Elizabeth—the whole ship goes by, and then comes the rudder. And there's a tiny thing at the edge of the rudder called a trim tab. It's a miniature rudder. Just moving the little trim tab builds a low pressure that pulls the rudder around. It takes almost no effort at all. So, I said that the little individual could be a trim tab. Society thinks it's going right by you, that it's left you altogether. But if you're doing dynamic things mentally, the fact is that you can just put your foot out like that, and the whole big ship of state is going to go. So, I said, "Call me Trim Tab."

YOU CAN
CHOOSE
COURAGE,
OR YOU CAN
CHOOSE
COMFORT,
BUT YOU
CAN'T HAVE
BOTH

Brene Brown

Fuller became so associated with this simple idea that "Call me Trim Tab" is inscribed on his gravestone in Mount Auburn Cemetery in Cambridge, Massachusetts.

You are the trim tab.

Your actions, however small, can ladder up to something bigger.

And if enough of us take action, maybe we have a fighting chance.

As the American cultural anthropologist Margaret Mead said, "Never doubt that a small group of thoughtful, committed, citizens can change the world. Indeed, it is the only thing that ever has."

This world isn't perfect, but perhaps we can leave it slightly better than we found it.

The difference is us. The difference is you.

How will you start today?

APPENDIX A

THE ROI OF PURPOSE

THE ROI OF PURPOSE

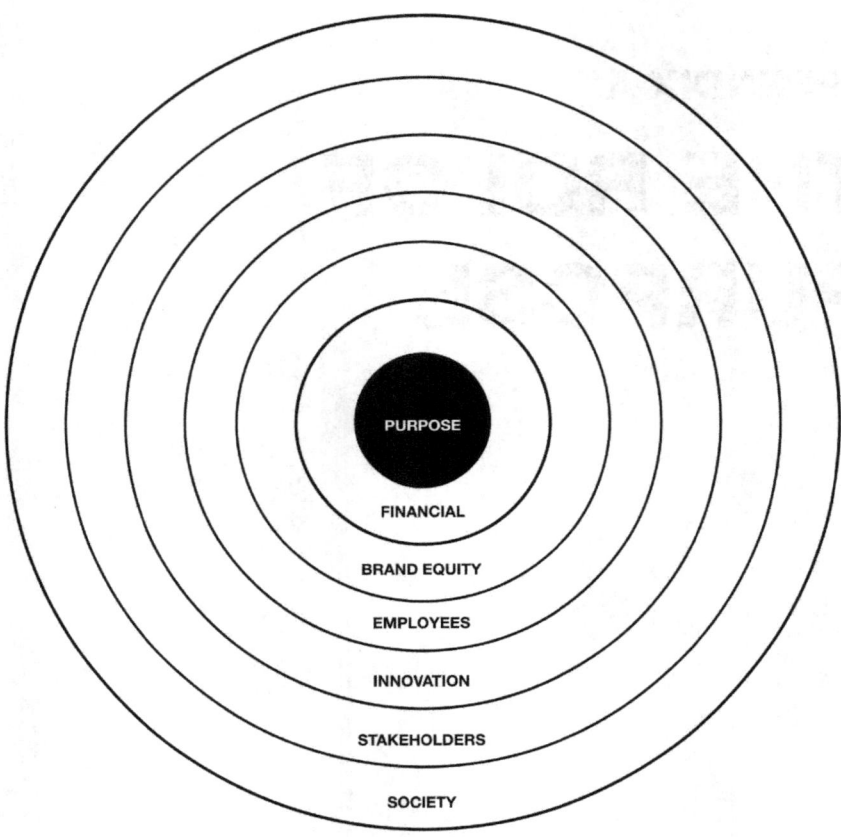

Financial: Profit, revenue, sales growth, market share, share price

Brand Equity: Purchase intent, advocacy, loyalty, price premium

Employees: Engagement, recruitment, retention, reduced turnover

Innovation: New products and services, improved and more efficient processes, new markets

Stakeholder: Customers, vendors, government, non-profit, corporate brand value

Society: Positive social and environment outcomes

A s more and more companies adopt a purpose-driven strategy, one of the key questions that needs to be addressed is how to measure the return on investment from a purpose-driven initiative. But the question is a complex one, since purpose affects so many different aspects of a company: consumers, employees, shareholders, and other stakeholders.

While we are no means an expert on the intricacies of business modeling, we offer a modest proposal on how to integrate the various metrics into a multidimensional model that attempts to truly "measure what matters" when it comes to calculating the return on purpose (ROP) for a company or brand.

Here are the key elements that we propose should be measured:

Financial: As we outlined in the principle "Purpose Must Be Profitable to Be Scalable," the model must measure the financial gains attributable to the initiative (since this is business, not philanthropy). For instance, when Adidas sells 11 million pairs of sneakers made of ocean plastic at $2 billion of revenue, that line item on a P&L is a clear indication of the financial success of the project. If the company is publicly listed and an initiative can be shown to have a direct impact on the share price (as in the case of Nike, whose Colin Kaepernick campaign ultimately surged 33 percent after taking a dip), there is also a case to be made for attributing that value to the model.

Brand: The impact of a purpose-driven initiative on the health of the brand is also another key area to be measured. There is no doubt that the brave stand Patagonia took in challenging President Trump burnished its brand in the eyes of its loyalists. And there is no doubt that Tesla's bold ambition to rid the planet of fossil fuels is part of why its customers are willing to pay a price premium for the brand. The silver bullet question that is most important is drawing a clear correlation between purpose and sales. Sometimes the correlation is easy to see: witness how Patagonia's sales jumped six times on the day following the announcement. However, given the complexity of the purchase funnel, we believe that at the very least measuring purchase intent (does this initiative make you more or less likely to purchase this brand?) is the closest proxy when trying to evaluate success.

In the age of "weaponized word of mouth" at scale via social media, the other crucial thing to measure is advocacy (does this initiative make you more or less likely to recommend this brand?). As we outline in the chapters about Tieks, positive word of mouth at scale is invaluable to a brand. If possible, brands should put into place bespoke pre- and postconsumer tracking or use existing models like Net Promoter Score to measure this sentiment. Other measures worth tracking are brand loyalty, lifetime value, and the openness to paying a price premium.

Employees: Often, as we saw in the chapters on LEGO and Chobani, one of the biggest upsides of purpose-driven initiatives is the effect they have on the employees of the company in terms of morale and motivation. While each company has its own metrics for measuring employee engagement, a common one worth measuring is the impact on turnover: Does the initiative make employees more or less likely to stay with the company? One of the world's leading corporate purpose platforms, Benevity's research shows that employees are 57 percent more likely to stay with a company that offers volunteering and fundraising opportunities, leading to significant cost reductions (the average cost of replacing an employee is 1.2 times their annual salary).

This is in addition to helping make it easy to recruit new employees, especially millennials and Gen Z, who are increasingly motivated by the opportunity to work for a company that creates meaningful social and environmental impact (leading to lower recruiting costs). As the importance of the employer brand (the term used to describe a company's reputation and popularity from a potential employer's perspective) continues to grow, purpose will become a key component to attract the best talent.

Innovation: Another undermeasured aspect of purpose initiatives is the effect they have on liberating employees to think innovatively on how everyone can add value to the company. In some cases, this has led to employees coming up with entirely new products or opening up new markets. Authentic, employee-driven innovation may be one of the most valuable outcomes that a purpose-driven culture can trigger.

A great example is the chapter on Microsoft employee Saqib Sheikh, who developed a Seeing AI app, which has enormous potential to create a new platform for products that drive accessibility. Or as we show in the chapter on Zappos Adaptive, a clothing line started by Zappos employee Saul Dave after a phone call with a customer revealed a hugely underserved new market.

Stakeholders: This is a somewhat broad bucket, which includes customers (retailers and distributors who may purchase your product to sell to consumers), suppliers (vendors who sell raw materials or produce your product for you), and society (government, nonprofits, and other actors whom the company has relationships with).

The benefits of a positive reaction to a purpose-driven initiative could be myriad, from more favorable trading terms to broader community acceptance and support. Ultimately all of this ladders up to corporate reputation, that invaluable intangible which can greatly affect the perceived brand value of a company.

Social: Finally, it is now becoming possible to measure the social and environmental benefits of an initiative in terms of not just outputs (the list of actions generated by the initiative) but outcomes (the actual benefits to local and global society). One of the pioneers in this field is our friend Lesa Ukman, whose Pro Social Valuation model is worth exploring because it is able to calculate a financial value to society generated by a social impact initiative.

For instance, if a corporate impact initiative leads to fifty thousand veterans getting jobs (as is the case with Activision's Call of Duty Endowment), we now have a way to accurately measure the reduction in cost to society in terms of welfare and support services, not to mention the economic upside caused by so many new entrants to the workforce.

While it is imperative to acknowledge that it takes many actors to create such systemic shift, if companies are able to correctly attribute that value and fold a proportion of it into the return on investment model, this makes the business case for doing good that much stronger and paves the way for future initiatives.

As companies search for a holistic approach, we hope this exploration can spark debate on how to measure economic, social, and cultural capital generated by purpose-driven company initiatives. We believe that, with time, our models for measuring the impact will become more sophisticated and standardized across, business allowing us for the first time to see how truly transformational this approach could be.

ABOUT
GOOD IS THE
NEW COOL

Good Is the New Cool connects and serves a global movement of world-changing entrepreneurs, creators, and innovators using business and culture as forces for good. We tell inspiring stories across books, films, and podcasts that show people how to use their talents and resources to create a better world. We also offer inclusive physical, digital, and virtual experiences to engage our community in meaningful dialogue on today's most urgent issues so we can all learn how to implement bold creative solutions that can lead to real social change.

We invite you to join our community by downloading the Good Is the New Cool app or visiting us at www.goodisthenewcool.com—our online home. It is a place where we all can connect, exchange ideas, and engage with content, products, and experiences that uplift our spirits and catalyze collective action for good.

ABOUT CONSPIRACY OF LOVE

Conspiracy of Love is the global brand purpose consultancy born out of our first book, *Good Is the New Cool: Market Like You Give A Damn.* We help leaders at Fortune 500 brands, innovative nonprofits, and world-changing start-ups to use purpose and love to motivate your employees, delight your customers, and make the world better.

Since inception in 2017, Conspiracy of Love has been privileged to work with iconic brands in many categories: trillion-dollar tech giants like Microsoft and Facebook; cutting-edge lifestyle brands like Adidas, Red Bull, the North Face, and Sonos; spirits brands like Bombay Sapphire Gin and Crown Royal; and universally loved food brands like Oreo and Skittles. We have also advised leading companies such as AB-Inbev, Miller Coors, Coty, Nestle Waters, and many others.

We are a certified B Corp, joining the global community of companies like Patagonia, Ben & Jerry's, Seventh Generation, and more who believe in business as a force for good.

To learn more about how we help leading brands discover, design, and deploy purpose-driven initiatives based on the principles in this book, please visit us at www.conspiracyoflove.co.

"Conspiracy of Love are at the forefront of a tectonic shift in the way brands do business."
                    —Brenda Fiala, Global VP Strategy, Bacardi Group

"We found them amazing to work with and have no hesitation recommending them as partners in purpose."
                    —Marion Delguette Saenan, Marketing Director, Oreo

"They helped us reach a highly successful outcome—the adoption of a transformational multi-year plan to help the company evolve and meet the needs of a new generation of purpose-led consumers."
                    —Nelson Switzer, Chief Sustainability Officer,
                    Nestle Waters, North America

"They did a phenomenal job and helped us create a playbook on how to do more good that will help our communities."
                    —Kim Mauller, Senior Insights Manager, Innovation
                    And Foresight, Molson Coors

Their speed, innovation and extensive network, and their ability to effectively combine purpose and brand made them an exceptional partner."
                    —Catherine Davis, CMO, Feeding America

"Conspiracy of Love are the real deal. Smart, empathetic, strategic and seasoned; they really know how to guide an organization to imagine and realize their essential purpose. They are indispensable partners in today's world."
                    —Tom Herbst, CMO, The North Face

"They instilled a belief in the team that we collectively have the power to inspire, unite, and ultimately create change. We loved working with them and continue to use his framework to guide our thinking."
                    —Tom Cartmale, Red Bull Media House

Good Is the New Cool: Market Like You Give a Damn

We are at a crossroads: either we can try to prop up the old, broken marketing model, or we can create a new model, one that is fit for the unique challenges of today.

—From *Good Is the New Cool*

Marketing has an image problem. Media-savvy millennials, and their younger Gen Z counterparts, no longer trust advertising, and they demand increased social responsibility from their brands—while still insisting on cutting-edge products with on-trend design. As always, brands need to be cool—but now they need to be good too. It's a tall order, and with new technology empowering consumers to bypass advertisements altogether, it won't be long before the old advertising-based marketing model goes the way of the major label.

If only there was a new model, one that allowed companies to address environmental, civic, and economic issues in a way that grew their brand and business, while giving back to society and rebranding branding as a powerful force for good. Enter *Good Is The New Cool*, a bold new manifesto from marketing experts Afdhel Aziz and Bobby Jones. In provocative, whip-smart, and streetwise style, they take aim at conventional marketing, posing the questions few have had the vision and courage to ask: If the system is broken, how can we fix it? Rather than sinking money into advertising, why not create a new model, in which great marketing optimizes life?

With seven revolutionary new principles—from "Treat People as Citizens, Not Consumers," to "Lead with the Cool"—and insights and interviews from a new generation of marketers, social entrepreneurs, and leaders of such brands as Zappos, Citibank, and the Honest Company, as well as the culture creators working with artists like Lady Gaga, Pharrell, and Justin Bieber, this rule-breaking book is the new business model for the twenty-first century, and a call to action for anyone committed to building a better tomorrow. This visionary book won't just change your business—it will change the world.

APPENDIX B

MORE INSPIRATION

We thought it may be a good idea to give you a list of resources that we have been using to inspire us in the movement of business as a force for good.

Reading: Books

Introductory Reading

- *Delivering Happiness: A Path to Profits, Passion, and Purpose*, by Tony Hsieh (CEO of Zappos)
- *Buy the Change You Want to See: Use Your Purchasing Power to Make the World a Better Place*, by Jane Mosbacher Morris
- *Humankind: A Hopeful History*, by Rutger Bregman
- *A Selfish Plan to Change the World: Finding Big Purpose in Big Problems*, by Justin Dillon
- *Green Giants: How Smart Companies Turn Sustainability into Billion-Dollar Businesses*, by Freya Williams
- *Drawdown: The Most Comprehensive Plan Ever Proposed to Reverse Global Warming*, Edited by Paul Hawken
- *All We Can Save: Truth, Courage, and Solutions for the Climate Crisis*, Edited by Ayana Elizabeth Johnson and Katharine K. Wilkinson
- *Do Purpose: Why brands with a purpose do better and matter more*, by David Hieatt.

Intermediate Reading

- *Manifesto for a Moral Revolution: Practices to Build a Better World*, by Jacqueline Novogratz
- *Thirst: A Story of Redemption, Compassion, and a Mission to Bring Clean Water to the World*, by Scott Harrison
- *Dare to Lead: Brave Work. Tough Conversations. Whole Hearts.*, by Brené Brown

- *Let My People Go Surfing: The Education of a Reluctant Businessman*, by Yvon Chouinard, et al.
- *The Upcycle: Beyond Sustainability-Designing for Abundance*, by William McDonough and Michael Braungart

Advanced Reading

- *Postcapitalism: A Guide to Our Future*, by Paul Mason
- *Reimagining Capitalism in a World on Fire*, by Rebecca Henderson
- *The Second Mountain: The Quest for a Moral Life*, by David Brooks
- *Capitalism: A Ghost Story*, by Arundhathi Roy
- *Abundance: The Future Is Better than You Think*, by Peter Diamandis and Steven Kottler
- *Doughnut Economics: Seven Ways to Think Like a 21st-Century Economist*, by Kate Raworth
- *Moral Capitalism*, by Steven Pearlstein
- *Perspectives on Purpose*, by Nina Montgomery
- *Purpose: The Starting Point of Great Companies*, by Nikos Mourkogiannis

Viewing: Documentaries

- *The Corporation*, by Joel Bakan and Jennifer Abbott
- *The New Corporation*, by Joel Bakan and Jennifer Abbott
- *The 13th*, by Ava Du Vernay
- *The New Breed—the Rise of the Social Entrepreneur*, by Pete Williams
- *The True Cost*, by Andrew Morgan
- *Waiting for 'Superman,'* by Davis Guggenheim
- *Wasted! The Story of Food Waste*, by Anna Chai and Nari Kye
- *Miss Representation*, by Jennifer Siebel Newsom
- *Rest in Power: The Trayvon Martin Story*, by Jenner Furst and Julia Willoughby Nason

Thanks and Acknowledgments

We are both truly grateful to the many amazing people who have supported our journey along the way, starting with our amazing team at Conspiracy of Love: Nadia Petrik, Helen Trickey, Lucia Slezakowa, and Veronika Monteith.

We thank our many Co-conspirators: LeKeith Taylor, Sara Vaughan, Trisha Stezzi, Ben Cleaver, Tom Evans, Chris Johns, Jerri Chou, Ruthie Schulder, Jessica Resler, Ant Demby, Lesa Ukman, Dana Bakich, Chuck Welch, and Will Travis.

Our incredible partners in developing the Good is the New Cool TV show: Mark Rubinstein, Arnie Zipursky, Dayna Zipursky, Marly Reed, and Klaudia Rekas at CCI Entertainment; Scott Budnick, Adrianna Ambriz, and Misha Schwarz at 1Communty; and Colin Reno at WME.

The dynamic duo of Shani Langi and Sharice Bellantonio of Usual Suspects, our partners in producing the Good Is the New Cool Australia conferences.

Our indefatigable podcast editor Natalia Rodriguez Ford and Michaella Solar-March and Joey Stevenson at Soho House for championing our events series there.

And for all the great work they have done behind the scenes, thank you to Mark Sperling, Zach Corzine, Ayanna Carter, Gordon Parks, Topfan, and Vulcan Media.

Afdhel: As always, thank you to my endlessly supportive wife, Rukshana, and our son, Nuri, for reminding me of the goodness in the world every day. Thank you also to my mother, Fathima Aziz, for giving me her gifts of drive and determination, and my late father, Shibly Aziz, for his gifts of moral courage and kindness. Thank you also to my closest friends Romesh Jayawickrama, Leigh Walters-James, Brenton Smith, and Ranidu Lankage for their constant encouragement and endless ribbing. Thank you to the wonderful team at Speakers Spotlight in Canada: Marnie Ballene, Catherine McCabe, Helen Fitzgerald, Marta Moher, and Dwight Ireland and Tori Mara and Caitie Bradley at Outspoken.

Bobby: First of all, thank you, Renee. I could not have done this without your unwavering love, encouragement, and support. Mom, I'm so fortunate to be able to share these milestones with you. Everything I do is to honor and thank you and Dad for all you have done for me. Lisa, thank you for being the best big sister anyone could ever ask for. Miles, every day you teach me how to express love and joy; you are my greatest gift.

Thank you to my DC, Direct Impulse, YARDStyle, Access, Peace First, GoodFellas, and Morgan State families. There is no way I can recognize every person by name who has been part of my journey, but just know that I am grateful for each of you who have loved, taught, and challenged me along the way.

I am particularly appreciative for the lessons instilled in me by Mama Fair, who taught me to pursue meaning over money; Cathy Hughes, who taught me that love and excellence go hand in hand in business and life; and Dickie and Jan Cox, who taught me to keep my eyes on the prize and keep God first.

Bibliography

"About Habana." *Cafe Habana*. Accessed January 30, 2021. https://www. cafehabana.com/story/

Aziz, Afdhel. "How Swell Is Riding the Wave of Impact Investing." *Forbes*. August 29, 2018. https://www.forbes.com/sites/afdhelaziz/2018/08/29/ how-swell-is-riding-the-wave-of-impact-investing/?sh=73ca97dad470.

"Benevity Study Links Employee Centric Corporate Goodness Programs to Big Gains in Retention." *Benevity*. May 31, 2018. https://www.benevity. com/media/media-releases/benevity-study-links-employee-centric-corporate-goodness-programs-big-gains.

"Bezos And Blackrock Are Pouring Billions into This $30.7 Trillion Trend." *Yahoo Finance*. August 18, 2020. https://finance.yahoo.com/news/bezos-blackrock-pouring-billions-30-230100473.html.

Campbell, Scott and Ashley Tully. "Eliminating Forced Labor Around the World, Starting with the Supply Chain." *SAP*. March 5, 2018. https:// news.sap.com/2018/03/eliminating-forced-labor-around-the-world-starting-with-the-supply-chain/.

*Certified B Corporation.*Accessed January 30, 2020. https://bcorporation.net.

"Corporate Governance: Business Roundtable Redefines the Purpose of a Corporation to Promote 'An Economy That Serves All Americans'." *BR Business Roundtable.* August 19, 2019. https://www.businessroundtable. org/business-roundtable-redefines-the-purpose-of-a-corporation-to-promote-an-economy-that-serves-all-americans.

Costello, Martine. "The Rise of Individual Impact Investors." *Impactivate.* July 26, 2018. https://www.theimpactivate.com/the-rise-of-individual-impact-investors/.

Cotton, Barney. "What Is Impact Investing and Why Is It on the Rise?" *Business Leader.* August 27, 2019. https://www.businessleader.co.uk/what-is-impact-investing-and-why-is-it-on-the-rise/72276/.

"Delta Airlines Mission and Vision Statements Analysis." *Delta Airlines.* Accessed January 30, 2021. https://mission-statement.com/delta-airlines/.

Edelman, Richard. "Edelman Trust Barometer Special Report on COVID-19 Demonstrates Essential Role of the Private Sector." *Edelman.* Daniel J. Edelman Holdings, Inc. Accessed January 29, 2021. https://www. edelman.com/research/edelman-trust-covid-19-demonstrates-essential-role-of-private-sector.

"15 Critical Insights into Gen Z, Purpose and the Future of Work." *WeSpire.* Accessed January 30, 2020. http://www.wespire.com/wp-content/uploads/2018/07/WeSpire_GenZ-2.pdf.

Fink, Laurence D. "BlackRock: Focus on Society and Profits." *The New York Times,* January 16, 2018. https://www.nytimes.com/interactive/2018/01/16/business/dealbook/document-BlackRock-s-Laurence-Fink-Urges-C-E-O-s-to-Focus.html?dlbk.

Friedman, Matthew. "Just Facts: As Many Americans Have Criminal Records as College Diplomas." *Brennan Center for Justice.* November 17, 2015. https://www.brennancenter.org/our-work/analysis-opinion/just-facts-many-americans-have-criminal-records-college-diplomas.

"5 Socially Responsible Investment Platforms That Help You Invest in Both Purpose & Profit." *The Good Trade.* Accessed January 30, 2021. https://www.thegoodtrade.com/features/socially-responsible-investing-platforms.

"Gallup Releases New Insights on the State of the Global Workplace." *Gallup* (Blog). October 8, 2013. https://news.gallup.com/opinion/gallup/171632/gallup-releases-new-insights-state-global-workplace.aspx.

Gelles, David. "He Ran an Empire of Soap and Mayonnaise. Now He Wants to Reinvent Capitalism." *The New York Times,* August 29, 2019. https://www.nytimes.com/2019/08/29/business/paul-polman-unilever-corner-office.html.

Helmore, Edward. "Fashion industry changes might help save the planet." *Taipei Times.* September 7, 2019. http://www.taipeitimes.com/News/editorials/archives/2019/09/07/2003721848.

"Increase the Effectiveness of Your Executive Team." *Center for Creative Leadership.* Accessed January 30, 2021. https://www.ccl.org/articles/leading-effectively-articles/increase-executive-team-effectiveness/.

Kaplan, Juliana. "14 countries that are paying their workers during quarantine and how they compare to America's $1,200 stimulus checks." *Business Insider.* May 8, 2020. https://www.businessinsider.com/countries-offering-direct-payments-or-basic-income-in-corona-crisis-2020-4

Longfield, Nicola. "Achieving growth in a sustainable economy." *KPMG.* Accessed January 29, 2020. https://home.kpmg/xx/en/home/insights/2020/02/achieving-growth-in-sustainable-economy.html.

Malle, Chloe. "Has Everlane Ushered in a Brave New World of Retail?" *Vogue*.February 21, 2019. https://www.vogue.com/article/everlane-new-world-of-retail.

Mandela, Nelson. "Sport has the power to change the world." *Laureus World Sports Inaugural Awards*. February 9, 2000. Monaco. Youtube Video, 04:35. https://www.youtube.com/watch?v=y1-7w-bJCtY.

Marr, Rhuaridh. "One Million Moms demands Oreo boycott over 'homosexual agenda' rainbow cookies." *MetroWeekly*. October 20, 2020. https://www.metroweekly.com/2020/10/one-million-moms-demands-oreo-boycott-over-homosexual-agenda-rainbow-cookies/.

Messerly, John. "Summary of Maslow on Self-Transcendence." *Reason and Meaning: Philosophical Reflections on life, death, and the meaning of life*. January 18, 2017. https://reasonandmeaning.com/2017/01/18/summary-of-maslow-on-self-transcendence/.

Moore, John. "The Patagonia Way to Customer Loyalty." *Brand Autopsy*. Accessed January 29, 2021. http://brandautopsy.com/2015/09/the-patagonia-way-to-customer-loyalty.html.

Murray, James. "HSBC: Companies focused on climate change 'outperformed' as virus spread." *GreenBiz*. April 6, 2020. https://www.greenbiz.com/article/hsbc-companies-focused-climate-change-outperformed-virus-spread.

"New Assessment Helps Employers Find Job Seekers Who Want to Be a Force For Good: Introducing the First Purpose Assessment for Recruitment." *B The Change*. January 16, 2020. https://bthechange.com/new-assessment-helps-employers-find-job-seekers-who-want-to-be-a-force-for-good-f9228f6adc8c.

"Organizational Change: 3/4 of Millennials Would Take a Pay Cut to Work for a Socially Responsible Company." *Sustainable Brands*. November 2, 2016. https://

sustainablebrands.com/read/organizational-change/3-4-of-millennials-would-take-a-pay-cut-to-work-for-a-socially-responsible-company.

Oxfam, "The 22 richest men in the world have more wealth than all the women in Africa." *Oxfam America.* January 20, 2020. https://www.oxfamamerica.org/explore/stories/22-richest-men-world-have-more-wealth-all-women-africa/.

Park, Leslie. "IBM Study: Purpose and Provenance Drive Bigger Profits for Consumer Goods In 2020." *IBM News Room.* January 10, 2020. https://newsroom.ibm.com/2020-01-10-IBM-Study-Purpose-and-Provenance-Drive-Bigger-Profits-for-Consumer-Goods-In-2020.

Pownall, Augusta. "'We're looking at a change of our total business' says IKEA sustainability chief Lena Pripp-Kovac." *DeZeen.* September 4, 2019. https://www.dezeen.com/2019/09/04/lena-pripp-kovac-ikea-circular-interview/.

Pfau, Bruce N. "Generational Issues: What Do Millennials Really Want at Work? The Same Things the Rest of Us Do." *Harvard Business Review.* April 7, 2016. https://hbr.org/2016/04/what-do-millennials-really-want-at-work.

"Retention: A Strategic Challenge." *Alex Charles: Search Partners.* Accessed January 30, 2020. https://alexcharles.co/retention-strategies/.

Sabanoglu, Tugba. "Global adaptive apparel market size from 2019 to 2025 (in billion U.S. dollars)." *Statista.* November 27, 2020. https://www.statista.com/statistics/875613/global-adaptive-apparel-market-size/.

Schwartz Tony and Christine Porath. "Opinion: Why You Hate Work." *The New York Times.* May 30, 2014. https://www.nytimes.com/2014/06/01/opinion/sunday/why-you-hate-work.html.

"Special Report: Brand Trust and the Coronavirus Pandemic: Edelman Trust Barometer 2020." Accessed January 30, 2021. https://www.edelman.com/

sites/g/files/aatuss191/files/2020-03/2020%20Edelman%20Trust%20Barometer%20Brands%20and%20the%20Coronavirus.pdf:1-28.

Spera, Mark. "The 10 Marketing Secrets to Everlane's Success." *Growth Marketing Pro (GMP)*. February 2, 2019. https://www.growthmarketingpro.com/ecommerce-marketing-manual-10-secrets-everlanes-success/.

Tabuchi, Hiroko. "'Worse Than Anyone Expected': Air Travel Emissions Vastly Outpace Predictions." *The New York Times*. September 19, 2019. https://www.nytimes.com/2019/09/19/climate/air-travel-emissions.html.

"To Affinity and Beyond: From Me to We, The Rise of the Purpose-Led Brand." *Accenture Strategy*. Accessed January 30, 2021. https://www.accenture.com/_acnmedia/thought-leadership-assets/pdf/accenture-competitiveagility-gcpr-pov.pdf.

Toomey, Russell B., Syvertsen, Amy K. andMaura Shramko. "Transgender Adolescent Suicide Behavior." *Pediatrics*142, No.4 (October 2018): 1-8.

Ubadhye, Neeti. "Google Employees Stage Worldwide Walkout." *The New York Times*. November 1, 2018. Video. 01:08. https://www.nytimes.com/video/technology/100000006192998/google-walkout-sexual-harassment.html.

"Unilever's purpose-led brands outperform." *Unilever*. June 11, 2019. https://www.unilever.com/news/press-releases/2019/unilevers-purpose-led-brands-outperform.html.

"U.S. Jobless Claims Pass 40 Million: Live Business Updates." *The New York Times*. Contributed by Ben Casselman, Patricia Cohen, Kate Conger, Maggie Haberman, Niraj Chokshi, Ben Dooley, Sapna Maheshwari, Geneva Abdul, Mohammed Hadi, Emily Flitter, Jim Tankersley, David Gelles, David Yaffe-Bellany, Tiffany Hsu, Carlos Tejada, Katie Robertson and Gregory Schmidt. January 20, 2021. https://www.nytimes.

com/2020/05/28/business/unemployment-stock-market-coronavirus.
html.

Vogt, Anna. "All hail the recent rise of frenemies." *Campaign*. April 14, 2020. https://
www.campaignlive.co.uk/article/hail-recent-rise-frenemies/1679919.

"Why Purpose." *Jim Stengel Company*. Accessed January 30, 2021. https://
www.jimstengel.com/purpose

Afdhel Aziz

Afdhel Aziz is one of the most inspiring leaders in the movement for business and culture as forces for good.

He is the Founder and Chief Purpose Officer of Conspiracy of Love, a global social impact marketing agency whose clients include iconic brands like Adidas, Red Bull, and Oreo, as well as Fortune 500 companies like Microsoft, Mondelēz, Diageo, AB Inbev, and Facebook.

Afdhel is the coauthor of *Good Is the New Cool: Market Like You A Give a Damn*, the best-selling book about brand purpose, published by Regan Arts (a division of Phaidon) in 2016.

He is a writer at Forbes, where he covers the intersection of business and social impact. He is also the author of 'China Bay Blues' (a book of poetry) and 'Strange Fruit' (a novel).

An inspirational keynote speaker, he has traveled the world and been featured at the Cannes Lions, SXSW, TEDx, Advertising Week, Columbia University, Conscious Capitalism, and more.

Born in Sri Lanka, he is a graduate of King's College London and the London School of Economics. He is now based in Los Angeles, where he lives with his wife and son.

Bobby Jones

Bobby Jones is an author, renowned international speaker, strategist, expert on conscious capitalism, and businessman who is on an inspiring mission to show individuals and companies around the world how to be forces for good.

With over two decades of senior leadership experience in purpose-driven marketing and in business, Bobby delivers keynotes, workshops, and consultations that provide leaders in business and culture with an essential road map for mastering the key principles of purpose, to drive growth and impact. Since the release of his best-selling book *Good Is the New Cool: Market Like You A Give a Damn*, in 2016, Bobby has helped people in over 140 counties to develop solutions to global challenges. He has delivered talks, consultations, and workshops to some of the biggest companies in the United States, Europe, Australia, and South America, as well as NGOs, celebrities, and changemakers around the globe. The tools he provides help these entities unlock their purpose—and grow their businesses and brands—by being of service to others.

Bobby is a native of Washington, DC and proud alum of Morgan State University. He lives in Brooklyn, NY with his wife and son.

CPSIA information can be obtained
at www.ICGtesting.com
Printed in the USA
JSHW031722290621
16399JS00002B/4